# The Listening Party

# Tim Burgess

# The Listening Party

ARTISTS, BANDS AND FANS REFLECT
ON OVER 90 FAVOURITE ALBUMS

# Volume 2

**DK London**
**Editor** Florence Ward
**Senior Art Editor** Anna Formanek
**Production Editor** Siu Yin Chan
**Senior Production Controller**
Louise Minihane
**Managing Editor** Pete Jorgensen
**Managing Art Editor** Jo Connor
**Publishing Director** Mark Searle

Packaged for DK by Emma Bastow
and Eoghan O'Brien
**Editor** Emma Bastow
**Designer** Eoghan O' Brien
**Curated by** Paul Stokes
**Image research** Matt Turner

DK would like to thank Matthew Yates for
proofreading and Helen Peters for indexing.

First published in Great Britain in 2022
by Dorling Kindersley Limited
DK, One Embassy Gardens, 8 Viaduct
Gardens, London SW11 7BW
The authorised representative in the EEA is
Dorling Kindersley Verlag GmbH. Arnulfstr.

124, 80636 Munich, Germany
Page design copyright © 2022
Dorling Kindersley Limited
A Penguin Random House Company

10 9 8 7 6 5 4 3 2 1
001–333136–Nov/2022

A CIP catalogue record for this book
is available from the British Library.
ISBN: 978-0-2415-8656-3

Printed and bound in Slovakia

For the curious
www.dk.com

Volume II of The Listening Party is dedicated, as
ever, to all the artists and fans who have joined
us over the past two and a half years – long may
our party continue.

To Nick Fraser, unsung superhero. And to
Andrew, Mat and Matt for their unswerving
dedication. To all the music creators out there
– keep going, we need you.

Tim x

The publisher would like to thank the artists
and contributors who haave made this book
possible. The publisher has endeavoured
to trace all copyright holders but if any have
been inadvertently overlooked, the publisher
would be pleased to make the necessary
amendments. This publication has not
been endorsed, sponsored or authorised by
any individual or organisation named in
the publication except the author.

This book was made with Forest
Stewardship Council ™ certified
paper—one small step in DK's
commitment to a sustainable future.
For more information go to
www.dk.com/our-green-pledge.

The publisher would like to thank the following for their kind permission to reproduce their photographs:

(Key: a-above; b-below/bottom; c-centre; f-far; l-left; r-right; t-top)

3 Pete Fowler. 5 Ben O'Brien (cr). 9 Jonathon Kingsbury. 15 Dave Haslam. 17 Getty Images: Ian Dickson / Redferns. 18 Getty Images: Andrew Hasson / Avalon (t). 19 Tim Burgess. 20 Tim Burgess (tr). Getty Images: Andrew Hasson / Avalon (b); Brian Rasic / Hulton Archive (tl). 21 both Tim Burgess. 23 Wendy Smith. 25 Getty Images: Andrew Benge / Redferns. 26 Gwenno Saunders. 27 Gwenno Saunders. 29 Getty Images: Brian Rasic / Hulton Archive (bl). 31 Getty Images: Jon Super / Redferns (b). 32 Getty Images: Madden / Redferns. 33 Tim Burgess. 35 Getty Images: Visionhaus / Corbis (b). 37 Getty Images: David Corio / Redferns (b). 39 Getty Images: Harry Herd / Redferns (bl). 40 Tim Burgess. 41 Getty Images: Hayley Madden / Redferns (t). 42 Getty Images: Kevin Cummins (cb); Andy Chislehurst (br); Andy Chislehurst (bc); Andy Chislehurst (bl). 45 Getty Images: Roberto Ricciuti / Redferns (t). 47 Shutterstock.com: ITV (b). 49 Getty Images: Hayley Madden / Redferns (b). 51 Getty Images: Joseph Okpako / WireImage (t). 52 both Róisín Murphy. 54 808 State. 56 all Disclosure. 59 Mark Chadwick. 60 R. Stevie Moore (l). Tim Burgess (r). 62 Baxter Dury. 63 Baxter Dury. 65 both Otim Alpha. 66 Ibibio Sound Machine. 67 Getty Images: Anthony Pidgeon / Redferns (bl). 69 Getty Images: Pete Still / Redferns (tr). @leema_seven (bl). 71 Getty Images: David Lodge / FilmMagic (b). 72 Neil Anderson. 73 Tim Burgess. 74 Getty Images: Matt Cowan (cb). Bicep (bl); Bicep (bl). 77 Steve Double for WarChild. 78 Getty Images: Martyn Goodacre / Hulton Archive (t). 79 Getty Images: Fred Duval / FilmMagic (bl); Martyn Goodacre / Hulton Archive (t). 79 Dave Rowntree (r); Salad (b). 81 Getty Images: Stuart Mostyn / Redferns (bl). 82 Getty Images: Louise Wilson (b). 84 Aaron Gilbert. 85 Getty Images: David Lodge / FilmMagic (b). 87 Getty Images: Rob Verhorst / Redferns (b). 88 Getty Images: Jean-Jacques BERNIER / Gamma-Rapho (b). 91 Getty Images: Avalon (cl). Toya (b). 92 Getty Images: David Wolff - Patrick / Redferns (bl) Tim Burgess (t). 97 Getty Images: Gus Stewart / WireImage (bl). 98 Getty Images: Lorne Thomson / Redferns (b). 100 Getty Images: Neville Elder / Corbis Entertainment (br). 102 Alamy Stock Photo: Tina Newbury / SJN (b). 105 Mark Bijasa. 106 both Uffie. 108 Getty Images: Terry Lott / Sony Music Archive (t). 110 Shutterstock.com: Andre Csillag (bl). 113 Getty Images: Michael Ochs Archives (cl). Simone Marie Butler. 115 Getty Images: Gareth Cattermole (bl). 116 Getty Images: Mark Westwood / Redferns (b). 118 Getty Images: Midori Tsukagoshi / Shinko Music / Hulton Archive (crb). Susanna Hoffs. 120 Chris Miller. 123 Getty Images: Barney Britton / Redferns (b). 125 Getty Images:

Shirlaine Forrest (l). 126 Rev Richard Coles. 127 Getty Images: Suzie Gibbons / Redferns (bl). 129 Getty Images: Burak Cingi (b). 130 Getty Images: Rune Hellestad - Corbis (bl). 130 Barry Gibb. 132 Alamy Stock Photo: dpa picture alliance (br). 133 Getty Images: Steve Rapport / Hulton Archive (t). 135 Shutterstock.com: Ilpo Musto (b). 136 Derek Riggs. 137 Alamy Stock Photo: dpa picture alliance (t). 138 Getty Images: Michael Ochs Archives / Stringer (bl). 141 A Winged Victory For The Sullen. 142 Belly. 144 all Belly. 145 Belly. 146 Getty Images: Fin Costello / Redferns (b). 147 Getty Images: Koh Hasebe / Shinko Music / Hulton Archive (bl). 149 Alamy Stock Photo: Allstar Picture Library (bl). 150 Getty Images: Roger Kisby (b). 152 Getty Images: GAB Archive / Redferns (tr). 153 Getty Images: David Corio / Redferns. 155 Tim Burgess. 157 Getty Images: Robin Little / Redferns (bl). 159 James Cameron. 161 Getty Images: David Corio / Redferns (t). 162 all Dry Cleaning. 164 Getty Images: Rob Verhorst / Redferns (bl). 167 Getty Images: Alexander Tamargo / Stringer (bl). 168 Getty Images: Samir Hussein / WireImage (b). 169 Sir Tom Jones. 170 Sir Tom Jones. 171 Getty Images: Samir Hussein / WireImage. 173 Avalon: Chris Walter / Photofeatures / Renta / Photoshot (b). 174 Getty Images: Mark and Colleen Hayward / Hulton Archive / Martyn Goodacre / Retired / Redferns (t). 176 Avalon (bl). 177 Getty Images: Gilbert Tourte / Gamma-Rapho (tr). 178 Getty Images: Paul Natkin / Archive Photos (b). 180 Getty Images: Redferns / Suzie

Gibbons. 181 Getty Images: Hulton Archive / Koh Hasebe / Shinko Music (b). 182 Tim Burgess. 183 Getty Images: John Keeble (br). 185 Sandra Vijandi. 187 Getty Images: Steve Jennings (bl). 188 Getty Images: Redferns / Richard Ecclestone (br). 189 Audioweb. 190 both Audioweb. 191 both Audioweb. 193 Getty Images: Hulton Archive / Caroline Gillies (br). 194 Getty Images: Michael Ochs Archives (bl). 195 Alamy Stock Photo: Pictorial Press Ltd (t). 197 Getty Images: Michael Ochs Archives (bl). 199 Robert Johnston. 200 Getty Images: Frank Hoensch / Redferns (b). 202 Getty Images: Redferns / Paul Bergen (br). 203 World Circuit. 204 World Circuit. 205 Getty Images: Redferns / Ebet Roberts (bl). 206 both We Are Scientists. 209 Getty Images: Redferns / Roberto Ricciuti (br). 210 Getty Images: Kevin Mazur (bl). 211 Getty Images: Robin Little / Redferns (br). 213 Getty Images: Mondadori Portfolio. 214 Getty Images: Michael Ochs Archives / Armando Gallo (b). 215 Getty Images: Redferns / Chris Gabrin (t). 216 Getty Images: WireImage / Chris Walter. 217 Getty Images: Michael Ochs Archives / Armando Gallo (t). 219 Getty Images: Redferns / Fin Costello (bl). 222 Getty Images: WireImage / Greetsia Tent (br). 224 Getty Images: Hulton Archive / Brian Rasic (b). 225 Getty Images: Hulton Archive / Martyn Goodacre (t). 226 both My Bloody Valentine. 227 Getty Images: Redferns / Ian Dickson (br). 229 all Garbage. 230 Garbage. 231 Garbage. 233 Getty Images: NBCUniversal / Paul Drinkwater (br);

WireImage / Michael Caulfield Archive (b). 235 Getty Images: Redferns / Paul Bergen (b). 236 Getty Images: Redferns / Mick Hutson (tl). 237 Getty Images: Redferns / Mick Hutson. 238 both Butch Vig. 239 Getty Images: Hulton Archive / Gie Knaeps (b). 240 Getty Images: Dave J Hogan (br). 242 Getty Images: WireImage / Shirlaine Forrest. 243 all Damon Albarn. 244 Getty Images: Redferns / Roberto Ricciuti (b). 247 Richard Clarke. 249 Jamie Treays. 251 Getty Images: Los Angeles Times / Gary Friedman (bl). 253 Kae Tempest

All other images © Dorling Kindersley, unless stated otherwise on the page featured.

For further information see:
www.dkimages.com

The tweets used for the John Lennon/ Plastic Ono Band Listening Party (pages 172-177) were excerpted from the book John & Yoko/Plastic Ono Band by John Lennon & Yoko Ono, published by Thames and Hudson (2020), including interviews with Tariq Ali & Robin Blackburn, Jonathan Cott, Robbie Dale, Mike Douglas, Kenny Everett, Barbara Graustark, Matthew Longfellow, Barry Miles, Andy Peebles, David Sheff, Howard Smith, Jann S. Wenner and Richard Williams, to whom we extend our grateful thanks.

✓ @Tim_Burgess
Stopped by the Queen Elizabeth Hall at
@southbankcentre ahead of our @LISTENING_PARTY
event later this month

✓ @BenIllustrator
New(ish) work!
I just updated the @LISTENING_PARTY project on my portfolio
with the new @bluedotfestival illustration!

Check it out on bentheillustrator.com

✓ @Tim_Burgess
We're getting together at @AbbeyRoad on Wednesday
with some very special guests - @Brixsmithstart
@Stephenhanley6 @simonWolstencr1 & @JohnLeckie7
- to listen to Bend Sinister by The Fall. You gang can join
in on twitter from 7.45pm (UK time) for all the usual
@LISTENING_PARTY fun

THE LISTENING PARTY.
LIVE AT ABBEY ROAD

NOVEMBER 10TH 2021
BEND SINISTER

Wednesday March 23rd
The Listening Party 2nd Birthday
Live from
Dolby HQ, Soho Square, London

HOSTED BY
TIM BURGESS
WITH VERY SPECIAL GUEST
JON HOPKINS
PRESENTING
MUSIC FOR
PSYCHEDELIC THERAPY
IN DOLBY ATMOS SOUND

JOIN US ON TWITTER FROM 8PM

Dolby

# Contents

# Foreword

In a time of fear and isolation, Tim Burgess came up with the notion of bringing us together through music. What if we all put aside our anxieties for a time, pressed play on our various devices, and in the same instant listened together as one to a beloved album? I can attest to the exhilaration, the euphoria of experiencing the Listening Party. In the midst of deep pandemic blues, music once more proved to be the bright light on a dark night.

Tim reached out to me in early December 2020, and we planned a Listening Party for the Bangles' second album *Different Light*. When the day rolled around, I was excited, but also nervous, my heart thumping, as I sat alone at my computer, eyeing the clock. I imagined music lovers and Listening Party lovers around the globe, poised to hit play at the exact same moment as me.

And then we did. I can still recall the rush of feeling when Manic Monday poured through my speakers. I was transported back to the 1980s. I was there again, standing alone in a dimly lit recording studio before a gleaming microphone. I remembered singing, "Six o'clock already I was just in the middle of a dream" that very first time with the red recording light on. How good and right it felt then, and how wondrous it was now, to listen together with Listening Partiers, all these many years later. What a joy it was to be spirited back in time: to feel those feelings again, to remember the camaraderie with my bandmates, and to experience a rush of gratitude for all the musicians, engineers and producers I've had the good fortune to make music with all these years.

That's the thing about music: it thrills and inspires and consoles us when we're down. Music reminds us of what it is to be alive, to be human, to be connected. I am eternally grateful to Tim for inviting us to his Party, and for bringing us together through music and song.

Susanna Hoffs

# Introduction

Sometimes a sequel isn't quite the equal of the original, but that's not the case with *The Listening Party* book you are holding in your hands right now. On the following pages you'll find a collection of some of the biggest names in music and a few others that might be new to you, with albums that might be familiar and others that will hopefully become firm favourites. We didn't need to resort to any gimmicks in Volume 2, but maybe Volume 3 will be in 3D, complete with pop up guitar solos and such like.

Our Listening Party family has grown over the last two years and wherever I go around the world, people are excited to talk about albums and artists they have discovered. We went from Twitter into the real world with The Listening Party live – starting with The Vaccines at Latitude Festival and taking in Abbey Road, with members of The Fall plus legendary producer John Leckie. Our first birthday party was spent at The Southbank Centre in London in the virtual company of Chris and Debbie from Blondie. That day saw the debut (and probably only ever) performance of The Listening Party Ensemble: myself with Nitin Sawhney, Mark Collins, Helen O'Hara and Tim Pope, with a live set that included Come On Eileen and I Want To Be A Tree – the internet confirmed that no band had ever tackled both those classics in a single gig before. Fast forward to our second birthday and for that party we headed to Dolby headquarters in Soho Square, London, for a mind blowing evening in the company of Jon Hopkins.

The Listening Party flourished in the dimly lit times brought about by the pandemic but once we could meet again in the real world, it has flourished in the new found light.

I've made friends in both the virtual and real world as I know many of you have, too. I've recorded and toured with some of those and met many more at festivals and events.

There are no plans to stop this Party that we've started and we have further adventures up ahead – festivals and venues contacting us all the time, along with artists, labels and managers enquiring how to get an album featured at one of our salubrious Twitter events.

So, take a bit of time to yourself, line up some of the albums featured in these pages and enjoy the stories and revelations about the songs and artists who make these brilliant records.

Tim Burgess

# A Note From Dave Haslam

I went to see Blondie (see page 214) in 1978 when I was 16. The event was overwhelming, the proximity to the band (it was a small venue), the volume banging through my body, the visuals, the onstage dynamic, the captivating presence of Debbie Harry.

Even waiting in line was exciting, surrounded by clusters of people and the chatter in the queue. Before the band came on, I was looking around, wondering who all these people were in the audience around me. We'd been drawn from different parts of the city, some people had travelled a long way, some had made a short bus journey. It was midweek (I had school the next day). I was happy to be among fellow fans. I had gone on my own: I had no girlfriend, but I had music. Looking back, despite the pangs of heartache, I was OK with that.

I had a thin tie on – I'd seen photos of the boys in Blondie, I knew that thin ties were part of their look. But some people were dressed far more outlandishly than me, of course. Checking what the people in the audience were wearing, I decided next time I was in town I'd buy some luminous yellow socks. I cringe a little now – in so many ways I didn't know what I was doing. But, on the other hand, I knew I was where I wanted to be; down near the front at a Blondie concert.

Blondie entertained and intrigued me. I wanted to know more about them, but there were no internet search engines, no one-click-and-everything-is-there. I'd found out a few things about them by the end of the year, and within 18 months I'd read half a dozen interviews in the music papers. For example, I discovered Hanging On The Telephone was a cover version.

Following clues in reviews and interviews, I started listening to other music associated with the venues Blondie had started out playing in New York; including Television and Talking Heads. Investigating the New York scene led me to the Velvet Underground and then Andy Warhol. A couple of three-minute Blondie singles introduced me to music and art that interests me to this day.

The interviews were interesting but there was always the journalist there, too. At school I learned a word for what would have been the case if there had been no journalist transcribing and editing and framing their words; the quotes would have been "unmediated". Kevin Rowland (see page 80) of Dexys Midnight Runners was a hero to me, and still is. He found the interview format irksome; he didn't want his words conveyed via a third party, so for a while he turned down interviews and put out statements about his music in advertisements in the music papers instead.

Fast forward through the decades to the Tim's Twitter Listening Party phenomenon when every evening we have a chance to discover more about albums from the musicians and hear directly from the artists themselves. Unmediated.

Scanning the schedule of forthcoming Party hosts, usually my attention is drawn first to groups I've been a fan of for years, like New Order and The Fall, and, of course, more recent favourites like Bicep (see page 74) and Jane Weaver (see page 24).

Jane Weaver turned out to be a wonderful Party host, explaining the circumstances of the recording, debates with her collaborators about which way the songs should go or how they should be recorded, her writing process, the evolution of the songs, the technical aspect and the instruments she'd used, influences from other artists that had gone into various songs – it was a delight to be guided through the songs in real time.

Jane told us her muse for the records was the painter Hilma af Klint. I realised I had seen her paintings but didn't know much about her so I spent half an afternoon finding out more. I love the idea of musicians drawing inspiration from visual artists, film-makers and poets, as well as other bands. And, of course, from their life experiences.

The Covid pandemic and the lockdowns left many of us struggling, didn't it? And no wonder; a challenging set of circumstances, our lives and the lives of our families and friends plunging into the unknown. Our opportunities to socialise were curtailed – my DJ diary emptied, and all of the live shows I was looking forward to were cancelled or postponed.

In the psychological chaos of Covid, there was some comfort in looking back, hanging on to memories of good times and music that helped mould life and our identity, and sharing our passion for albums from our past. You can lose your way in life but your favourite music never leaves you.

It was in this spirit that I made a point of seeking out the Listening Parties dedicated to *Steve McQueen* by Prefab Sprout (see page 22), My Bloody Valentine's *Loveless* album (see page 224), Japan's *Tin Drum* (see page 146), early Cure albums, and ABC's *The Lexicon of Love* (see page 42). When I heard Poison Arrow and The Look of Love from *The Lexicon of Love* album, I realised I still knew every single word, which is kinda crazy when I'm also at that age when you forget the names of people I see every day.

I've always been curious about the present and hopeful about the future, and made a date to be around for Listening Party events for the debut album by Working Men's Club (see page 98), Tim Burgess's own *I Believe* album (see page 30), and *New Long Leg* by Dry Cleaning (see page 162). I bet everyone who has followed Tim's Listening Parties has at some point discovered a new album to love.

The Listening Parties have been a great way to catch up on records I'd not heard before, or things I'd missed out on, sometimes very belatedly. If you have a busy life you probably don't get the time to go exploring. In the lockdowns I had more time than ever before. Ok, I thought, time to catch-up, and find out what was all that fuss about *Philophobia*, and *Oh, Inverted World*. And in I jumped. And I love the glee with which Tim announces something perhaps unexpected, and definitely exclusive; I'm thinking of the evening we spent with Bonnie Tyler (see page 88).

I felt part of a great community joining Tim's Twitter Listening Parties, and just as I was all those years ago at the Blondie show, I was excited as strangers gathered for Blondie's *Parallel Lines* Listening Party.

Chris Stein and Debbie Harry contributed thoughts and insights and memories and they were joined by photographer Bob Gruen who took (and posted) some incredible photos in Blondie's early career. There I was sat at home, as Debbie explained the genesis of the guitar riff in One Way or Another, the story of Picture This and Fade Away and Radiate. In addition to Bob's visual memories and explanations, Chris Stein also posted pictures from the archive of his own great photos. This was more than I could have dreamt of back when it took me several years to discover the band's basic story.

It's become a joy to realise how much care and enthusiasm is shown by many of the artists who host Listening Parties. They listen again to their records – in the case of older albums, maybe for the first time for decades – reassess and re-appraise them. And sometimes the producers are present too, or photographers who were around and documenting what was happening.

Some artists are more sensitive than others but none of them want their work disappearing into a black hole; musicians want people to hear the songs. In addition, many thrive on that love fans may develop for an artist's music. It's a kind of love, isn't it? It's definitely a kind of connection.

The Listening Parties are a form of socialising; during Covid lockdowns, it was heartening to be able to make a date with fellow fans, and fill our otherwise empty diaries. A sense of community is so important to us. At a venue, or online. Experiencing something unfolding in real time, together.

Beyond the specifics of Covid lockdowns, it strikes me that many of us feel a form

Beyond the specifics of Covid lockdowns, it strikes me that many of us feel a form of isolation in our lives. Some people cut off from the kinds of communal bliss live music brings; perhaps through lack of cash or lack of opportunities or being geographically distant from venues hosting the music you love. Perhaps you're uncomfortable in some way with meeting or gathering with people. You feel cut off. But you've discovered music.

I love these words from writer Maya Angelou: "Music was my refuge," she wrote, "I could crawl into the space between the notes and curl my back to loneliness." Tim's Twitter Listening Parties have given us a route to connect to deep musical, cultural, communal experiences. You're a music enthusiast. You're not alone.

Dave Haslam

# Tellin' Stories
## The Charlatans
Beggars Banquet, 1997

⚑ Few albums have been subjected to such scrutiny as The Charlatans' *Tellin' Stories*. Released just under a year after keyboard player Rob Collins was killed in a road accident while making the record near Monmouth, fans and friends awaiting the album were all aware of the shadow cast over its creation. Yet out of this darkness, what emerged rippled with an artistic strength and courage that not only captured one of the keyboard player's finest performances, but collectively saw The Charlatans reach a new creative high-water mark. Yes, the sense of loss was there – the playing on Area 51 and Rob's Theme, in particular, will ensure the keyboard player's life and talent will never be forgotten – but so too is the positive, powerful efforts of all five Charlatans (Jon Brookes on drums, Mark Collins on guitar (**@markcharlatan**), Martin Blunt on bass, Tim Burgess on lead vocals (**@Tim_burgess**) and Collins), which ensured the resulting album paid the greatest possible tribute to Collins: it took his band to a new level.

PHOTOGRAPHY:
Tom Sheehan

---

**LISTENING PARTY**

**28 MARCH 2020**

### 1. WITH NO SHOES

✅ **@Tim_burgess**
The "With No Shoes" phrase came from watching [TV show] Kung Fu: Caine vs 5 Men. Caine never wore shoes even when he was climbing mountains – I always thought about his strength of conviction – kept us in good stead I think. Richard [March] from Bentley Rhythm Ace provides some loops. Tom Rowlands [from The Chemical Brothers] fitted the final piece of the rhythm jigsaw as the very last bit of production on the whole record – in fact if he hadn't, it's fair to say this song wouldn't have made it. It's unique: 5 verses 3 choruses. Nice guitar Mark. That's Martin Duffy [from Primal Scream] on the keyboards. A beautiful human being and possibly the saviour of this record and our band. Wow. I've missed this song.

✅ **@markcharlatan (Mark Collins)**
Asked our management to find a secluded place in the Lake District for Tim and myself to go and make noise 24/7 and get some ideas together.

They found us a couple's holiday chalet complex with loads of neighbours and had us booked in as Mr and Mrs Burgess.

### 2. NORTH COUNTRY BOY

✅ **@markcharlatan**
Demo done at Tim's flat in Chalk Farm. Recorded at Rockfield and Monnow Valley studios. Think I suggested it be called Country Boy. Good call Tim. My mug on the single cover not Chris Rea.

✅ **@Tim_Burgess**
I've told this story before but it bears repeating. We saw the budget for the video and instead of getting actors, designers a venue etc. We spent it on flights to NYC and hotels. And the video is us just walking around and getting in a cab, etc. IT WAS PRETTY EPIC there was not much of a plan I remember [the director] Lindy [Heymann] grabbing me and Mark and literally begging us to walk down the street and be filmed – we were having too much of a good time.

**@Tim_Burgess**
Mark and I checked into a rented house in Windermere with everything we needed i.e. cider, skunk, noodles, wine and records. We brought a few CDs and a guitar, bass, synth, a mouth organ plus a portable 8 track digital recording equipment. We were in paradise.

### 3. TELLIN' STORIES

 **@markcharlatan**

Another idea brought back by me and Tim after our bromantic break in the Lakes recorded on my cassette 8 track machine (top bit of kit at the time). Really came to life when Rob got into it supplying extra chords and great melody ideas.

 **@Tim_Burgess**

Another from Windermere though it was not fully formed and it was called Laughing Gravy (Mark is a big Laurel and Hardy fan – his named his son Stan). Jon was a big Laurel & Hardy fan too. Both him and Rob really took a shine to this song – Rob reshaped my melody which meant I had to rewrite all of the lyrics. Mark had to insert the whole guitar riff pre chorus that goes along with the drums (Rob & Jon's idea). We did this by editing blank tape into the two-inch master tape. Which was a major, major tech job and only would be done as a last resort, [producer] Dave Charles was about as skilled as you could get at this kinda thing he was a master of his trade – we were always in very good hands.

### 4. ONE TO ANOTHER

 **@Tim_Burgess**

WHAT! A! SONG! This is essentially The Charlatans Vs The Chemical Brothers – it all started at The Heavenly Social. There were countless remixes and numerous appearances on each other's records. It really was a story within a story. Tom came to Rockfield – The Quadrangle studio to be exact – and brought a few gadgets: a sequencer and a synth and a sampler. In one of two days he'd shaped Tellin' Stories (Laughing Gravy) Only Teethin' (changed the sound of the congas completely) and One To Another (clocks, dinosaur sounds), triple tracked Rob's digital piano and doubles that with a real piano recorded and about 5 microphones in every corner of the room and put Mark's guitar through a synth. He took it back to London to mix it with [fellow Chemical Brother] Ed Simons and Steve Dub. By the time they finished it we had moved to Monnow Valley studios down the road. We had dinner, made margaritas, built a spliff and turned the volume up. BOOM!!!! It blew the speakers up & that was the end of that. Time for a dance.

South Country Boys… The Charlatans at Stanbridge Farm Studios in Sussex, April 1997.

@markcharlatan

Reminds me of Rob and days and days in a rehearsal room somewhere in Staffordshire going over and over the intro riff. Maybe into week two I suggested it might be good with another bit.

@robinturner [Robin Turner, author, then band's PR]

This song really feels like Rob's swansong. Was ready to go around to Knebworth [The Charlatans supported Oasis on the second night] way up front of the album. We were talking to @TheFace Magazine about a big feature. When Rob died, we became the cover. Remember my Dad driving me and Chloe [Walsh, PR] from Newport station (my hometown) to Monnow Valley two days after Rob had died. Tabloid hacks waiting patiently at the top of the drive #wankers

Martin Blunt and Jon Brookes, "Friends again" following a frank exchange of views on The Charlatans' musical direction during the recording session.

## 5. YOU'RE A BIG GIRL NOW

@Tim_Burgess

Two of my favourites at the time Bob Dylan and Lovin' Spoonful had songs called Big Girl Now so I felt I had to join the club. My favourite lyrics on the album. "Acoustically Heavenly" [a series of acoustic sets run by Heavenly Recordings] was a beautiful thing. Tash from the label and Beth Orton, ably assisted by Chloe, who along with Robin Turner did the bands' PR (and worked at Heavenly), organised shows at The Crown and Two Chairmen pub in Soho. Me and Mark debuted this song there, along with some Charlatans' classics, Just When You're Thinking Things Over, Here Comes a Soul Saver plus Silver Train by one of my 'Heavenly' favs [the band] East Village. I remember [ABC's] Martin Fry and [Dexys'] Kevin Rowland were there. That night was awesome.

@markcharlatan

First foray into open G tuned guitars. Thanks Keith [Richards]. Martin Duffy on piano. We spent ages sticking drawing pins into the hammers on the piano to give it that honky tonk feel.

## 6. HOW CAN YOU LEAVE US

@Tim_Burgess

The song was prophetic. Rob and Martin had come up with a brilliant Faces style stomp and the chorus came first. After Rob had died – going through all the pieces he left, it was really apparent that he was very close to this song. A total credit to the band that we fitted all the pieces together in such a carefully constructed way. Martin Duffy came to visit until the record was done, Primal Scream gave us as much time as we needed to finish this incredible record that we'd started. I love them for that.

## 7. AREA 51

@Tim_Burgess

Planned as the B side of North Country Boy, but after the circumstances we felt this song in particular really showcased Rob's skills – the middle bit where it all seems to take off made us think about space. If you ever meet Martin Duffy ask him about aliens. Me and Duffy spent a lot of time making spaceships out of hub caps, taking photographs and sending them to the Fortean times. Mani [then in Primal Scream] might have been involved in some of these fun times too.

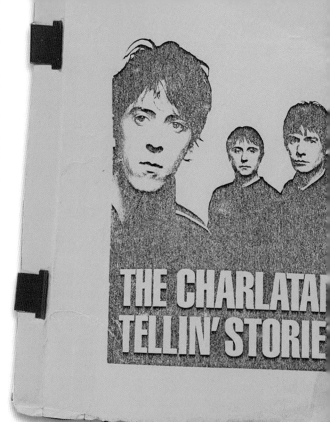

THE CHARLATA
TELLIN' STORIE

(top left) Mark Collins on guitar; (middle) the band's touring schedule and gig ticket from 1997; (right) a "smashed" Tim Burgess (model's own words).

One To Another. Taken outside the studio in April 1996, one of the last times Rob Collins (far left), was photographed with The Charlatans.

GLOUCESTER LEISURE CENTRE
Bruton Way, Gloucester

SJM Concerts present
**THE CHARLATANS**
plus special guests
**Friday 2nd May 1997**
Doors open 7.00
Ground Floor £12.00
Subject to Booking Fee
**STANDING**

N⁰ 927

TO BE RETAINED
exchanged or money refunded

### 8. HOW HIGH

**@Tim_Burgess**

Caine from Kung Fu back in the forefront of my mind here. Also a hip hop record by Method Man and Red Man with a few borrowed lines here and there. Sing along if you can keep up.

**@markcharlatan**

My vocal debut doing the ooo ooo ooo's.

**@Tim_Burgess**

Mark returned to Chalk Farm and we tried to make something like a Sergeant Pepper (reprise) Mixed with Barstool Blues by Neil Young and something from Don't Stand Me Down by Dexys. We thought of songs like this as collage songs where it's all about fitting the pieces together. Everyone always asks about the [yellow] jacket in the video. It belonged to the stylist. I never saw it again. If it was mine I'd have deffo let you borrow it.

### 9. ONLY TEETHIN'

**@Tim_Burgess**

Marvin Gaye inspired rhythms provided once again by Tom Rowlands. Rob and Tom really clicked on this one and Rob had pretty much finished all of his parts except the middle 8. Lyrically inspired by the goings on in my version of London – the city had become my city. We've only ever played this live once or twice. Were you there?

### 10. GET ON IT

**@Tim_Burgess**

Gene Clarke meets Dylan and The Band, or at least that's what we were (I was) hoping for. Martin Duffy plays the keys on this one. I really love the lyrics. I really wanted to connect with the people. I imagined listening to it on headphones. Put your hands in the air if you're listening on headphones. Oh! I forgot how much I love this song. People at work, people who were going through personal issues, people who would maybe listen to this song late at night before going to bed. I think it connected in a way some of our other songs didn't.

### 11. ROB'S THEME

**@Tim_Burgess**

I think about this song a lot. We put it on the record because Rob was working on it separately and we never heard it in completed form until after he died. These days things have taken on new meaning. I often think he was predicting the future, like he knew something was going to happen. I dunno but it's quite a thing to have made this track just before he died (is that too heavy handed?). That child you hear is Rob as a toddler. A perfect closing track.

# Steve McQueen
## Prefab Sprout
Kitchenware, 1985

⚷ Ethereal is a word that gets attached to a lot of 1980s guitar music… and it is possibly Prefab Sprout's fault. Still putting your finger on the Country Durham band's tender yet atmospheric songs, led by chiming guitars and a mix of voices that seemed to glint with sunlight, is a tricky one. Labelling it one way, fails to capture the other facets of Paddy McAloon (guitar/vocals), Neil Conti (drums), Martin McAloon (bass – **@CulpaFeliks**) and Wendy Smith's (keyboards/vocals – **@wendyfinnandmax**) music, it's just so ethereal… and yet as their second album *Steve McQueen* demonstrates, listeners' heart strings cannot remain unpicked when they hear it. Seeing as many others have failed to truly express the essence of this beautifully unique band, it was only right that Martin McAloon and Wendy Smith had a go…

**PHOTOGRAPHY:**
John Warwick

LISTENING
PARTY
**1 APRIL
2020**

### 1. FARON YOUNG

✔ **@wendyfinnandmax (Wendy Smith)**
Track 1 a homage to American singer Faron Young. Paddy is a bedroom musician. Song writing is his solitary (& prolific) occupation. He's with us in spirit tonight.

✔ **@CulpaFeliks (Martin McAloon)**
Antiques! Paddy needed a word not regularly heard in songs, so Mick Salmon our original drummer said Antiques. The crazy Fairlight chuntering at 2.18 was Thomas [Dolby, producer] pretending to be in Frankie playing Two Tribes (we'd been warming up with it while setting up the mikes) it ended up staying.

### 2. BONNY

✔ **@CulpaFeliks**
Think I've been playing Bonny since I was 16 or 17 – it's always been there… like a fingerprint or perhaps even a toenail - some expressions take me back!

### 3. APPETITE

✔ **@CulpaFeliks**
Thomas had me sing the bass line of Appetite using cut up lyrics from other songs in order to remember the rhythm of what I'd just played in rehearsals – I can only remember one of those lines "I'm in with the in-crowd" 26 seconds in at the words "hears the gun"

### 4. WHEN LOVE BREAKS DOWN

✔ **@wendyfinnandmax**
We made tape loops of my voice over a couple of octaves, creating the ethereal vocal backing track by playing the loops on the mixing desk. When Love Breaks Down, our first hit single, was released 342 times before rocketing to No 25 in the charts.

### 5. GOODBYE LUCILLE #1

✔ **@CulpaFeliks**
 The first time I heard Goodbye Lucille, Paddy sat at a piano and my brother Michael and his mate Paul Dent were chiming in on the Johnny Johnny refrain – it may have even been a waltz but that's possibly a mix of sentimentality and senility on my part.

### 6. HALLELUJAH

🔵 **@wendyfinnandmax**
Steve McQueen songs include a glittering roll call of stars, Faron Young, Hayley Mills and George Gershwin. Prefab Sprout's Hallelujah, recorded at Marcus studios, is ALMOST as iconic as Leonard Cohen's Hallelujah made infamous through John Cale & Jeff Buckley's versions.

### 7. MOVING THE RIVER

🔵 **@CulpaFeliks**
Moving The River is a strange song for me as I feel I know everyone in it and also, it arrived shortly after I'd had a good ticking off from my bro over a woman – almost word for word! Bizarre that! Not that it's about me, God forbid.

### 8. HORSIN' AROUND

🔵 **@CulpaFeliks**
The middle of Horsin' Around from 2.20 is priceless – Paddy's chords, Wendy's voice the arrangement, the glockenspiel that Thomas plants between the action, the brass stabs and Neil just letting the whole thing float – absolutely stunning.

### 9. DESIRE AS

🔵 **@wendyfinnandmax**
Desire As is my favourite track on Steve McQueen, I love the vocals. The demo was as good as the final track. Far from the eyes that ask me...

### 10. BLUEBERRY PIES

🔵 **@CulpaFeliks**
Lies Lies Blueberry Pies was something I remember my brother Mick used to say and laugh about – I'm still laughing.

### 11. WHEN THE ANGELS

🔵 **@CulpaFeliks**
Steve McQueen's estate never officially commented on the album title, it was nervousness in a notoriously litigious nation, that sparked the name change. Almost thirty years later I did correspond with Steve's first wife Neile who was lovely.

🔵 **@Tim_Burgess**
This album came out when I'd left school and was about to leave home. It still makes me think of endless possibilities and future excitement.

⬇
**@wendyfinnandmax**
This was the era of the wild moustache, that evolved into the era of the long and silver beard.

# Modern Kosmology
## Jane Weaver
Fire Records, 2017

Delving back into the life of 20th-century Swedish artist Hilma af Klint and revelling in the sound of analogue synths (some rescued from secondhand shops), musical alchemy saw Jane Weaver use scenes of the past to present a glimpse of the future with *Modern Kosmology*. Living up to the vision and scope of its title, the former Misty Dixon member's ninth solo album boasts constellations of hypnotic rhythms, spectral vocals and even a cameo from Can's Malcolm Mooney. Living up to her name, Weaver (**@JanelWeaver**) spun The Listening Party a truly intricate tale about the influences behind this galactic record.

**ARTWORK:**
Andy Votel

**LISTENING PARTY**
**10 APRIL 2020**

### 1. H>A>K

✓ @JanelWeaver

It's the acronym for Hilma af Klint, my muse for the record. I was strumming along on a bass guitar so then kept it. It was early on but I knew it would be the first track because it was quite sonically heavy.

### 2. DID YOU SEE BUTTERFLIES?

✓ @JanelWeaver

Visually I was referring to the Victorian penchant for Entomology Frames, collecting butterflies and then displaying them, trapping something beautiful and natural to document it.

### 3. MODERN KOSMOLOGY

✓ @JanelWeaver

Alongside the story of Hilma af Klint, I was reading about astronomy and Modern cosmology is the study of the history of the universe, so I just drew on that as Kosmology being the history of your own universe, about being hopeful and mindful etc and using your power for good vibes.

### 4. SLOW MOTION

✓ @JanelWeaver

I bought a Roland Juno from Cash convertors in Doncaster (!) and had to carry it through the town centre in the rain. I had been after one for ages, I love 80s synths. They are so powerful and great for pop stuff. Slow motion was one of the first songs I wrote on it.

### 5. LOOPS IN THE SECRET SOCIETY

✓ @JanelWeaver

The vocal theme is inspired by Hilma af Klint and the fact that she had to form a secret society to contain her work as it was 1900s Sweden and only men were celebrated for abstract art ideas. She worked with 4 other female artists called 'de fem'. They would have meetings and call upon spirit guides to channel energy to create their art!!

### 6. THE ARCHITECT

✓ @JanelWeaver

The theme is mainly about patriarchal gatekeepers and how even in art they will try and influence your creative autonomy. It doesn't matter if it's the 1900s or now, the theme is still applicable and relevant re equality and fighting for the cause.

### 7. THE LIGHTNING BACK

✓ @JanelWeaver

Title is kinda based on my mum saying she got struck by lightning when she was little!! She could taste metal in her mouth…!

### 8. VALLEY

 @JanelWeaver

At the time I was listening to things like Inner Space (Can) - Agilok and Blubbo, The Electric Prunes' Release of an Oath plus Serge Gainsbourg. I was writing about the landscape and energy from nature, I guess I wanted to do something atmospheric and organic as opposed to electronic, more spiritual. I wrote it on the beach in Anglesey, I went on my own to get my word's together and sit by the sea.

### 9. RAVENSPOINT

 @JanelWeaver

The demo of this was pretty messy. I'm playing violin very badly, I wanted it to sound like a Kommune jam in a Swedish forest, or Holy Mountain. I sent it to Malcolm Mooney from Can, to see if he'd be interested in doing a spoken word thing. Luckily Malcolm was coming to the UK so we managed to record his amazing voice.

### 10. I WISH

 @JanelWeaver

I started recording this at [studio] 80 Hertz [in Manchester], again changing the drums and adding a mini pop drum machine, I think. In Eve Studios [in Stockport] we recorded the Juno, the [Korg] Polyensemble etc. It's the end of the record and I love singing this live. This is probably the song where I've felt like crying on stage. I have no idea why. I like the wailing bit at the end! And then it goes back to H>A>K!

@JanelWeaver
I wrote most of the words in Anglesey in September 2016, I used to go there as a kid. I really have to go away to finish words, I have bags of paper, files and notes and have to get them together.

# Le Kov
## Gwenno
Heavenly Recordings, 2018

Growing up as one of the only four people in Cardiff who could speak Cornish might not have seemed helpful at the time. Indeed, Gwenno says she once subsequently chastised her parents for focusing on the language of the Cornish peninsula rather than albums by David Bowie and the like. In fact, her mother quietly believed she would discover those records without any help, and when those predictions came to pass Gwenno Saunders (**@gwennosaunders**) soon found herself making her own music, first with trio The Pipettes and then as a solo artist. And a knowledge of Cornish has subsequently proved incredibly useful. Turning to the neglected language, just at the moment government funding for it was cut, the singer-songwriter employed its words as the foundation for her second solo album *Le Kov*. Working with producer husband Rhys Edwards (also **@gwennosaunders**), by intertwining Kernewek (Cornish), analogue synths and, er, cheese, Gwenno takes us on a dreamy and otherworldly musical journey.

**PHOTOGRAPHY:**
Michal Iwanowski

**@GaryTwisted**
Gwenno is quite rightly musical royalty here in Cardiff (and Wales). This is Clwb Ifor Bach, in Cardiff where I work. [Mural by Mark James, spray painted by Rmer, Zadok and Karm.]

⊘ **Rhys Edwards**
@gwennosaunders

The piano hook is definitely a deep rooted @thecharlatans influence. So what a great opportunity to thank Tim Burgess personally.

→

Jamming. Gruff Rhys of Super Furry Animals recorded guest vocals for *Daromres y'n Howl (Traffic in the Sun)* in Gwenno's son's bedroom. Here are his "notes on traffic frustrations".

### 1. HI A SKOELLYAS LIV A DHAGROW (SHE SHED A FLOOD OF TEARS)

⊘ **@gwennosaunders**

I was thinking of the land of Cornwall as a female entity, she's crying with frustration at being almost forgotten. We made this album in the fog of early parenthood, on next to nothing (bar the small advance I got to split between us).

### 2. TIR HA MOR (LAND AND SEA)

⊘ **@gwennosaunders**

This was the first song I wrote for the album after watching [art critic] James Fox's Art of Cornwall doc and being completely inspired by Peter Lanyon's approach to painting and his love for Cornwall.

### 3. HERDHYA (PUSHING)

⊘ **@gwennosaunders**

I'm standing on Marazion beach looking out at the sea and imagining the Utopia of #LeKov against a backdrop of the rise of fascism and regressive politics in the UK. '

### 4. EUS KEUS?

⊘ **@gwennosaunders**

What can I say about this one? Cheese is my FAVOURITE food, this is a 17th century Cornish harvesting phrase I found in a book, and the song pretty much wrote itself.

### 5. JYNN-AMONTYA (COMPUTER)

⊘ **@gwennosaunders**

This started off as an acid techno track when I wrote it (!) then Rhys developed it into something that evokes the Weimar Republic for me, at least. There's a clear historical link between the two approaches I think!

### 6. DEN HEB TAVES (MAN WITHOUT HIS TONGUE)

⊘ **@gwennosaunders**

The chorus line 'The man who has lost his tongue has lost' comes from a phrase noted by Welsh Botanist/Antiquarian Edward Lhuyd in 1700. It's about what you lose when a language dies.

### 7. DAROMRES Y'N HOWL (TRAFFIC IN THE SUN)

⊘ **@gwennosaunders**

It's about all of the holidaymakers on their way down the A30 in a traffic jam. Synth intro is by our little boy, who was one year's old at the time.

### 8. AREMORIKA

⊘ **@gwennosaunders**

The ancient name of an area which includes Brittany today. I wanted to celebrate the historical links between Brittany and Kernow. The old trade, cultural and linguistic links – if we were more aware of them, would we feel so isolated?

### 9. HUNROS (A DREAM)

⊘ **@gwennosaunders**

It's a lullaby that I wrote for our little boy, it came together quite quickly and is quite close to the demo version… Side note - it doesn't make him go to sleep. A failure perhaps?

### 10. KOWETH KER (DEAR FRIEND)

⊘ **@gwennosaunders**

First verse is a poem written by German linguist Georg Sauerwein who spoke 75(!) languages, with one of them being Cornish. This is written for his friend who he couldn't see and who wasn't feeling well. Nothing had been written in Kernewek for a century, and I think it's such a beautiful use of language, to try to lift someone's spirits with a poem.

# *The It Girl*
## Sleeper
Indolent, 1996

⚓ That Louise Wener went on to enjoy a career as a novelist will be no surprise to anyone who has heard Sleeper's records. With songs illuminated by detailed portraits, carefully sketched situations, cinematic atmospheres and smoldering emotions, almost every song penned by the band feels like it could have been a novella, with relationship snapshots intermingling with tales of the sexual habits of Neil Armstrong's childhood neighbours. Instead, though, Wener, Jon Stewart (guitar), Andy Maclure (drums) and then bassist Diid Osman, poured these narratives into songs that became some of Britpop most engaging moments. With Sleeper revived since 2017 and recording again, Maclure (**@AndyMaclure**), Stewart (**@jonsleeper1**), Wener (**@ReaLouisewener**), and the album's producer – the iconic Stephen Street (**@StreetStephen**) – used the Listening Party to revisit *The It Girl*, though this time the story was the record's own creation.

**ARTWORK:**
Joe Magee

---

**LISTENING PARTY**

**3 MAY 2020**

### 1. LIE DETECTOR

✅ **@ReaLouisewener**
This might be my favourite vocal on the album. A song about mistrusting women who defy stereotypes.

### 2. SALE OF THE CENTURY

✅ **@ReaLouisewener**
Andy and I stayed up all night writing Sale. We lived in a little flat near Hampstead and went up to [the] heath to watch sun rise afterwards. And we thought, you just have that feeling, this is a good one.

### 3. WHAT DO I DO NOW?

✅ **@ReaLouisewener**
Remember working on this track in pre-production rehearsals with @StreetStephen and being so chuffed that he liked it. He added an extra chord in somewhere I think! Elvis Costello recorded a stripped back version after we supported him on tour in America. Huge honour.

✅ **@AndyMaclure**
Flash back to @StreetStephen punching fist into hand to keep verse it time.

### 4. GOOD LUCK MR GORSKY

✅ **@ReaLouisewener**
An apocryphal story goes with this song, but it's really about suburban claustrophobia giving way to escape and the grandest plans.

✅ **@jonsleeper1**
there's also a band in the usa who named themselves after the song, too.

### 5. FEELING PEAKY

✅ **@ReaLouisewener**
US version of album starts with this. I wanted this to be a single at the time, but don't think anyone else did. Doesn't have a sung chorus but that's what I liked about it. Sounds peak Britpop though?? Is that a good thing? Or not?

### 6. SHRINKWRAPPED

✅ **@ReaLouisewener**
"And then we watch the spooks on the news playing chess with the cynics, hope you die in the arms of your shrinks in your clinics." The media we inhabit now. More spooks and cynics? Or less? Discuss. Alienation mixed with insomnia.

### 7. DRESS LIKE YOUR MOTHER

◉ **@ReaLouisewener**

Another short and furious burst of energy to take us back up again. Thin girls with bruises. Style mags. Hype. It was all stylised heroin chic or ladette imagery in the 90s wasn't it? Calling bullshit to both!

### 8. STATUESQUE

◉ **@ReaLouisewener**

Our most trying to sound like Blondie moment! I even did the Debbie Harry jaw wobble in the video. On purpose.

⬇

**@ReaLouisewener**
Grew up watching old B/W movies with my dad and he gave me the "It Girl" phrase. First used for the actress Clara Bow. It Girls became a 90's "thing" again after the album came out.

### 9. GLUE EARS

◉ **@ReaLouisewener**

More domestic claustrophobia. A reoccurring theme for me. The lyrics trip over each other. I like that. Holding hands with gloves on….emotion felt through layers. Not committing.

### 10. NICE GUY EDDIE

◉ **@ReaLouisewener**

When we were writing and demoing all the tracks had working titles from reservoir dogs characters. Nice guy Eddie is the only one that stayed! A story song. Like Vegas and Inbetweener. I like odd relationships. The broken ones. Don't find traditional love songs easy. Such a skill to write emotion directly. Wrap my feelings +flaws in characters. Gave my anxieties to them. Process them that way!

### 11. STOP YOUR CRYING

◉ **@ReaLouisewener**

This man lives in the ocean, he puts his favourite clothes on, drifts away…. About that 90s drugged up euphoria and narcissism…. So many people lost inside it and then complaining about it. Wanting fame, a curious definition of love.

### 12. FACTOR 41

◉ **@StreetStephen**

I can imagine Elvis Costello singing Factor 41…

◉ **@ReaLouisewener**

Been sooo good to play live since we started playing again.

### 13. CLICK…OFF…GONE

◉ **@ReaLouisewener**

A slow down ending song. All the albums have one. Lots in here. Notes of grief, losing my dad. And burying hurt in visual, filmic images. Lots of different emotions and feels on this album! Hopefully takes you on a bit of a journey.

# I Believe
## Tim Burgess
PIAS Recordings, 2003

PHOTOGRAPHY:
Tom Sheehan

ARTWORK:
Soap Design Co.

✦ Sometimes you've got to try something new. Like, inviting the entire world over via Twitter to listen to your record collection… and then everyone else's. However, The Listening Party was not Tim Burgess' first leap into the unknown. While The Charlatans will be forever linked to Northwich near Manchester, for a long period Mr Burgess was a Los Angeles resident. Swapping countries, though, was not the only step into new territory, as time on the West Coast created the circumstances and the urge that led to the first record bearing the name Tim Burgess on the cover. Indeed solo album *I Believe* was, in many ways, a direct consequent of LA life, as time spent at famous (and only) LA pub The Cat & Fiddle led to a chance meeting with Linus Of Hollywood who served as producer. "We recorded in Linus' flat on the corner of Franklin & La Brea," Tim recalled for his Listening Party. "I lived in the hills up from Franklin and Cahuenga. I walked to the flat everyday. We recorded all the basic tracks in Linus Of Hollywood's apartment and then took the masters to other musicians we thought would be amazing to have on the album." From that flight to LA to walking every day, this journey proved very fruitful.

**LISTENING PARTY**
**6 MAY 2020**

### 1. I BELIEVE IN THE SPIRIT

◉ **@Tim_Burgess**
I really wanted to stay in Los Angeles for a while, I moved there in 1998 and had been constantly travelling. I needed some time at home. But I started writing and felt the need to record. One of the many reasons I settled in LA was because of its rich musical heritage. I had friends who were working with Van Dyke Parks, one of my friends was the daughter of Delaney and Bonnie and the spirit of Gram Parsons was all around.

### 2. HELD IN STRAPS

◉ **@Tim_Burgess**
Quite an angry song about starting something and leaving a trail behind a fire starter who starts too many fires without someone wafting the flame or indeed putting any out. "I feel like I've just been laid, by the whole world and it's face is red. I lead like I need to be led and it's never frightful". Quite a nice bit in the middle…reminding myself not to worry. It's tough being a Gemini sometimes. Then it's back to being angry ;)

### 3. ONLY A BOY

**@Tim_Burgess**

Lyrics inspired by the homeless kids in Los Angeles. There are lines about regret and fairness "if I were only a boy again I would build a new shelter for all my friends to live in and I swear it would be no less grand than the place I am in"

### 4. WE ALL NEED LOVE

**@Tim_Burgess**

Aw c'mon! This is a great song, right? Singalong with this one. I was always holding out that a band like One Direction would cover it, so more people would know the song ;) I always liked the sentiment in this song I was going for a universal Burt Bacharach style song. Like what all the boy bands go for...

### 5. OH MY CORAZON

**@Tim_Burgess**

Wrote the lyrics at the Cat n Fiddle pub one afternoon after working the song out with Linus. I always love the scene in On The Road where Jack and the Mexican girl have a brief 15 page affair. Kerouac wrote, "A pain stabbed my heart as it did every time I saw a girl I loved going in the opposite direction in this too big world." Fun Fact: The song Oh My Corazon was once name-checked by Richard Osman on Pointless.

**@richardosman** (Richard Osman)

Love that song!

### 6. BE MY BABY

**@Tim_Burgess**

Over time this has become my favourite track from the album. It seems to have a far-reaching lyric and lots of people have mentioned how much they like it. Was trying to reach high Kate Bush with a side order of Beach Boys.

Only a boy. Tim onstage at the 2003 Move Festival in Manchester.

Believe in magic.
Tim Burgess and his solo band performing the album in London in 2003.

## 7. YEARS AGO

✓ **@Tim_Burgess**

The Charlatans came to my house. Mark was the first to arrive... by about 5 hrs. We hadn't seen each other for months. After an hour or so I showed him a new idea. We finished the song before the rest of the band arrived. It's only a short one.

## 8. SAY YES

✓ **@Tim_Burgess**

Influenced by my favourite Curtis Mayfield as was Only A Boy and I Believe In The Spirit. Curtis spoke to me – not really, metaphorically and metaphysically. Feel free to dance this one...

**@Tim_Burgess**
Years ago was kinda inspired by this record xx love Marc [Bolan]

Tyrannosaurus Rex

My people were fair and had sky in their hair... But now they're content to wear stars on their brows

## 9. LOVE TO SPEND THE NIGHT

✓ **@Tim_Burgess**

The first song to be written for the album, and the only song in the album credited to me on my own. The first demo of this was over 8mins long and I recorded it very late with an engineer called Josh The Goth in a studio on Sunset Blvd – it was my first experience of a one on one with just me on acoustic guitar. It was a gorgeous studio. The incredible Stand-up bass by Bruce Witkin – he was the bass player for The Kids, Johnny Depp's band before he was an actor.

## 10. PO' BOY SOUL

✓ **@Tim_Burgess**

Felt quite Dylan(y) at the time. My situation was that I was in a UK band and was living in LA – it definitely wasn't without its complications. I had many, many conflicting feelings about my situation. I hope I explain it in this song which I feel now is about escape. But escape from Who? What? Maybe I don't think I ever want to know. That brrrrum brrrrrum sound at the start, I still use it. Mainly when playing cars with Littlest B.

## 11. ALL I EVER DO

✓ **@Tim_Burgess**

This will always remind me of Josh Schwartz. Josh was the electric guitarist when we played live. One of the best guitarists I've ever seen. Sadly he passed away a couple of years ago at home in LA after a long illness. The end section became a kind of freestyle extended monolith and this song took on a a whole new meaning – almost the meaning of life. Will always remember those days touring in clubs, and in arenas with Stereophonics and Rolling Stones [wow did I really just say that].

✓ **Tim_Burgess**

This album and Listening Party goes out to Josh Schwartz. My friend, in another dimension.

# Joy As An Act Of Resistance
## Idles
Partisan, 2018

Dentist, carer, barman… just some of the day jobs members of Idles were doing when they came to record their second album. Perhaps another career we should add is would-be Charlatan. "Forever [by The Charlatans] was one of the first basslines I ever learned," Idles bassist Adam 'Dev' Devonshire told the Listening Party. "Absolutely bangs. Big love to you, Tim." Not only did this record allow Idles to e-meet a hero, but its success meant it was also the one that allowed Devonshire along with Joe Talbot (vocals), Mark Bowen (guitar), Lee Kiernan (guitar) and Jon Beavis (drums) (all **@idlesband**) to finally focus on music – good news for ears, possibly bad news for the teeth of Bowen's patients. The reason for the slow abandonment of "proper" jobs is also the key to Idles strength. The Bristol band took their time, not only honing their own music, but building up a word-of-mouth endorsement among fans that has imbued their audience with a unique zeal for their rambunctious yet melodic rock.

**ARTWORK:**
Partisan Records

---

**LISTENING PARTY**
**10 MAY 2020**

### 1. COLOSSUS

⊘ **@idlesband**
Dev: Sounds strange to hear Collosus at this pace. It was a conscious decision to slow the song down for live purposes to add intensity and set the tone for gig.

### 2. NEVER FIGHT A MAN WITH A PERM

⊘ **@idlesband**
Bowen: Joe said he wanted a song like a knife so I started playing the intro and we wrote the song in about 10 mins after that. We recorded the BVs separately and our producer got it wrong, so you are actually hearing both.

### 3. I'M SCUM

⊘ **@idlesband**
Bowen: I'm scum: I recorded my guitar part with Joe shouting through a PA speaker into the pickups of my guitar.

### 4. DANNY NEDELKO

⊘ **@idlesband**
Dev: Think Jon, Lee and I wrote the basis of Danny... during a writing session where we were struggling to come up with anything good. This popped out at the end. Joe and Danny had a pact they'd write a song about each other, so he knew it was coming x

### 5. LOVE SONG

⊘ **@idlesband**
Jon: Love Song was Bobo's [Bowen] idea of us writing a techno tune. Love Song is one of the most enjoyable songs to play live. Except maybe that one time when Joe and Bobo kept the breakdown going for about 15 minutes.

### 6. JUNE

⊘ **@EssexChef [fan]**
Do you know whose wedding is on the album cover?

@idlesband

Jon: We got in contact with the guy who owned the photo, it was their uncle's wedding from the 60s.

### 7. SAMARITANS

@RoyKemmers [fan]

I'm a sociology lecturer at a university. I use Samaritans' lyrics on 'the Mask of Masculinity, is a mask that's wearing me' in my lecture on gender identity and (toxic) masculinity. Perfect fit with Goffman's dramaturgical perspective.

@idlesband

Dev: That is amazing! And that also gives me something to read up on! Cheers prof!

### 8. TELEVISION

@idlesband

Dev: Seeing the reaction Television gets when we play it live is a fucking beautiful thing.

### 9. GREAT

@idlesband

Bowen: I wrote the solo to try to sound like a pompous national anthem, I played it to Lee and he was jumping up and down, got me to play it again, then played the thirds up making it sound like queen. Wild stallions!

@idlesband

Lee: I can confirm this to all be true :) I am also wearing a Brian May T-shirt as we speak...

### 10. GRAM ROCK

@idlesband

Bowen: We wrote this in a room in Heidelberg with the beautiful hills around us. The only rule was we had to say yes to everyone's ideas. I had been listening to Jesus Lizard on the way there and I wanted to play slide and in open D. We tried to fit as many chords as possible in.

### 11. CRY TO ME

@idlesband

Dev: Cry To Me [a Solomon Burke cover] was initially thought of as a b-side when we finished it but it made so much sense on the album, it had to go on.

### 12. ROTTWEILER

@idlesband

Jon: Joe's vocals of "Keep Going" was just to us on the headphones as we played this live to give us the energy to continue, I remember laughing as I was smashing seven shades of Hell into my cymbals.  It was so good we kept it in.

Socials. Idles' Joe Talbot gets close to the fanbase in Manchester, 2018.

# The Brown Album
## Orbital
FFRR, 1993

✠ Despite being named after a motorway, there is nothing prosaic about Orbital. Christened after the 'London orbital' M25 because of the ad hoc acid house parties that would suddenly erupt around it in the early 90s, brothers Paul and Phil Hartnoll were deeply embedded in the era's dance counter culture that fused hippy ideals, new sampling technology and the rise of club drug ecstasy to inspire a 'second summer of love'. The Kent pair's self-titled second album – often dubbed The Brown Album because of the shade of its simple artwork – was not only a key expression of acid house, but it was also one of the scene's first properly released albums. Pioneers artistically and culturally, Orbital were also innovators technically as they created this long, unfolding record at a time when tape and digital technology was in flux. "It wasn't easy putting this altogether like a DJ mixed record back then," Paul (**@orbitalband**) explained as he began his Listening Party. "You have to bear in mind we were doing this in a small project studio, we had to record the tracks onto different stereo pairs of a digital 8 track…" In so many different ways, the results were revolutionary.

**ARTWORK:**
Grant Fulton

**LISTENING PARTY**
**14 MAY 2020**

### 1. TIME BECOMES

⦿ **@orbitalband**
This opening was designed to twist people's minds! It's the same as the opening on our previous album (until the loop point) it was a kind of psychedelic play on making you feel like you'd put the wrong album on, or gone back in time.

### 2. PLANET OF THE SHAPES

⦿ **@orbitalband**
This was the first track recorded in the new strongroom studio we set up. This album was started in my parents' house in Dunton Green, Kent, but properly recorded and written in our first London studio, the room on the stairs at the Strong Room. We moved in after going on our first proper tour, supporting Meat beat Manifesto in the USA, what a trip! I'd hardly left Kent at the point.

### 3. LUSH 3-1

⦿ **@orbitalband**
Named by my friend Clive coming into the room and stating loudly while I was writing it "thats lush that is" very easy...

### 4. LUSH 3-2

⦿ **@orbitalband**
We seem to do this a lot, make a dubby part 2 of a track. I always remember Underworld recording in the studio bellow us, and Darren Emerson loving the drums on this. I know him already from going to the Drum Club on Thursdays but this was when we first met Rick and Carl. Such lovely people.

### 5. IMPACT (THE EARTH IS BURNING)

☑ @orbitalband

Does any one know where that vocal is from? I remember the film, I remember sampling it but I have no idea what its called! The survival vocal in a minute is also from the same film. it was a french film dubbed into English which is why it was so clear.

### 6. REMIND

☑ @orbitalband

Another Meat Beat Manifesto connection, this is an instrumental version of a remix we did for them. the original track was called Mindstream. We basically did a re write but with the vocals on the rcmix, then re mixed the remix for our own album. It was all so free back then!

### 7. WALK NOW...

☑ @orbitalband

Here we go, Australia 92. Never been there before, but my mate Jim lived with a load of DJs who were doing the party and got Orbital into do it. It was a fantastic 7 weeks of my life!

### 8. MONDAY

☑ @orbitalband

This originally had the idea of having the b side to the Jane single, It's A Fine Day, over the top. Its called red sea red sky. It fits perfectly. While we were thinking about it Kirsty [Hawkshaw] and Opus 3 put out a version of the same track so we thought we'd leave it. As we'd already utilised It's A Fine Day on Halcyon!

### 9. HALCYON + ON + ON

☑ @orbitalband

This track was originally written and recorded on a Sunday night after a BIG week end, mellow and slightly jaded.

### 10. INPUT OUT

☑ @orbitalband

Open University! [sampled] It's all we had to watch late at night when I was young! It was a good episode as far as I remember, no idea what they were trying to teach me but I was transfixed.

@orbitalband
PETE WATERMAN was a hero to us in that he let us have the Opus 3 sample [in Halcyon + On + On] for the price of a lunch with Pete Tong! Pete was our record label boss.

# *A Steady Drip, Drip, Drip*
## Sparks
BMG, 2020

**ARTWORK:**
Galen Johnson

⚓ Brothers Ron and Russell Mael (both **@sparksofficial**) are a unique pop phenomenon. It isn't just the fact that the Californian siblings have been making pop music together since the late 1960s, nor that Sparks have recorded 20-plus albums of enduring quality – and once staged a 21-date residency in London playing a different record each night. What makes Sparks truly a one-off is the music they have been making for the last half century or so. Who else writes songs about love and suburbia, National Crime Awareness Week and owning The BBC, that become pop gems adorned with soaring vocals, swirling synths and cutting-edge production (the pair count disco pioneer Giorgio Moroder among their collaborators)? Novelist Ian Rankin, who joined the playback, tweeted "I once sat at the same table as the brothers at an awards do – what a buzz that was. Musically impressive from their earliest days and refusing to rest on any and all laurels. Inspiring." We can't offer you dinner with Ron and Russell, but having them tell some stories about one of their records is the next best thing…

LISTENING
PARTY
**20 MAY
2020**

### 1. ALL THAT

✅ **@sparksofficial**
Russell: The intro… Might be the first time we've used a saxophone in a song since Music That You Can Dance To. Very touching lyrics from Ron.

### 2. I'M TOAST

✅ **@sparksofficial**
Russell: Nice crunchy guitars from Evan Weiss and Eli Pearl, both of whom you saw on tour with Sparks the last time around. And you'll see again on the next tour.

### 3. LAWNMOWER

✅ **@sparksofficial**
Russell: Alexa, how about playing Lawnmower next? We didn't know there was an Andover in the UK [the lyric is "My girlfriend is from Andover, Andover"]. There are several Andovers in the US, though.

### 4. SAINTHOOD IS NOT IN YOUR FUTURE

✅ **@sparksofficial**
Russell: Electronics and acoustic guitars galore. Any suggestions for those who won't be anointed with sainthood in their future? Ron likes mentioning UK awards in his lyrics for some reason. BAFTA in this one. Mercury Prize gets namechecked in Things I Won't Get by [spin off supergroup with Franz Ferdinand] FFS.

### 5. PACIFIC STANDARD TIME

✅ **@sparksofficial**
Ron: Not every song about the West Coast need be sunny – this is a foggier view of our home.

### 6. STRAVINSKY'S ONLY HIT

✅ **@sparksofficial**
Ron: The most fractured song of all time – dangerous if you attempt to dance to it. Stravinsky moved to LA and actually lived about 15 minutes away from each of us in Brentwood. Some critics have said I've started looking more and more like Stravinsky, I hope that's a compliment.

### 7. LEFT OUT IN THE COLD

✓ **@sparksofficial**
Russell: Winnipeg rocks! [they sing "Winnipeg is where I'm living/Cold as hell, it's unforgiving"] We've never been to Winnipeg. But it still rocks.

### 8. SELF-EFFACING

✓ **@sparksofficial**
Russell: Ron is self-effacing. FACT. Listen to drummer Stevie Nistor absolutely slamming it in this one! Stevie Nistor has been playing drums with Sparks since 2006, show him some respect! Ron Mael on cheesy organ!

### 9. ONE FOR THE AGES

✓ **@sparksofficial**
Ron: Ok, it's about an accountant's dreams, but don't hate on it for that.

### 10. ONOMATO PIA

✓ **@sparksofficial**
Russell: "onomatopoeia" NOUN: the formation of a word from a sound associated with what is named (e.g. cuckoo, sizzle). But in our song the woman is named Onomato Pia because of her unique communication flair. Get it?

### 11. IPHONE

✓ **@sparksofficial**
Ron: PARENTAL ADVISORY: EXPLICIT CONTENT "Put your fucking iPhone down and listen to me." This tweet is brought to you by 'Twitter for iPhone.' You're probably too occupied with your iPhone to listen to this song. We'll get back to you later.

### 12. THE EXISTENTIAL THREAT

✓ **@sparksofficial**
Russell: Sorry again that this has taken on extra meaning in these strange times.

### 13. NOTHING TRAVELS FASTER THAN THE SPEED OF LIGHT

✓ **@sparksofficial**
Russell: This song actually has two choruses. At the end, in the last cycle of the song, both choruses are laid on top of each in counterpoint. And just for fun, we decided to double-time the instrumental.

### 14. PLEASE DON'T FUCK UP MY WORLD

✓ **@sparksofficial**
Ron: Children's choir vocals provided by the Coldwater Canyon Youth Choir. (No, it's not Russell doubled over and over again.) We Are The World for the year 2020.

In the pink. Ron (sitting) and Russell Mael.

✓ **@Tim_Burgess**

Sparks blew my mind as a kid – no band got close to their sheer off the wallness.

# *Nixon*
## Lambchop
City Slang, 2000

To kick off the Listening Party for Lambchop's *Nixon* album, a GIF of luxuriant, golden honey pouring into a bowl was tweeted – a simple declaration that this was a visual representation of the smooth richness of frontman Kurt Wagner's voice. No arguing with that one. And that video of honey actually captured much more than just the Nashville band's vocals. "Gold" is virtually the first word you hear on the record, as the touching, almost naively simple hope of The Old Gold Shoe opens the album, and golden is the best way to sum up *Nixon*'s spirit.

Emanating a hazy warmth across its ten songs, the record is an embracing hug of golden brass, golden vocals, golden emotions, golden strings and solid gold songs. There's a dash of country twang, an understated pinch of indie cool and some life-affirming, big soul vibes which are, well… golden.

"We were a collective of like-minded individuals content to gather together to have a great time," wrote Wagner (**@lambchopisaband**) during the Listening Party of the source of the atmosphere Lambchop captured on tape. "Making records a part of it was contagious."

With songs such as You Masculine You and The Distance From Her To There, flourishing with swirling strings, gently chopped guitars and Wagner's simple yet affecting vocals, the record felt truly timeless from its very first play, while with the album's centrepiece track, the bittersweet bliss of Up With People, Lambchop had created a song for the ages.

ARTWORK:
Wayne White

| | |
|---|---|
| 1 | The Old Gold Shoe |
| 2 | Grumpus |
| 3 | You Masculine You |
| 4 | Up With People |
| 5 | Nashville Parent |
| 6 | What Else Could It Be? |
| 7 | The Distance From Her to There |
| 8 | The Book I Haven't Read |
| 9 | The Petrified Florist |
| 10 | The Butcher Boy |

Get on up (with people). Kurt Wagner onstage with Lambchop at Somerset House London, in 2009.

**@Tim_Burgess**
Burgess & Wagner. Two uncompromising cops with great record collections. New drama for BBC2, Fridays 10pm.

LISTENING
PARTY
**25 MAY
2020**

**@lambchopisaband (Kurt Wagner)**

[Producer/engineer/owner of Beech House studio] Mark Nevers' influence and production on these tracks cannot be understated. At the time his influences were Joe Meek [Beech House studio partner], John Kelton and the Ramones and that's about it. Ok, maybe Lou Reed too.

**@Tim_Burgess**

I have played this album 1000s of times. Drunken, high, elated and deflated but there is something so solid about Kurt Wagner and at this moment his merry fellow chops' of 11 members.

**@Tim_Burgess**

You Masculine You. A Favourite, the fragility of the falsetto. Impeccable. My main inspiration for Wonderland.

**@MrTomGray [gomez]**

I, like so many others, discovered @lambchopisaband with Up With People. I think it was on a @CitySlang sampler I stole from the storeroom of our dutch label.

**@Tim_Burgess**

Its fair to say Nixon was the most important influence for my input in The Charlatans' LP Wonderland. Hold tight and you'll see x

**@lambchopisaband**

Thanks to Tim for this and bringing the focus back to listening to albums cover to cover. It's why we make them.

# The Lexicon Of Love
## ABC
Neutron, 1982

⚑ When it comes to music, Sheffield always seems to have a way of doing different… better. Pulp, Warp, Arctic Monkeys, The Human League and Richard Hawley are among its artists who have changed the flow of creativity in the UK, and when it comes to 1980s pop, ABC are there, flying Steel City's "do differently" flag too. While London and Birmingham might have been epicentres of New Romanticism's emergence out of punk, Martin Fry and his band evolved something new and entirely cinematic among Sheffield's concrete housing estates. Their debut album, *The Lexicon Of Love*, is the expression of this spirit mixing style, funk, protest and dancefloor glamour to devastating effect. "Let the opening credits roll," declared Fry (**@ABCFRY**) as he dusted off his Lexicon for the Listening Party. "Ladies and gentlemen welcome to *The Lexicon of Love*, bring your own popcorn!"

**ARTWORK:**
Eric Bailey

✍ ABC are presented with discs marking 250,000 sales (not streams!) of Poison Arrow in 1982.

↓ **@Birmingham_81** (below) My £1.50 ticket to see ABC at Birmingham's Holy City Zoo in October 1981 – the week that Tears Are Not Enough was released. Every person packed into that tiny club knew they were going to huge; (below left) Here are my badges which are almost 39 years old.

The Zoo
presents
A.B.C.
on
MONDAY 19th OCTOBER
The Holy City Zoo, Water Street
Birmingham

With ticket £1.50          10 p.m. - 2 a.m.
Without ticket £2.00

## 1. SHOW ME

@ @ABCFRY (Martin Fry)

"Once I needed your love but that was just one thing left on your mind..." Just about sums up the whole album. Here come the castanets. There simply aren't enough tunes with castanets.

## 2. POISON ARROW

@ @ABCFRY

Poison Arrow is the ultimate love revenge tune. Recorded at Sarm East on Brick Lane. Underneath a wig shop. Pre-hipster Brick Lane. It was a dangerous place at night.

## 3. MANY HAPPY RETURNS

@ @ABCFRY

The intro's a bit Raymond Chandler on shoestring. We had an early song called Boomerang about [a] guy going back to his girlfriend, to the scene of the crime. I guess this grew out of that. I sound about 12. Anne Dudley played the electric piano solo. One of the few solos permitted on the album. We were very post punk and anti-solos. We had a manifesto. We were very opinionated back then.

## 4. TEARS ARE NOT ENOUGH

@ @ABCFRY

Recorded at Polydor studios at 1 Marble Arch originally. Our first single. Reached 19 on the charts. Trevor [Horn, producer] tarted Tears up a bit. To say the least. The harpsichord solo in the middle eight gave it a Louis Quatorze feel. Trevor Horn was brilliant throughout. He had a habit of getting the best performance outta you. You could never second best him.

## 5. VALENTINE'S DAY

@ @ABCFRY

Big Brit funk ambitions on display here. Engineered to sound great in Sheffield nite spots like Penny's, Craisy Daisy, The Limit on a Monday night and the Penthouse to name but four. We had a night out with Trevor in Sheffield to show him the importance of the 12inch mix at Penny's, Disco John DJ-ing.

## 6. THE LOOK OF LOVE (PART ONE)

@ @ABCFRY

Bowie hung out [at] the sessions at Good Earth studios. He was visiting Tony Visconti during his Baal phase. He suggested to Trevor that I should keep leaving unanswered answer machine messages in the bit which ended up being a monologue. We'd do anything to avoid a guitar solo.

## 7. DATE STAMP

@ @ABCFRY

Living in Sheffield you felt invisible, off radar and undetected. I guess that's where all that peacock flamboyant new romantic stuff came from. A generation saying Look at Me. That's where the gold suit definitely came from.

## 8. ALL OF MY HEART

@ @ABCFRY

We recorded the strings at Abbey Road. Trevor said that if we added full orchestra it would go to number one. He gave me an IOU for a million pounds as a guarantee. The single got to number 6 so I never got to cash it in. Anne Dudley's string arrangement are incredible. When Trevor asked who should do the arrangements Anne raised her hand and volunteered. I think it was one of the first things she worked on. Her piano playing on this is sensational.

## 9. 4 EVER 2 GETHER

@ @ABCFRY

Can I hereby claim that I invented the 4 ever way of spelling stuff? This predates Prince and I Would Die 4U. I saw the chorus lyric on the wall of the lift at Hyde Park Flats in Sheffield. I lived at 99 Roland Row. A very synth type of address if you think about it. Just goes to prove you can find romance in the strangest of places, there's poetry everywhere, in amongst the concrete.

## 10. THE LOOK OF LOVE (PART FOUR)

@ @ABCFRY

Here comes The Look Of Love part 4. There were 3 more versions of the Look Of Love. Credits roll. More Pizzicatos and a fond farewell. Ladies and Gentlemen, thank you for your kind indulgence.

# *I'm All Ears*
## Let's Eat Grandma
Transgressive, 2018

⊥ Aside from bands with family members, Rosa Walton and Jenny Hollingworth (both **@thelegofgrandma**) might have some sort of record for inter-band, long-term friendships. The pair met while in the reception class at their Norwich primary school and have been making music together since they were 13. However they have come along way from early compositions like The Angry Chicken… well sort of. The duo's second album *I'm All Ears*, is an assured, emotionally mature dazzling record of dark synths, intoxicating loops and passionate vocals. Yet it also possesses a vibrant sense of fizzy energy and good fun, that you suspect The Angry Chicken shared too. Walton and Hollingworth – along with a several of their collaborators, including The Horror's Faris Badwan (**@FARISADAMBADWAN**) – revealed how they hatched this beast of an album.

**ARTWORK:**
Yanjun Cheng

---

**LISTENING PARTY**
**29 MAY 2020**

### 1. WHITEWATER

🔘 @thelegofgrandma
Rosa: I have the best memory of Jenny & I being in my bedroom the day after we got back from Secret Garden Party, Jenny beginning to write this track and me lying in bed having a nap, and thinking how cool the track sounded in my sleep.

🔘 @thelegofgrandma
Jenny: After working on so many pop songs I think I really wanted us to write something different and instrumental. I imagined we were writing music for a horror film opening sequence. Maybe that's how I felt after such an intense weekend!

### 2. HOT PINK

🔘 @thelegofgrandma
Jenny: We wrote this track & It's Not Just Me with [late producer and artist] SOPHIE and Faris Badwan [The Horrors]. At the time me and Rosa were both really frustrated with a lot of the sexism we had been subjected to when we had been touring "I, Gemini" and decided to translate that into lyrics.

🔘 @FARISADAMBADWAN (Faris Badwan)
Sophie Rosa Jenny & I worked on Hot Pink together – I remember when the song was a really early sketch the original lyric was "slime green" or "lime green" ha ha. But when Hot Pink came up it was immediately a keeper.

### 3. IT'S NOT JUST ME

🔘 @thelegofgrandma
Rosa: We started writing this song at SOPHIE's house in LA & it's got a really sunny, bright feel about it because of that – it's always really interesting to me how the environment you write a track in is reflected in the music. We'd come straight from SXSW, and I was figuring out how to navigate my first proper relationship whilst also touring.

### 4. FALLING INTO ME

🔘 @thelegofgrandma
Jenny: We really wanted to write a dancey track, and so every time one of us made a new version of Falling Into Me we'd invite the other one round and make them dance to it all the way through to see if it was upbeat enough.

All the better for seeing you... Let's Eat Grandma's Rosa Walton and Jenny Hollingworth (with drummer Remi Graves) onstage in Glasgow in 2018.

### 5. SNAKES & LADDERS

⊘ @thelegofgrandma

Jenny: In 2015 we went to see Portishead at Latitude which, alongside our tour manager Lee always playing Protection by Massive Attack in the van, had a massive impact on me, and inspired me to get into trip-hop. This track started out as an assignment I did for college where we had to study a genre and then write a track in the style of it. We then re-used the lyrics and melody from it and made it into a different song.

### 6. MISSED CALL (1)

⊘ @thelegofgrandma

Jenny: There's a lot of lyrics on the album about phone calls and we thought this bit of music sounded like a ringtone, and would make a nice little interlude.

### 7. I WILL BE WAITING

⊘ @thelegofgrandma

Rosa: It was autumn when we wrote this track, and I always get this thing in autumn where I feel very nostalgic and think back to all the autumns that have passed. This track is very reflective, likc you're seeing an overview of a period of life in retrospect, and feeling relief that things are starting to change.

### 8. THE CAT'S PYJAMAS

⊘ @thelegofgrandma

Jenny: It felt like there was a distinct lack of cats on the album, so we thought we'd add one.

### 9. COOL & COLLECTED

⊘ @thelegofgrandma

Jenny: This song was written at college and is about the crushing insecurity of being a teenager and liking someone who you don't think could ever like you back.

### 10. AVA

⊘ @thelegofgrandma

Rosa: We wanted to write about mental health, it being a theme in our lives with us and our friends. Ava is about the pain of not being able to reach someone you love when they're struggling, and coming to the acceptance that sometimes there's only so much you can do.

### 11. DONNIE DARKO

⊘ @thelegofgrandma

Jenny: Donnie Darko is still my favourite track that we've released. A lot of time has passed since we wrote the lyrics but they still feel really relevant. The music soars but the lyrics are about loneliness & losing control.

# *Force*
## A Certain Ratio
Factory, 1986

After the impact of Joy Division, there was the danger that all the bands on the same indie label, Factory, might permanently live in that artistic shadow. The fact the opposite happened is in part down to the taste of the label's co-founder Anthony H Wilson, and, of course, each act's own unique spirit. After all, *A Certain Ratio*'s music is too joyful to live in the darkness. Embracing the post-punk starkness that bands from Greater Manchester seemed to ooze in the early 1980s, Jeremy Kerr (vocals/bass – **@jez_kerr**), Andy Connell (keyboards – **@andyconnell**), Martin Moscrop (guitars/synth/trumpet – **@martinmoscrop**), Anthony Quigley (saxophones) and Donald Johnson's (drums – **@Dojo007**) addition of tropical rhythms and bold brass ensured a dazzling heat emanated from their songs, infusing minds and bodies with vibrant energy.

**ARTWORK:**
Johnson Panas

**LISTENING PARTY
4 JUNE 2020**

### 1. ONLY TOGETHER

**@martinmoscrop**
This was the first of ACR's albums where Jez took on full time singing duties and I know Jez dislikes his vocal on this track but I love it. It was Andy Connell's only full album with us and his input is immense on keys. [Andy Connell left ACR after this record to focus on Swing Out Sister]

**@jez_kerr**
I tried listening to the album, but I couldn't get past the first few words. This is my first listen in 35 years. I've never liked hearing my voice back, prior to this album I just stood in a corner and played the bass.

### 2. BOOTSY

**@martinmoscrop**
Named after Bootsy Collins because of Jez's backwards bass line and the working title stuck. When we demoed this we thought the chorus would sound good with a female vocal. Andy and Corinne were in the early stages of Swing Out Sister so we asked her.

**@swingoutsister (Corinne Drewery)**
If I sound nervous on Bootsy its because it was one of the first times I'd been in a recording studio.

### 3. FEVER 103°

**@andyconnell**
Haha – that intro..the Akai S900 demo disc! Shakuhachi and frogs. Sounded like the future. Didn't sound like the future a few weeks later when Peter Gabriel put the bugger all over Sledgehammer.

**@martinmoscrop**
Never has a title been so relevant than now. Moody verse with a very poppy chorus, something ACR have always been quite good at.

**@jez_kerr**
Title pinched from Sylvia Plath, my all time favourite writer

### 4. NAKED AND WHITE

**@martinmoscrop**
The first time I got to use my Korg Guitar synthesiser. This was also Tony's first full album with us and his soprano sax lines are all real hooks. He worked very closely with Andy Connell and they had a strong Zawinul/Shorter (Weather Report) feel.

### 5. MICKEY WAY

**✓ @Dojo007 (Donald Johnson)**
Here we have the Akai S900 doing its thing again (The Rhino's) as we called them the Ooh & ahh which was my voice via some FX that was sampled into the machine & triggered live on my bass drum & snare as we recorded the song.

### 6. AND THEN SHE SMILES

**✓ @jez_kerr**
I pinched the title and some words from the novel Less Than Zero by Brett Easton Ellis. It's the only tune for me that started on an acoustic guitar, probably why it's quite a repetitive chord progression, the guitar only had 2 strings, the E and the G.

### 7. TAKE ME DOWN

**✓ @martinmoscrop**
Another moody one and whenever we produce something moody, Donald always uses rim shots. It has a very rocky chorus which was a new thing for ACR at the time.

### 8. ANTHEM

**✓ @Dojo007**
Love this dreamy soundscape...

**✓ @andyconnell**
My favourite I think. Completely out of character.. I got to play that lovely piano in Yellow and have a DX7 break. Bit of a Hermeto tribute later on too.

**✓ @martinmoscrop**
Another bad acid trip ending. We were always good at those.

### 9. SI FIRMI O GRIDO

**✓ @Dojo007**
Got ya whistles ready for the next track...

**✓ @andyconnell**
That riff. Donald's brother Derek had a nifty little playing style on the clarinet. Chipping, he called it. I'd never seen it but I loved it, so this was my slightly cack-handed attempt at something similar.

**✓ @martinmoscrop**
Si Firmi A live favourite and we always work the audience into a frenzy with this at the end of our set. It contains 2 WW2 chants my Dad taught me, the brass line, get out of bed, you lazy buggers and the chant, I had a good job and I left. My Dad should get a writing credit.

Funked up: A Certain Ratio live on The Tube, January 1986.

# The Decline Of British Sea Power
## Sea Power
Rough Trade, 2003

⚓ From line-up changes to a new name, a switch of hometowns to staging a Listening Party for every one of their albums, Sea Power are a band who keenly embrace the new. Originally from Kendal in Cumbria, Martin Noble (guitar), Matthew Wood (drums) and brothers Yan (vocals/guitar) and Hamilton Wilkinson (bass) (all using @SeaPowerBand) relocated to Brighton when they formed their band, before going on to release an impressive eight albums – with Abi Fry on viola and cornet player Phil Sumner augmenting the line-up – together. In that time they've also staged memorable shows that have involved cymbals thwacked by foliage and a nightly stage invasion by a giant bear (well, bear costume). They also embraced the Listening Party, though in very Sea Power fashion as they have opted to do every record but not in order. Aptly their final party of their initial run was for their first album, *The Decline Of British Sea Power*, released before the group removed the national prefix from their name, so batten down the hatches for a record which launched a thousand songs (well, Sea Power are getting close to that mark)…

**ARTWORK:**
Alison Fielding

---

LISTENING PARTY
6 JUNE
2020

### 1. MEN TOGETHER TODAY

✓ @SeaPowerBand
Noble: This choral intro was taken from the middle eight of blackout, and then layered up with more vocals. It was lovely to [be] getting my younger brother to sing some parts. We enjoyed the cheeky factual/homoerotic song title.

### 2. APOLOGIES TO INSECT LIFE

✓ @SeaPowerBand
Noble: Apologies to Insect Life was one of the very few songs BSP have created from jamming.That was back when me and Woody had a flat in Portslade above a butcher's shop. We'd get together and play for ages, loud and wild. Good times.

### 3. FAVOURS IN THE BEETROOT FIELDS

✓ @SeaPowerBand
Noble: This one was a real latecomer to the album. Almost didn't make it on there. Glad it did. A nice 'little' number.

### 4. SOMETHING WICKED

✓ @SeaPowerBand
Phil: I just love this song. The mystic of it. I only found out the meaning of some of the words/lyrics a couple of years later from Yan. It just got better and better. Keep guessing!

### 5. REMEMBER ME

✓ @SeaPowerBand
Noble: Yan wrote nearly all of Remember Me. He wrote the brilliant opening guitar riffs. Hats off to Yan!

### 6. FEAR OF DROWNING

☑ **@SeaPowerBand**

Yan: Fear of Drowning was written during the floods in Lewes and after a strange hallucination of chaos on the beach being watched floating in the sea of Brighton.

☑ **@SeaPowerBand**

Noble: My wife Vicky recorded the sea to the start of Fear of Drowning. I think [it] even gets a credit on the album. Another nice memory.

### 7. THE LONELY

☑ **@SeaPowerBand**

Yan: The Lonely is one of 3 songs co-written by Geoff Goddard from beyond the grave. The best piano player who ever lived and probable writer of hit Telstar.

### 8. CARRION

☑ **@SeaPowerBand**

Noble: The electronic hi-hat in Carrion was inspired by Salt n Pepa's 'Push it'. It was also the first album i ever stole. Sorry mum.

### 9. BLACKOUT

☑ **@SeaPowerBand**

Noble: I loved the Suede song My Dark Star and saw some similarities between Blackout and that song. Some songs on this album have 'Timpani Drum Rolls' on them. Blackout, Lately, etc. They are played on a really basic Casio Keyboard, of course. Budget Timpani, alright!

### 10. LATELY

☑ **@SeaPowerBand**

Yan: The first song I ever wrote on the piano. Wooden Horse the second! Couldn't play though but came out ok. One hand at a time. [At the epic end] We were gonna throw the kitchen sink in [this] but it was already broken from playing percussion on it with a heron.

### 11. A WOODEN HORSE

☑ **@SeaPowerBand**

Noble: It was a real pleasure to have Geoff Goddard, one of Joe Meek's co-writers, work alongside us, washing dishes in the University Canteen [our pre band job]. He came to one of our shows and he loved this song. I love it too. Great work, Yan.

Green shoots. Sea Power performing their debut album at the 2003 Reading Festival.

# Lighting Matches
## Tom Grennan
Insanity, 2018

⚡ In an era when algorithms seem to have as much say in success as actual rhythms, Tom Grennan is a timely reminded that pop music should be more than a box-ticking exercise. Emerging from a teenage indie record collection, the Bedford singer-songwriter first struck through as a guest vocalist on Chase & Status's *All Goes Wrong*. His smokey, powerful voice was there for all to hear, but Grennan also had his own vision to back it up. While happy to combine his own ideas with co-writers in the pursuit of songs that speak to millions, he is no pop puppet as a raw beating heart underscores all the collaborations that make up his debut album *Lighting Matches*. Yes, he makes music he wants the masses to hear, but he wants them to feel something real too. Proof of that passion – and its impact – was the Listening Party Grennan (**@Tom_Grennan**) staged for his first record. Not only did he move fans and people new to his music alike, he also moved himself. "I'm actually in tears here," he wrote as he returned to 12 songs that really have changed his life. "Thanks for saving me everyone. I mean that from the bottom of my heart."

**PHOTOGRAPHY:**
Olivia Rose

---

**LISTENING PARTY
9 JUNE 2020**

### 1. FOUND WHAT I'VE BEEN LOOKING FOR

✔ @Tom_Grennan
I went into a writing session with Jordan Riley, and it just seemed to fall out of the sky. It's weird because at the time I wasn't having it all. Jordan came up with the hook and it was done within an hour. I sent it across to my manager Dan Dawkins and didn't really think anything of it as I moved on to the next day. He was proper gassed, as was my A&R Ali. When i revisited in a different head space it actually blew me away. When Sky Sports Super Sunday picked the track up it was all systems go, my two loves collided, music and football.

### 2. ROYAL HIGHNESS

✔ @Tom_Grennan
I was in a studio off Tottenham Court Road with the writer/producer team Laconic. I randomly saw the word royal highness on a sticker which was randomly stuck a draw in the studio. BOOM.

### 3. BARBED WIRE

✔ @Tom_Grennan
Written with my guitarist Danny Connors in Northampton at Stalker Studios. He actually brought the chorus to the table but the rest of the song was emo as fuck, so I attacked the chorus from scratch and cooked up a treat.

### 4. RUN IN THE RAIN

✔ @Tom_Grennan
To me it's about finding your way in the world when you are down on your luck, and fighting against the odds to succeed. Noel Gallagher was in the studio next door and advised me to stop smoking like a chimney as it will fuck my voice for recording.

### 5. ABOARD

✔ @Tom_Grennan
Probably my favourite song on LIGHTING MATCHES. It's about loyalty but it's also about not letting anything get in your way when you are on a roll.

On fire! Tom Grennan performing live in Sheffield in 2018.

### 6. LIGHTING MATCHES

◉ @Tom_Grennan

Weirdly despite being the title track of the album, it might be my least favourite on the record. songs about starting something new and lighting a match to create a fire, no matter what the end game maybe.

### 7. LUCKY ONES

◉ @Tom_Grennan

One of my favourite songs. About two people who are lucky to find love and are deeply lost in cupid's arrow. Drowning in the good stuff of love this is. Ruins the heart strings.

### 8. SOBER

◉ @Tom_Grennan

It's about me and my relationship with drink and also my struggle with being sober in love if that makes sense? Produced by one of the greats Fraser T Smith. He brought the fire on the production side, a proper joy to share a studio with him.

### 9. I MIGHT

◉ @Tom_Grennan

Written by the American legend Diane Warren – she's probably the most successful American writer of all time. Diane is the funniest person I've ever met, proper wild. Diane had the songs for years and after hearing me sing in the room pulled it out of a draw and said 'you're the voice I've been waiting for', which was a massive confidence boost.

### 10. MAKE 'EM LIKE YOU

◉ @Tom_Grennan

Wrote this sing with Joel Pott who was in the band Athlete, Joel is super sound. The song's about a robot world and I'm the only human left in it, everyone else is manufactured. Writing that out sounds mental ha ha ha, but I know what I mean.

### 11. SOMETHING IN THE WATER

◉ @Tom_Grennan

The song is personal to me. I had been beaten up and was suffering with depression, and this song was a message to myself that there was something better for me than this existence. I needed to pick myself up and get going. writing the lyrics were super cathartic to me.

### 12. LITTLE BY LITTLE LOVE

◉ @Tom_Grennan

Last song I wrote for the record with Joel Pott, and I felt that I was really beginning to hone my craft as a writer. Felt like a big Oasis song to me. Imagine Liam Gallgher singing this song supported by the boss Bonehead and Noel Gallagher!

# *Statues*
## Moloko
Echo, 2003

Róisín Murphy (**@roisinmurphy**) is the unofficial queen of Listening Parties… nah, actually it's official! Her enthusiastic typing has given us vibes and insight into her glitter-flecked solo albums, each a sophisticated dancefloor- and mind-filler, making her playbacks some of the biggest hashtag hoots we've enjoyed. Though everyone wondered what would happen when she agreed to revisit *Statues*, the final album by her first band, Moloko. A true break-up record, not just for the group but because her relationship with co-leader Mark Brydon had ended too, while *Statues* shimmers like Moloko's other releases, it is underscored by a real sadness. Would it be a case of tissues at the ready? Well, there were tears… but there was laughing and dancing too; this was still a Róisín Murphy Listening Party after all. "Very proud, happy we made it through," she declared of this bittersweet album for her. "Perfect end to the most incredible few years of my life…"

PHOTOGRAPHY:
Elain Constantine

"Vintage Zandra Rhodes In case you're wondering…" revealed Róisín Murphy of her outfit, as she and Mark Brydon were swept up ahead of making Moloko's final album.

## 1. FAMILIAR FEELING

@roisinmurphy

Spectacular arrangement! Dramatic intro. What has she got? She's got the lot! My goodness what an intro! I'd forgotten. Eddie Stevens there playing his massive organ, Mark on bass... I can see him playing it! Paul Slowly on drums. We gave Eddie Stevens full rein with the strings on this record, you should have seen him conducting a full orchestra to his own arrangement, genius spidery wizard that he is.

## 2. COME ON

@roisinmurphy

I used to like it when [guitarist] Dave Cooke used to sing 'Half past three and it's time for tea, and a mini roll on the side' in rehearsal. I love a mini roll. You can hear Mark singing along with me on the talkbox, which is a very basic kind of vocoder where you have a big tube from the synthesiser straight into your mouth. The sound is generated from tube in your mouth. Plenty of spit down that tube.

## 3. CANNOT CONTAIN THIS

@roisinmurphy

This is one of my favourites, feels like a baby cos I had to fight for it. The incredible Arik Marshall who I met when I sang with Macy Gray at Brixton Academy at her request. One of the most amazing musicians I've ever seen at work. He came into the studio, sat down and pleasured the guitar. Fully. It's the slight wonkiness of the song we were unsure of. But it's that, that makes it timeless.

## 4. STATUES

@roisinmurphy

This song is almost too hard to talk about, it's really Mark's song. He wrote the vocal melodies and most of the lyrics, along with the music as he always did. Might be the best thing we ever did.

## 5. FOREVER MORE

@roisinmurphy

What can I say about Forever More? I really have to give it to Eddie Stevens on the arrangement here, astonishing. When it came to making an edit for the radio it was almost impossible. It's a perfect song for me to sing live. I LOVE singing this song live.

## 6. BLOW X BLOW

@roisinmurphy

The balance between the live musicians and the electronic is pretty perfect. There was a very great deal of thought and attention that went into mixing this record. Everything about this album was massive. No expense spared. It almost killed us.

## 7. 100%

@roisinmurphy

A touch camp this one. I took a long time trying to sing 'je t'adore'. French is not natural to me! I felt dead sophisticated when I'd accomplished it. Oh my god I can just see Eddie absolutely molesting the keyboards on this outro.

## 8. THE ONLY ONES

@roisinmurphy

This for me is one of the best tracks on the record, everything in the pocket – it sits just right and I love the mad middle section. This is the thinking man's choon, trust me! There's plenty of references in my lyrics that people wouldn't be looking for, I was well aware that the title of this song is also the name of a fantastic band.

## 9. I WANT YOU

@roisinmurphy

Francois Kevorkian [DJ and producer] said he absolutely loved this album, he said it reminded him of Hear My Dear by Marvin Gaye!!!!! Which was also a breakup album. Of course Marvin has a song called I want you. It's one of my favourites of all time. She's got the lot! Oh my God I sound like I'd do anything, if only I were as much of a pushover in real life. Mind you I've had my moments.

## 10. OVER & OVER

@roisinmurphy

Oh God no! I can't take it. Too much drama! Seriously though what about these strings for fuck's sake? What about these drums too, one of my all time favourite drum takes. It was astonishing to see him do that. Paul Slowly forever.

# ex:el
## 808 State
ZTT, 1991

⚑ A nexus of crossing musical cultures and a signpost for the future, 808 State's album *ex:el* really captured a moment of creative fluidity. Pioneers of the late 1980s electronic music scene, the Manchester band featuring, at the time, Graham Massey (**@state808**), Martin Price, Darren Partington and Andy Barker, had made the most of the burgeoning sampling technology and digital recording equipment to create a landscape of light melodies and crystalline beats that not only attracted crowds to the dancefloor but grabbed the attention of their fellow artists. Enthralled by their vision, New Order's Bernard Sumner provided guest vocals on this record, while in terms of an 808 statement for their future they also recruited the vocalist from Icelandic band The Sugacubes just before she was due to make a solo album. That was, of course, Björk. 808's remaining member and head of State, Massey, provided a glimpse of the creativity that was in the air when they first spread out *ex:el*.

**ARTWORK:**
Tony Panas & Trevor Johnson

Music Complete. New Order's Bernard Sumner onstage with 808 State (see Spanish Heart, right).

## 1. SAN FRANCISCO

◉ **@state808 (Graham Massey)**
Titled after a passing resemblance to the theme tune to The Streets Of San Fransisco, 70s TV cop show. The discordant lead line played on the Mini Moog by our label boss Trevor Horn.

## 2. SPANISH HEART

◉ **@state808**
Bernard had already appeared with us live earlier on in 1990 when we supported Happy Mondays at G Mex – he sang Magical Dream.

## 3. LEO LEO

◉ **@state808**
We had [dub record label] On-U Sound vibes in mind while writing this – I remember we went and mimed to Leo Leo on Granada Reports – Bob Greaves Xmas Party  on local TV just after we finished mixing it.

## 4. QMART

◉ **@state808**
We met Bjork on the set of The Word in London – she played us some brass band demos of what would become Debut with a view to writing beats later in the year. We asked her to come up to Manchester and experiment in the studio.

## 5. NEPHATITI

◉ **@state808**
The two Nephatiti samples come from a museum record and a performance of Wayne Shorter's Nephatiti by the group Circle. We are the Music Makers is from Willy Wonka, later to be used again by Aphex Twin. That phrase subsequently adopted as an electronica community website.

## 6. LIFT

◉ **@state808**
Called that because it referenced lift muzak – anodyne futuristic – Barry White meets Kraftwerk. Taking a few turns on the way. We always had a camp track on our albums.

## 7. OOOPS

◉ **@state808**
The first track with Bjork. Again the Casio Midi Guitar and Acoustic Guitar. She went wondering around Cheadle Hulme in the rain to write the lyrics. She came back with a tin of sprouts and ate them out of the can.

## 8. EMPIRE

◉ **@state808**
Called Moogsville/Bounty on the track sheet. Trying out a new drum machine called an Alesis SR16 – we do love our mellotron flute sounds.

## 9. IN YER FACE

◉ **@state808**
Sums up those times perfectly for me – future facing and powerful and a pop smash.

## 10. CÜBIK

◉ **@state808**
This was written and related as a B side to In yer face and EP of Dance earlier that year – Tommy Boy got some good dance floor feedback from the New York Clubs and we re lined it up to be a single.

## 11. LAMBRUSCO COWBOY

◉ **@state808**
We were chasing a similar vibe with this track. Darren was christened The Lambrusco Cowboy by Big Ron our manager after his favourite tipple.

## 12. TECHNO BELL

◉ **@state808**
I heard an awesome live version of this recently performed by [New Orleans style band] Mr Wilson's Second Liners again in a street parade situation – a lesson in rhythm.

## 13. OLYMPIC

◉ **@state808**
This was commissioned by Manchester City Council in 1990 for the City's bid for the 2000 Olympics. Manchester [found out it had] lost the bid at the first open air gig at Castlefield Arena in the Centre of Manchester. Coronation Street stars wept and [Australian airline] Qantas' windows got smashed when Sydney Australia won. Great gig though. One of many for us on that sacred site. A version of this became the theme to The Word on Channel 4.

# *Settle*
## Disclosure
PMR/Island, 2013

Before he became an auctioneer, Howard and Guy Lawrence's dad played in several rock bands. Fortunately, they took influence from only one of his jobs, so rather than house clearances, it's house music that brought the brothers together as Disclosure. With their mother's work as a session musician further enhancing the family's musical reputation, it was always a fair bet that creating exciting new sounds as DJs and producers was always going to take precedence over trading in antiques. The Surrey brothers do, though, possess the ability to uncover a gem or two as their debut album *Settle* proves, boasting an array of key samples and guest vocalists that range from Sam Smith to Jessie Ware. Celebrating the seventh birthday of their debut record, the Lawrence brothers (**@disclosure**) Settled up with a little help from Twitter.

ARTWORK:
Roxie Pandora

## 1. INTRO/WHEN A FIRE STARTS TO BURN

**@Tim_Burgess**

When A Fire Starts To Burn

**@disclosure**

Right! & it starts to spread! @ericthomasbtc is the MAN!

## 2. LATCH

**@disclosure**

We're Latched on!

**@TheTalesOfRyan [fan]**

Zed Bias sample oi oi

**@disclosure**

Well spotted!

## 3. F FOR YOU

**@disclosure**

Absolute throwback!

## 4. WHITE NOISE

**@disclosure**

White noise – opened every show on our Caracal tour with this one. Always gets the vibes started.

## 5. DEFEATED NO MORE

**@disclosure**

Wrote this together with [Friendly Fires'] Ed Macfarlane above our dad's auction house, as we did with many of the songs on Settle. No central heating or running water. Spiders everywhere!! it was grim but we were lucky to have that space.

## 6. STIMULATION

**@disclosure**

Little known fact, the vocal is actually the incredible Lianne La Havas singing A Long Walk. She literally sung it acapella in front of our drooped jaws. We took it, chopped it up & boom!

## 7. VOICES

**@disclosure**

Garage garage garage. No shame haha played this at nearly every DJ set we played for 3 years straight. Memories!! Shouts to [vocalist] Sasha Keable.

## 8. SECOND CHANCE

**@disclosure**

FACT – Kelis on the sample… and now, she's on track 1 of our 3rd album! Funny how life works.

## 9. GRAB HER!

**@disclosure**

Our all time favourite J Dilla on the vocal sample.

## 10. YOU & ME

**@disclosure**

Jimmy Napes [producer] and Eliza Dolittle [vocals]! That's Guy singing bv's too ;) his big moment lol

## 11. JANUARY

**@disclosure**

January with Jamie Woon! We wrote this and then went for a banging pub lunch. Been good mates ever since - still think about that day every 22nd Jan. Also… biggest Jamie fans EVER still. Check his 2 albums if you haven't already. Insanely good.

## 12. CONFESS TO ME

**@disclosure**

The banger of the bunch [with Jessie Ware]. Remember Noel Gallagher saying he loved this song to us at Glastonbury but we didn't play it that night. He said 'show was good… but it could have been better' lol classic. Jessie Ware's new album just dropped too. In love with the final song in particular. Check it!

## 13. HELP ME LOSE MY MIND

**@disclosure**

Last tune! Help Me Lose My Mind ft. The wonderful Hannah from London Grammar.

(far left)
**@disclosure**
Think this picture was taken just as we finished making our song You & Me. Jimmy Napes [producer] and Eliza Doolittle [vocals]!

(left top and bottom)
**@disclosure**
Guy signing the first Settle vinyls. That took a while!

# Levelling The Land
## Levellers
China, 1991

✠ If there was one band who understood the collective power of the Listening Party, then it was the Levellers. Named after a movement from the English Civil War that argued for equal rights, the Brighton band are famed for a cooperative approach that tapped into the communal free party scene that emerged at the same time as they formed. The music on Mark Chadwick (vocals/guitars), Simon Friend (guitars/vocals), Jeremy Cunningham (bass), Jonathan Sevink (fiddle) and Charlie Heather's (drums) second album embraces both their influences and their times as it pumps up their folkish roots with an all-embracing expression of freedom – encapsulated in many ways by the indie disco anthem and record opener One Way. To celebrate the album, Mark Chadwick (**@levellermark**) threw a free party of the listening kind.

**ARTWORK:**
Jeremy Cunningham

LISTENING
PARTY

9 JULY
2020

**1. ONE WAY**

✅ **@levellermark (Mark Chadwick)**
It's all about the boom boom, and the chorus, the lyric was from a Dutch fan who just said there's only one way etc.

**2. THE GAME**

✅ **@levellermark**
The chorus was inspired by Ennio Morricone who passed this week. Belter!

**3. FIFTEEN YEARS**

✅ **@levellermark**
We recorded this a few weeks after [the main session] up in London, it fitted so it went on the later represses. Jez bass hero on this track.

**4. THE BOATMAN**

✅ **@levellermark**
This always sounds really slow now, we recorded this one on the studio stairs for that chilled hippy vibe man. Jon and myself cycled to the studio Ridge farm north Sussex. Oh yes, there was the free parties back then, thus this bit with Steve B on dodge…

**5. LIBERTY SONG**

✅ **@levellermark**
This one came out of a few jams, before and the middle came out of nowhere in the studio, angry fellas.

**6. FAR FROM HOME**

✅ **@levellermark**
This one was the most fun to record as I recall, came just after [producer] Al Scott said 'It's all shit and I'm going to bed.' We stayed up and practiced this.

**7. SELL OUT**

✅ **@levellermark**
Singer actually singing a song.

### 8. ANOTHER MAN'S CAUSE

🔘 **@levellermark**
Love Si's harp on this, he and Jon worked really hard on the instrumental middle still blows my mind.

### 9. THE ROAD

🔘 **@levellermark**
This songs about all the people we meet on the road up until we got to record it in Ridge Farm, which had a swimming pool. Happy days.

### 10. THE RIVERFLOW

🔘 **@levellermark**
Is that blood? Sweat? Maybe. No, it's Charles Charlie Charles, playing the double kick drums on this one.

### 11. BATTLE OF THE BEANFIELD

🔘 **@levellermark**
Last one, thanks everyone, that went by very fast, but real great tune from the pen of Si to end on, and happy days then. Here's to happy days in the future. PEACE.

↓

**@levellermark**
The view of the studio from the desk upstairs, Ridge Farm Studio plus animals.

# Phonography
## R. Stevie Moore
Vital, 1976

With at least 300 released albums to his name, R. Stevie Moore's sobriquet as the "Godfather of home recording" feels something of an understatement. The Nashville singer-songwriter is a one man lo-fi music industry. Self-recording and self-releasing much of his material, his prolific DIY approach is anything but amateur and there is a great, inventive artistry to Moore's work. His limited home recording set-ups inspires him to push in bold creative directions as he innovates and enthrals. *Phonography* was his first "official" album, collecting together recordings from the self-released opening salvos *Stevie Moore Often* and *Stevie Moore Returns*, and Moore (**@RStevieMoore**) delivered a frantic, improvised and idiosyncratic Listening Party worthy of the spirit behind the early creative bursts that launched an artist whose influence is writ large across the DIY scene and beyond today.

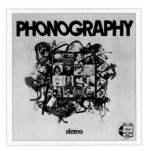

**ARTWORK:**
Vital Records

← California Rhythm. R Stevie Moore celebrates the release of his first "proper" album.

○

@Tim_Burgess
Me and the amazing
R Stevie Moore.

## 1. MELBOURNE

✔ **@RStevieMoore**

All instruments 'n all by the composer. Melbourne has no real connection to the city. Just a title. No, never been.

## 2. EXPLANATION OF ARTIST

✔ **@RStevieMoore**

PHO-NOG-RAPHY is a solo work, overdubbed on Sony & Teac 1/4 track stereo tape recorders at leisure. The artist used Hagstrom & Gibson electric guitars, a Fender bass, Univox and Elka synthesizers, Magnus chord organ, Victor spinet piano, Premier drums, and various toy devices.

## 3. GOODBYE PIANO

✔ **@RStevieMoore**

Recorded November 5, 1975. Goodbye piano – you're too overweight for me to take you with me/ Into the hills, where rings are round the collar/ They tell me not to worry 'bout the dollars/If it were not for you, I wouldn't bother, so. Caught THE RESIDENTS' ears with Goodbye Piano, and they lived happily ever after.

## 4. EXPLANATION OF LISTENER

✔ **@RStevieMoore**

Convo with found tape.

## 5. CALIFORNIA RHYTHM

✔ **@Tim_Burgess**

Anyone been to an @RStevieMoore live show??? (Maybe you saw me playing percussion)

## 6. I'VE BEGUN TO FALL IN LOVE

✔ **@RStevieMoore**

I CANT KEEP UP BEGINNING TO FALL IN LOVE AGAIN!

## 7. THE SPOT

✔ **@RStevieMoore**

Fake news advert banking for euros and tories.

## 8. I WANT YOU IN MY LIFE

✔ **@RStevieMoore**

ALL TIME TOP HIT

## 9. I WISH I COULD SING

✔ **@RStevieMoore**

I WISH I COULD SING

## 10. THEME FROM A.G

✔ **@Tim_Burgess**

High five to the high priest of lo fi.

## 11. THE VOICE

✔ **@RStevieMoore**

THE VOICE? SELF-OBSSESSED? DAMN STRAIGHT!

## 12. SHOWING SHADOWS

✔ **@RStevieMoore**

Search the video on YouTube for this one.

## 13. SHE DON'T KNOW WHAT TO DO WITH HERSELF

✔ **@RStevieMoore**

Influences 1974-76? SPARKS, ROXY MUSIC, 10CC, ELO, ROY WOOD, PILOT, MACCA, QUEEN, GUSTAV MAHLER

## 14. THE LARIAT WRESSED POSING HOUR

✔ **@RStevieMoore**

Again, find the wonky video!!

## 15. I NOT LISTENING

✔ **@RStevieMoore**

Whew, thank god that's over!!!

## 16. MR. NASHVILLE

✔ **@RStevieMoore**

Many thanks to Harry Palmer, Ira Robbins, Jon Child, Chris Cutler, and Victor Lovera. Tim, you are a Godsend. xoxo @thirdmanrecords reissue? Jah Quite??

## 17. MOONS

✔ **@RStevieMoore**

NOT LO-FI. LO-IF. D.I.WIFI. Today is a highlight of my life. Take care of yourselves, everybody. Take care of me. CIAO NOW.

# Prince Of Tears
## Baxter Dury
PIAS, 2017

It's 3am… In another light, with others eyes this club might look a bit shabby. Frayed at seams, stained, smelly, sticky, suffocated by oppressive prosaic music and would-be playboys. Tonight though, it's a palace, because it's 3am and for the first time in ages… months, you're not at home. Alone. That is where you have been because someone broke your heart. Actually, they didn't just break it. They shattered it leaving shrapnel-like memories of your old relationship scattered around your life, ready to stab you in your rawest wounds when you least expect it, dragging you back down into the despair as you keep trying to climb away from. But not tonight… because it's 3am and you're out. You're holding court. So ignore the reflux rising up your throat, the table of half drunk glasses and the sweet, alcohol-infused sweat peppering your forehead, you are the coolest person here. Tonight you can be anyone you want: rogue or royal. You've got the swagger, the danger, the grace, the charm. Your confidence is back and your internal monologue is helpfully reminding you that you're NOT thinking about the person who broke your heart… No… You're not thinking about them… Definitely not… Because this is your new life, your new domain… This is your heartbreak. You are the Prince Of Tears.

Delusional and hopeful. Loving but injured. Full of vitriol, though brimming with forgiveness. Intensely personal yet brutally accessible. Baxter Dury's fifth album proved both a private meditation into the very real relationship breakdown he experienced just before writing this album and his most ambitious work to date. *Prince Of Tears* was not just a title, it was a mind-set, a melodrama, a catharsis, a comedy… a family album. "This one is slightly more bedded in real feelings," Dury (**@baxterdury**) coyly admitted as the Listening Party for his most candid album started. Those feelings were "a bit of common heartbreak," he revealed on *Prince Of Tears*' release. "You can have loads of ideas

PHOTOGRAPHY:
Tom Beard

| 1 | Miami |
|---|---|
| 2 | Porcelain |
| 3 | Mungo |
| 4 | Listen |
| 5 | Almond Milk |
| 6 | Letter Bomb |
| 7 | Oi |
| 8 | August |
| 9 | Wanna |
| 10 | Prince of Tears |

(←)
**@baxterdury**
This is a posey pic of me pretending to direct the orchestra.

@baxterdury
Mike Moore [co-producer], Dani [Spragg, engineer], Joe [Davies, conductor] and moi.

or get all political, but actually there's nothing more simply damming than heartbreak and nothing else is more life-changing," he suggested. "You could get shot and split up with your girlfriend in the same week and you'd still think about your girlfriend. So that happened, but I used it." Opening with the stunning rebound groove of Miami, for his record's woe Dury initially wrong foots us. His epic prose poem weaves its way between disco keys, '70s cinematic strings and heartbeat bass offering the listener the chance to tumble down the rabbit hole into Dury's anti-Wonderland.

Our heartbroken narrator has reinvented himself as a foul-mouthed, cocksure ladies man, but his confidence is only the product of alcoholic excess, fatigue and emotional repression, and after the opener's stunning crescendo the rest of *Prince Of Tears* reveal the real emotional depths heartbreak has left him in.

"Amazing how strong Miami is in hindsight, but I still like the rest," tweeted Dury, who for whom the Listening Party was like walking through a hall of mirrors for emotion, revisiting the warped, strange reflections he had created of himself in song three years earlier.

"It's like badly funded Channel 5 doc," he tweeted of the alternative narratives that infuse each of album's snapshots. Not that the *Prince Of Tears* is a bleak affair. Underscoring these "biographical film soundtracks for an imaginary film about myself, which is fictional" is a wry humour and inspired wordplay. As heartbreak fades on the record (and happily in real life), the faux over confidence of Miami is replaced at the end of the album by optimism. A counter point to the nocturnal emotional delusion of Miami, the equally cinematic strings of the closing the title track leaves the record facing a hopeful dawn. Dury's heartbroken narrator is not out of his hole yet, but there's a wisp of closure and the first thoughts of *tomorrow*. It is like a morose pop song version of the beach at the end of *La Dolce Vita*. The light has come, obsession is slipping and the world somehow feels bigger and brighter again.

LISTENING PARTY

24 JULY 2020

@baxterdury
I love these songs a lot even though it's more a shopping list of uncomfortable moments. This all really happened.

@baxterdury
I'm not very good at spelling or singing or cooking. I sound good on twitter though.

@stoksie (Paul Stokes, journalist)
Prince Of Tears is a really subtle & effective closer. It's not out of the hole, but there's a wisp of optimism so the emotional credits can start to roll. It's the heartbreak, morose pop answer to the beach at the end of La Dolce Vita. Bravo.

# *Gulu City Anthems*
## Otim Alpha
Nyege Nyege Tapes, 2017

✠ With the joyful spirit that surges through Otim Alpha's songs it is easy to see why he became such a successful wedding singer in his native Uganda. Nuptials, and the parties after them, can draw an attendance well into the thousands, so someone with adungu-playing skills and infectious vocals is clearly a must for any newlyweds. Though when Alpha wasn't performing at these parties – or at funerals – he was augmenting the Uganda musical tradition with new, electronic elements he created by recording on his computer. These recordings slowly won him a following beyond his own borders, to the point that 11 year's worth of material was brought together as the album *Gulu City Anthems*, gaining the singer international acclaim.

With his country's experience of disease and a litany of wars – including ongoing campaigns by armed rebels – part of the strength of Alpha's music is that he also confronts the realities of Uganda life alongside his more celebratory tracks. "Gulu is where I was born. It's in northern Uganda and it just became a city," Alpha (**@OtimAlpha**) tweeted of this record's connection to his home. "The album is called *Gulu City Anthems* because it tells the story of what is happening in Gulu, the good and the bad." Alpha paints a musical picture as vivid as it is euphoric.

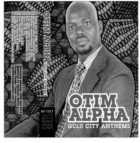

**ARTWORK:**
Nyege Nyege Tapes

LISTENING
PARTY
**26 JULY
2020**

### 1. GANG BER KI DAKO

✓ @OtimAlpha
This song is telling my brother to get a woman to stay with, because here we believe when a home has a woman that is a good home.

### 2. ANYOMO LABEL (PAILYEC)

✓ @OtimAlpha
This is a wedding song. The groom is telling his clan that today he's married the woman he loves, In Uganda weddings are really big, with 100s or 1000s of people. I write a song for the couple and perform it. People have a lot of fun.

### 3. BILABER

✓ @OtimAlpha
This is a funeral song. We also compose songs after people die to remember them with. In the past, there were wars in Gulu between [warlord] Joseph Kony and his LRA [Lord's Resistance Army], and Yoweri Museveni, the president of Uganda. Many people lost their lives and up to now there are many people still missing or suffering because of what happened.

### 4. LOK LOBOCWERO CWINYA

✓ @OtimAlpha
I wrote this song because I see too much suffering around me. In Uganda for example I see a lot of orphans who have no family to support them, no education, sometimes nowhere to get food.

### 5. TOO WIYE MING

🔘 **@OtimAlpha**

This is another funeral song, Anywar is the name of the man who died and his family asked me to write it. Too means death, I was saying death is a jealous person.

### 6. TONI G

🔘 **@OtimAlpha**

In our culture you can marry as many women as you can take care of. This is a story about a man who was married to four women but he didn't take care of them.

### 7. WILOBO LANYI

🔘 **@OtimAlpha**

This is a song with a message for young people. In my country we've had a problem with HIV and other sicknesses, so many young people have been getting those problems because they keep running with different men or women. In this song I'm telling young people if you get someone who loves you with a true heart, even if they're young, they're old or they have no money, stay with them.

### 8. COO OROMO

🔘 **@OtimAlpha**

This is [a] song for when there was a big fight, men were fighting and the message was going to women and children at home that they should not worry. Our men are strong and we have reserve forces, I'm saying, we will still win.

### 9. CAM KI LAWOTI II

🔘 **@OtimAlpha**

This song is saying let's be nice to each other, if you have something little share with your friends, especially when you are eating food & your brother is hungry. Instead of eating alone, share.

### 10. AGIKI NE TYE

🔘 **@OtimAlpha**

This is about how some people think nothing changes but you have to work hard & something will happen. I was sending a message that if you listen, in this world nothing is permanent, don't give up.When the war was happening here many people were so worried that nothing would change, but I was telling them everything will have an end.

### 11. KODI PA BARIKIYA (KWAN)

🔘 **@OtimAlpha**

This is a song about a guy called Dr Anyala, he got a masters, PhD, he had been studying since primary school, he was always concentrating on studying. He really wanted to become someone and now he's finished. He told me to compose a song about his name because he was saying it's good for people to know how good school is.

🔀 **@OtimAlpha**

My favourite instrument is an adungu – I love the sound and the way it looks.

⬇ **@OtimAlpha**

Uganda is beautiful & there are many places for tourists to visit too.

# *Doko Mien*
## Ibibio Sound Machine
Merge Records, 2019

PHOTOGRAPHY:
Dan Wilton

Fuelled equally by West African folk tales and cutting-edge electronics, Ibibio Sound Machine's music exists thanks to the global exchange of ideas and art. Yet the London band possesses a strong, irrepressible identity all of their own too. With an initial cultural exchange between frontwoman Eno Williams (**@IbibioSound**) and John McKenzie (bass), Tony Hayden (trombone/keyboards), Scott Baylis (trumpets/keyboards) and Max Grunhard (saxophone/keyboards), Ibibio Sound Machine injects Afrobeat, post-punk, African disco and funk and electronics experiments to weave its own jubilant sonic tapestry. The London-born Williams' upbringing in Nigeria adds an additional edge to the band's passionate lyrics, mixing folk stories recounted by her mother, with personal experience and inspiration from modern visual artists like the late Jean-Michel Basquiat, to create songs that swap effortlessly between English and Ibibio (a language used around Nigeria's southern cost). Staging a Listening Party for their third album *Doko Mien* (which means "tell me"), Ibibio Sound Machine's musical sunshine shone brightly.

**@IbibioSound**
About this time, roughly a year ago, we were partying with everyone at @bluedotfestival.

They work very hard. Ibibio Sound Machine onstage in Oregon in 2019.

LISTENING
PARTY
**26 JULY
2020**

## 1. I NEED YOU TO BE SWEET LIKE SUGAR

**@IbibioSound (Eno Williams)**
First track. I Need You To Be Sweet Like Sugar, kinda self-explanatory. I sing in Ibibio, the native language from my part of South-Eastern Nigeria. There are hundreds of dialects in Nigeria, I felt it was important to represent where I'm coming from in my music.

## 2. WANNA COME DOWN

**@IbibioSound**
About how much we look forward to seeing you [live] all again.

## 3. TELL ME (DOKO MIEN)

**@IbibioSound**
This one actually came from an argument I was having with the guys about how I should be singing a particular track we were writing. So I was like "tell me how you want me to do it then!"

## 4. I KNOW THAT YOU'RE THINKING ABOUT ME

**@IbibioSound**
Ok not exactly party vibes, but it's about how social media is both a blessing and a curse.

## 5. I WILL RUN

**@IbibioSound**
Who do you run to in times of trouble?

## 6. JUST GO FORWARD (KA I SO)

**@IbibioSound**
It's a mantra about perseverance. No point thinking about yesterday, gotta move on and accept change, especially right now!

## 7. SHE WORK VERY HARD

**@IbibioSound**
This is a folk story about the dangers of being enslaved by money. A girl loves a friend's necklace, borrows it from her and then loses it. I draw a lot from stories I heard as a child.

## 8. NYAK MIEN

**@IbibioSound**
Means "let me be", letting go of every negativity and only allowing positive vibes in your head. Hope you're all keeping your spirits high!

## 9. KUKA

**@IbibioSound**
This song was conceived by our trombonist @trombony [Tony Hayden], he definitely bagged himself a properly appropriate Twitter handle!

**@SharmanSomerset [fan]**
Even more so if he's really skinny!

**@IbibioSound**
Not as much as he used to be!

## 10. GUESS WE FOUND A WAY

**@IbibioSound**
This is kinda about the idea of speaking to people in a language most don't understand, but that music has its own power of communication.

## 11. BASQUIAT

**@IbibioSound**
This was a piece we got asked to write for the closing of the first Basquiat exhibition at Barbican in London [in 2017], so we tried to convey something of what we felt about his life and work in a song. Was the closer of our set... when we had gigs!

67

# *Velveteen*
## Transvision Vamp
MCA, 1989

⚓ There have been signature moves, but a signature shade of lipstick? Exploding across screens in the late 1980s, from Saturday morning TV to Top Of The Pops and beyond, Transvision Vamp frontwoman Wendy James could not be ignored. However, while her pink lips might have made the first impression, it was her band's pop art sounds that lingered in minds. A mix of Nick Christian Sayer's fuzz-filled guitars, hooky choruses and James' cooler-than-thou vocals, with their second album Velveteen, Transvision Vamp – completed by bassist Dave Parsons and drummer/keyboard player Tex Axile – skilfully straddled the divide between video-driven mainstream success and something more edgy. Donning her signature shade, James (**@THEWENDYJAMES**), who once got Elvis Costello to write an entire record for her and now has her own band, returns to Transvision Vamp's trashy pomp for a Listening Party every bit as frenetic as Velveteen itself.

**PHOTOGRAPHY:**
Peter Ashworth

---

**LISTENING PARTY
5 AUGUST 2020**

**1. BABY I DON'T CARE**

✅ **@THEWENDYJAMES**
WE'RE ON!!!!!!!

**2. THE ONLY ONE**

✅ **@THEWENDYJAMES**
The actual video is shot in the Ladbroke Grove TABERNACLE... this amphitheater in Italy is massive and rarely allowed to be in... I can't remember where....

**3. LANDSLIDE OF LOVE**

✅ **@THEWENDYJAMES**
The Pink Lipstick!! btw... that was a thing!

**4. FALLING FOR A GOLDMINE**

✅ **@THEWENDYJAMES**
This was actually from NICK SAYER'S first band Midnight & The Lemonboys... You know Nick Sayer and his previous band were headed for success, they were touring with @U2 and he slipped a disc and was laid up for 9 months during which time, @u2 become famous and Nick's band

disbanded! THIS SONG is lovely!!!!! I became friends with Bono when I made the Elvis Costello [written] record Now Ain't The Time For Your Tears.

**5. DOWN ON YOU**

✅ **@THEWENDYJAMES**
I think we were quite tough actually... so much attitude in 1989!! I am LOVING down on you!!!!!!! fuck... need to start playing this in gigs again!!!!!!

**6. SONG TO THE STARS**

✅ **@THEWENDYJAMES**
It's sensational! listening now, it's clear to see why this album resonated with everyone, EVERY SONG!!!!!! wow.

**7. KISS THEIR SONS**

✅ **@THEWENDYJAMES**
I'm pretty sure that guitar part in KISS THEIR SONS is borrowed from???????/ addicted to love????/ Robert Palmer??????? or?????/ I love it... it's about the UK music press... I think.......... I'm sure....

Visionary. Wendy James onstage in Hammersmith in 1989.

### 8. BORN TO BE SOLD

**@THEWENDYJAMES**

Remember [video for] this in BARCELONA on the RAMBLAS!! I love the dancing girls and the old lady in it... Spain was good for TVV... legendary ..

### 9. PAY THE GHOSTS

**@THEWENDYJAMES**

Fuck - it's an amazing album!!!!!! THANK YOU ALL FOR REMINDING ME!! Maybe I'll do a gig playing the WHOLE OF VELVETEEN TOP TO BOTTOM... wow... yeah... my blood's up... I could do this easily...

### 10. BAD VALENTINE

**@THEWENDYJAMES**

ok BAD VALENTINE... I have to tell you: THE BASS is upright bass by Herbie Flowers who played on Lou Reed's Walk On The Wild Side, isn't it heaven!!!! He lives in Brighton and plays one man shows on a Sunday... go and see him! he's one of the music business legends... and a true gent!

### 11. VELVETEEN

**@THEWENDYJAMES**

wow... recorded at TOWNHOUSE STUDIOS on the Goldhawk road!!! West London! #VELVETEEN IS MAGNIFICENT!!!!!!!!! THANK YOU ALL... FOR MY WHOLE LIFE! THANK YOU!!!!!!! This is awesome!! I love it! thank you! what a brilliant thing you've got going here... it's such a pleasure!!!!!!!

**@leema_seven [fan]**

I'm thinking of going platinum #velveteen

**@THEWENDYJAMES**

where the hell did you get that?!! when I left London I left my platinum and gold discs outside, stupidly and they were gone in the blink of an eye.. West London, probably ended up at RECORD AND TAPE EXCHANGE NOTTING HILL GATE... xo

# *Infinity Land*
## Biffy Clyro
Beggars Banquet, 2004

**ARTWORK:**
Chris Fleming

⚓ Considering their festival bill-topping, arena-touring status, it is hard to remember a time when Biffy Clyro were thought of as a weird little outfit. Of course, with eccentric characters inhabiting their lyrics and a love of bold imagery, the Scottish trio are anything but the definition of run of the mill, but when they first emerged, Simon Neil (vocal/guitar – **@BiffyClyro**), Ben Johnston (drums – **@amphibiben**) and James Johnston (bass – also **@BiffyClyro**) were something of a fringe act. Take the cover of their third album for example, it features a mouse wearing a gas mask… Ok. Biffy's move from this outsider realm – without compromising the integrity or their vision – to become one of the world's biggest rock acts has been largely accomplished by people simply hearing and loving their songs. Brash and in the best rock traditions, there is such a welcoming, warm core to their songs that fans seem to fall for passionately when they hear them – so much so, even *The X Factor* borrowed their 2010 single Many Of Horror (When Worlds Collide) to provide winner Matt Cardle with a Number 1.

Among those who were key in getting people to give Biffy Clyro a listen was the British journalist Daniel Martin, who passionately wrote about the band for NME, eventually getting them on the cover of the music weekly several times, which in turn led to more radio and live exposure.

"Dan was such a supporter of our band. He gave us our first ever good review in NME and fought our corner for a long time," explained Biffy's Neil at the start of what would prove to be a very different and very emotional Listening Party. Stunning his family and friends – along with many others in the music industry – Martin had passed away suddenly aged 41 just a month earlier, prompting Biffy to stage the playback of *Infinity Land* in his honour. "Dan was always wanting to turn *Infinity Land* into a comic or something. Wish we had," added the singer, explaining the choice of tribute. The Listening Party shined a light on one of Biffy Clyro's often overlooked but crucial albums, something Daniel Martin would truly have loved.

LISTENING
PARTY
19 AUGUST
2020

Mon the Biff. James
Johnston, Simon Neil
and Ben Johnston.

### 1. GLITTER AND TRAUMA

**@BiffyClyro**
Simon: Opening and closing songs are the most
important. Figure them out, the album will tell you
what it wants.

**@amphibiben (Ben Johnston)**
We started the album this way because we wanted
people to think they'd got the wrong CD by a
different band. We sure made ourselves easy to
like didn't we? Si got flung around by a giant man
in the video for this, that wasn't acting. Love it.

**@BiffyClyro**
James:  I still have a scar from the video!

### 2. STRUNG TO YOUR RIBCAGE

**@BiffyClyro**
Simon: I wanted to write a song that used every
feet on the guitar. This is it!

**@amphibiben**
Such Fond memories of recording this at Monnow
Valley Studio with the mighty [producer] Chris
Sheldon in under three weeks! So much fun and
an incredible studio too.

### 3. MY RECOVERY INJECTION

**@BiffyClyro**
Simon: A reggae groove was so wrong it was right.
Dan Martin would compare this record to Girls
Aloud. I love how his mind worked. As passionate
about both. We had fun shooting this video in
Austin, Texas. Like an acid trip.

**@amphibiben**
I'm guessing this song wins first prize for daftest
video, but what a joy to shoot over in Austin,
Texas. Pretty much the hottest I've ever been. Si's
acting is phenomenal of course. Still one of my
favourite outros ever.

⬆
**@tourmanagerneil
(Neil Anderson)**
Only One Word
Slow-Mo video, filmed
just outside of London
in late November
2004. Paul Williams.
The fourth single.

## 4. GOT WRONG

◉ @BiffyClyro
Simon: My hair recedes at the horns!

## 5. THE ATROCITY

◉ @BiffyClyro
James: The Atrocity was my first go at fretless bass – not easy!

◉ @amphibiben
I remember getting to use my wee spring drum on this track, lovely tone.

◉ BiffyClyro
Simon: It's spreading from my lungs! This song fell out quickly. Find that hard to believe listening back

## 6. SOME KIND OF WIZARD

◉ @amphibiben
I don't remember feeling like we made weird music back then.

◉ @BiffyClyro
Simon: This felt like a straight song to us. We wanted it be the "big single" Fleetwood Mac vibes. Hats off if you clap in time.

## 7. WAVE UPON WAVE UPON WAVE

◉ @amphibiben
I remember Jamie Lenman [frontman of rock band Reuben] playing this song with us at King Tuts in Glasgow and completely nailing it. He did however add his own harmonies... cheeky boy. I always loved the fleetin serenity here. Harmonics galore.

◉ @BiffyClyro
Simon: An attempt at Beach Boys...

## 8. ONLY ONE WORD COMES TO MIND

◉ @BiffyClyro
Simon: This still feels good. This might be our heaviest outro ever. Pure Pantera!

## 9. THERE'S NO SUCH MAN AS CRASP

◉ @BiffyClyro
Simon: Male voice choir!! We recorded this drunk on a Saturday night.

◉ @BiffyClyro
James: The great Chris Sheldon let me record Simon's vocals for 'Crasp' what an honour.

◉ @amphibiben
Si and James recorded this one weekend whilst Chris was home in England. Turned out pretty damn good!

## 10. THERE'S NO SUCH THING AS A JAGGY SNAKE

◉ @BiffyClyro
Simon: John Peel debuted Jaggy. It blew our minds. This was my attempt at Bohemian Rhapsody. We didn't get close exactly... we found another destination.

◉ @BiffyClyro
James: Jaggy is still one of my favourites to play live – love it.

## 11. THE KIDS FROM KIBBLE AND THE FIST OF LIGHT

◉ @BiffyClyro
Simon: Kibble's opening riff has every fret on the guitar played at the same time. Reverse of Strung To Your Ribcage. All these titles would appear to me at night. Pictured strange B movie posters. Gareth [Jones] from Tetra Splendour [Welsh band

also called People In Planes] on trumpet. We then asked everyone to sing in extreme accents. Listen closely.

⊘ **@amphibiben**
How many accents can you hear in this ensemble coming up?

### 12. THE WEAPONS ARE CONCEALED

⊘ **@BiffyClyro**
Simon: A fade in... More trumpet. Hard to resist. It was hard to play this slow.

⊘ **@amphibiben**
60s metal with trumpets, of course. Once again with this album, you've no idea where the song is going next. I love it so much.

⊘ **@BiffyClyro**
Simon: This album is about constant movement.

Biffy Clyro staged their listening party in honour of the late journalist Dan Martin, who was an early champion of the band.

⊘ **@Tim_Burgess**
It's beautiful to remember our friends through the music they loved. It means they never really go away.

### 13. PAUSE IT AND TURN IT UP

⊘ **@amphibiben**
You could swim in this song. Beautiful. X

### 14. TRADITION FEED (HIDDEN TRACK)

⊘ **@BiffyClyro**
Simon: This is nightmare folk music!

⊘ **@amphibiben**
Should have put huge drums on this.

⊘ **@BiffyClyro**
James: This has been an amazing trip down memory lane, and very emotional... miss and love you guys.

⊘ **@BiffyClyro**
Simon: Straight up, we would not be where we are without Dan's love, support and understanding. He made us believe in what we were doing. Forever grateful. Love you Dan. Miss you Dan. You were a special, sweet soul.

# *Bicep*
## Bicep
Ninja Tune, 2017

Having begun life as a night out when the duo DJ-ed all over town, then a music blog unearthing and sharing Italio disco and techno gems, *Bicep* "the album" by Bicep "the band" was a much-anticipated affair. Childhood friends Andrew Ferguson and Matthew McBriar (both **@feelmybicep**) had steadily built their reputation with a series of releases on influential dance labels, including their own Feel My Bicep, before finally landing their self-titled debut. Filled with sleek, pleasure-seeking electro the Belfast duo have found favour with audiences on and off the dancefloor, as they created tracks that dancers could lose themselves in while also making sonic space ripe for headphone explorers. Exactly three years on from *Bicep*'s release, the pair threw a Listening Party to celebrate the flexing of Bicep from blog to band.

ARTWORK:
The Royal Studio

Flex. Bicep onstage at Coachella Festival in 2017.

**@feelmybicep**
All that gear made at least one appearance on the album.

## 1. ORCA

◉ **@feelmybicep**

Orca is probably the last one we finished on the album, it all came together fairly quickly if memory serves us well. All the melody in this track is comprised of 3 or so layers all gated together off our 909 hats, their distinctive choke gives the vocals a very unique open and close rhythm. We've tried this since and never sounded as good.

## 2. GLUE

◉ **@feelmybicep**

This one was was started a few years before we even started working on the album but had sooo many different iterations before we eventually ended up here. We actually did the drums and then vocals first, only recording the pads at the very very end which is the opposite to how we normally work. Silkie Carlo who recorded the vocals is a civil liberties and privacy activist.

## 3. KITES

◉ **@feelmybicep**

Was recorded pretty much in one go on a modded korg poly 800s and (then) new modular setup, it's a mix of running triggers through the vcf on the mod and running another through the modular and effecting it through that.

## 4. VESPA

◉ **@feelmybicep**

Samples an old documentary about counter cultures in Northern Ireland… add into that a lot of tape and phaser passes.

## 5. AYAYA

◉ **@feelmybicep**

Haha funny listening back how happy we were writing this. You really realise after writing for a few years how hard it is to get into that care free state. We used the yamaha dx200 on this, which we spent over 2 years trying to get on ebay, ours came from Russia… They seem more common now but at the time they were like gold-dust.

## 6. SPRING

◉ **@feelmybicep**

Looking back probably a bit too long for an album track this one haha, def a nod to our more dancefloor stuff before this.

## 7. DRIFT

◉ **@feelmybicep**

We recorded this when we bought our new tape echo, at the time we were looking @ natural tape phasing and lots of experimental artists like Basinski & Steve Reich. Mixing polyrhythms & time signatures we were unnatural with at the time.

## 8. OPAL

◉ **@feelmybicep**

Really wanted to make a bigger melody and really strip back the drums for a track, funny – thanks to Four Tet how this one has really grown post release of the album.

## 9. RAIN

◉ **@feelmybicep**

Another rhythm experiment, layering 3 separate wonky tape delay recordings of the juno 60 together, super simple but was such a nightmare to mix from all the tape noise. Even the vocal took forever to get the resonance out of it.

## 10. AYR

◉ **@feelmybicep**

Another track with Amy Spencer and still a fav of ours, that adds a slightly different flavour to the album. The drums are actually mostly our voices through our make noise erbe-verb [synth module], such a fun hands-on reverb to mess with.

## 11. VALE

◉ **@feelmybicep**

We did so so so many versions of this, the final version ending up a lot more stripped out than we probably ever intended. It's a bit of a nod to Miami freestyle with a UK twist.

## 12. AURA

◉ **@feelmybicep**

The original unreleased Bicep, it definitely took the edge off finishing the album in a sense because we knew this one was already being anticipated quite heavily online. This was originally a beatless track, we never considered it having drums when we wrote the melody. We were listening to a lot of new wave and 80s synth stuff at the time.

# Help
## Various Artists/War Child
Go!, 1995

ARTWORK:
John Squire

⚔ "I wrote it for breakfast, recorded it for lunch, and we're putting it out for dinner," declared John Lennon (see page 172) of the speed which his Instant Karma! single made it from his mind to the record shops. Although not quite as quick as Lennon's blueprint – it was a week rather than a day, though even The Beatle wasn't as fast as he claimed – this speedy philosophy was the guiding principle behind the *Help* album put out by charity War Child in 1995.

Having witnessed news reports from the Balkan war while off ill, record company exec Tony Crean and friends from the industry got together to make a record to raise funds for children impacted by the conflict. Because of the urgency of the crisis, everyone who took part was asked to record their track on Monday 4 September 1995 and get it mixed the next day, so the album could be in the shops by the following Saturday (9 September). Happily, plenty of artists were up for the challenge, including Blur, Oasis, Portishead, Sinead O'Connor, Paul McCartney, Manic Street Preachers, The Charlatans, Radiohead and more, and their contributions meant the album sold 70,000 copies on that very first day on sale. Marking 25 years since the record's rapid release, War Child (**@WarChildUK**) and many of the artists involved came together for a special Listening Party.

LISTENING PARTY
9 SEPTEMBER 2020

### 1. OASIS: FADE AWAY

✅ **@WarChildUK**
This opening track #FadeAway on HELP was also the first one finished. Oasis got their gear set up the night before so as soon as the clock hit midnight they could start recording. They were finished by 8am. This acoustic version features Noel Gallagher on lead vocals. Noel also found time to appear on the final track on the album #ComeTogether, conduct interviews, do a photoshoot and drop Fade Away off at Radio 1 for its first play by Jo Wiley.

### 2. THE BOO RADLEYS: OH BROTHER

✅ **@SiceBooRadleys (Simon Rowbottom)**
I love that "Oh Brother" is a song that isn't available anywhere else but the HELP album. It makes it really special. I remember the mad scramble to get the track mixed and finished before the deadline. It was such a great idea to have it recorded and out within a week. Wish we could have done that with all our songs.

### 3. THE STONE ROSES: LOVE SPREADS

✅ **@WarChildUK**
This is the only recording of 'Love Spreads' with Robbie Maddix on drums. He took the place of Reni who had left the band in March 1995. The album cover is an original piece of artwork created by [the band's guitarist and artist] John Squire for HELP.

### 4. RADIOHEAD: LUCKY

✅ **@WarChildUK**
The first appearance of #Lucky by @radiohead was on HELP. The band wanted to donate their best track which appeared two years later on OK Computer. The band were so happy with the track produced by Nigel Godrich they used the exact same version on OK Computer.

### 5. ORBITAL: ADNAN

⊘ **@orbitalband**

I recorded that vocal from the news on the morning of recording. It was so sad about a [Yugoslav] Dad losing his son. We took the whole 'do it in one day' literally. We wrote and recorded it in one go.

### 6. PORTISHEAD: MOURNING AIR

⊘ **@WarChildUK**

This made it's first appearance on HELP efore being included on Portishead's self-titled second album.

### 7. MASSIVE ATTACK: FAKE THE AROMA

⊘ **@WarChildUK**

Fake The Aroma is a reworking of Karmacoma with Daddy G replacing Tricky's vocals which featured on the original. Robert Del Naja aka 3D also donated an original piece of artwork that was used on the inner sleeve.

### 8. SUEDE: SHIPBUILDING

⊘ **@matosman (Mat Osman)**

We'd been searching for something that we felt would fit the situation. Something beautiful but sombre, political but not ranting. And we all loved Shipbuilding. I knew the Elvis Costello version first but it's Robert Wyatt's version that's always stuck with me. So fragile. So real.

### 9. THE CHARLATANS VS. THE CHEMICAL BROTHERS: TIME FOR LIVIN'

⊘ **@Tim_Burgess**

What a song. Was a real pleasure to record. Gotta love Sky Stone. Hooch!!! Was drink of choice. I recorded my vocals at 6am. Tapes were picked up at 7pm. Then we headed to the Boardwalk (in Manchester) for a night out.

### 10. STEREO MCS: SWEETEST TRUTH (SHOW NO FEAR)

⊘ **@WarChildUK**

This came three years after the band's No.2 UK album Connected, the band weren't creating a lot at the time and were inspired by the sense of purpose to write The Sweetest Truth for HELP in 24hrs.

⊘ **@StereoMcs_Rob_b (Rob Birch)**
Hey it was fun.

### 11. SINÉAD O'CONNOR: ODE TO BILLIE JOE

⊘ **@midnighttone (Tony Cream at Go! Discs who organised the project)**
Always remember Sinead's producer John Reynolds dropping it into Abbey Road and casually saying 'just finished, see if you can use it...' Blew us all away.

### 12. THE LEVELLERS: SEARCHLIGHTS

⊘ **@WarChildUK**

Jeremy Cunnningham [Leveller's bass player]: Searchlights is a song about the struggles of being an immigrant, written by our friend Rev Hammer. It's a tune Simon [Friend, guitarist] always used to belt out in soundchecks so when war child asked us for a track it seemed like the perfect one.

*Help* album press release from 1995.

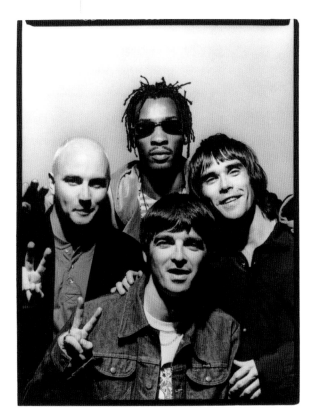

CLOCKWISE FROM TOP:

ROBBIE MADDIX, IAN BROWN, NOEL GALLAGHER     SICE
(STONE ROSES)     (OASIS)     (BOO RADLEYS)

**WAR child**

**HELP**

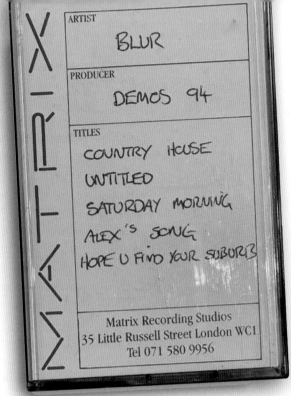

ARTIST
BLUR

PRODUCER
DEMOS 94

TITLES
COUNTRY HOUSE
UNTITLED
SATURDAY MORNING
ALEX'S SONG
HOPE U FIND YOUR SUBURB

Matrix Recording Studios
35 Little Russell Street London WC1
Tel 071 580 9956

(↑)

(Above) Linda McCartney at Abbey Road studio during the recording of *Help*.

(Above right) Home taping. The original Blur demo tape that would be adapted for their War Child track.

(→)

(Opposite top) Paul sandwich. Weller and McCartney pictured with Warchild organiser Tony Crean.

(Opposite bottom) Brian Eno, the executive producer of *Help*.

**13.** MANIC STREET PREACHERS:
RAINDROPS KEEP FALLIN' ON MY HEAD

⊘ @WarChildUK

This was the first track the Manics recorded after the tragic disappearance of Richey Edwards. The track was originally written by Burt Bacharach and Hal David for the classic western Butch Cassidy and the Sundance Kid

**14.** TERRORVISION:
TOM PETTY LOVES VERUCA SALT

⊘ @WarChildUK

Terrorvision: Loved this day, loved being part of this album… top tunes, top bands. Please get involved again, the suffering doesn't ever go away. Peace and love from Terrorvision.

**15.** THE ONE WORLD ORCHESTRA:
THE MAGNIFICENT

⊘ @WarChildUK

The One World Orchestra was Jimmy Cauty and Bill Drummond of The KLF, the track is a drum and bass reworking of [The Clash's] The Magnificent Seven with vocal contributions from Serbian DJ Fleka of radio station B92. Drummond and Cauty had originally wanted Robbie Williams to provide the vocals but he was unavailable as he was on holiday with his mum in Turkey.

**16.** PLANET 4 FOLK QUARTET:
MESSAGE TO CROMMIE

⊘ @WarChildUK

The Planet 4 Folk Quartet were [DJ and producer] Andrew Weatherall (RIP) and [producer] Dave Harrow who teamed up to create Message To Crommie as part of HELP.

Dave Harrow: I played all the instruments including the melodica, we recorded the track in Manchester. The track was made up on the spot, as that's how we usually worked, and recorded very quickly.

**17.** TERRY HALL AND SALAD:
DREAM A LITTLE DREAM OF ME

⊘ @salad_band

Terry [Hall, The Specials] asked us to be involved with him, I sat with him in a tiny office listening to records, he played Mamas & Papas, Dream A Little Dream Of Me and I was hooked. He then drove me home in his jeep. Star struck much? Yes definitely…

**18.** NENEH CHERRY AND TROUT: 1, 2, 3, 4, 5

⊘ @WarChildUK

Neneh Cherry: This record was a LONG time ago in another life before the life before this one. We were hanging out in Stockholm & working with the

late great Christian Falk. Christian took us to the ABBA studio where the original ABBA keyboards were still housed & we decided to make the tune there. An old nursery rhyme came to mind & the tune was born.

### 19. BLUR: EINE KLEINE LIFT MUSIK

🔵 @DaveRowntree (Dave Rowntree, Blur)
Damon had a studio in Busspace – Victorian bus depot in Notting Hill, which had Wonky upright piano that wouldn't tune – you can hear it on the track. We had a demo called I Hope You Find Your Suburb – which hadn't made it on to an album. We re-purposed it as an instrumental.

### 20. THE SMOKIN' MOJO FILTERS: COME TOGETHER

🔵 @WarChildUK
Come Together was recorded at Abbey Road. The Smokin' Mojo Filters are Paul Weller, Paul McCartney, Noel Gallagher, Steve white and Steve Cradock.

# *My Beauty*
## Kevin Rowland
Creation, 1999

⚓ Having written many songs that have changed other people's lives with Dexys Midnight Runners (see *The Listening Party* volume 1 for an album packed full of these) as the 20th century drew to a close Kevin Rowland wanted to share some of the tracks that had saved his.

This should not have been controversial thing. As someone who has freely admitted getting involved in music probably kept him away from a life path that might have led to prison, you can bet an album of Rowland covering some of his favourite music would feature some truly powerful songs. Yet when *My Beauty* was released in 1999, an album the artist appeared on the cover of and performed while wearing a dress, there was a sad backlash. Crowds pelted him with bottles at the Reading Festival until he sharply talked them down, while critics mocked the record on release. Fortunately, 20 years on from the confidence-questioning reception, *My Beauty* has quietly become a firm favourite among many music fans. To celebrate this long overdue acclaim, Kevin Rowland (**@DexysOfficial**) was joined by producer James Paterson (**@JamesMPaterson1**) to stage a Listening Party that allowed everyone to finally bask in the record's great beauty.

**LISTENING PARTY**
**1 OCTOBER 2020**

### 1. GREATEST LOVE OF ALL

✓ **@DexysOfficial (Kevin Rowland)**
Greatest Love sounds, well, great :} I'm hearing this anew. It's weird.

✓ **@JamesMPaterson1**
The Greatest Love of All, I really get it now. Kevin's voice, the arrangement, Pete's magical powers, it's spiritual.

### 2. RAG DOLL

✓ **@DexysOfficial**
Fucking great strings from Fiachra Trench!

✓ **@JamesMPaterson1**
When Kevin asked me to co produce this LP, I thought he was having a laugh. I'd not been out of rehab for that long and was still without confidence, but he promised me copious cups of tea, Kevin's tea is second to none. I used to have to carry my Atari plus monitor in a bag, on the train to Brighton. That was kind of satisfying and heavy man. Kev would meet me and I felt like I was involved. It was exciting. We worked hard in between cups of tea.

### 3. CONCRETE AND CLAY

✓ **@Tim_Burgess**
Nobody but nobody does a talking interlude/intro in a song better than Kevin Rowland. There, I said it.

### 4. DAYDREAM BELIEVER

✓ **@DexysOfficial**
I changed the lyric on the chorus from Sleepy Jean to Little G to my old school friend Little G. Still don't like that break down on day Dream Believer. I like the rest of it though. It's a great groove, love the harmonica and backing vocals.

**5.** THIS GUY'S IN LOVE WITH YOU

✅ **@DexysOfficial** (Kevin Rowland)
Incredible bass playing from John Mackenzie {RIP}. Lovely strings on This Guy! Amazing guitar throughout the album playing from the mighty Neil Hubbard on guitar!

**6.** THE LONG AND WINDING ROAD

✅ **@DexysOfficial**
All the fuck wits who said I was crazy when I released this 'shit album' are very quiet lately. You know who you are.

**7.** IT'S GETTING BETTER

✅ **@Tim_Burgess**
It's Getting Better an absolute highlight. Helped with my times of trouble.

✅ **@huwstephens** (Broadcaster and DJ)
Very proud that I have signed copy of this album on cd, as I asked you to sign it in BBC Wales, Cardiff the year it was released Kevin. Lots of love and thanks for the music.

✅ **@DexysOfficial**
Ah. Nice one man :}

**8.** I CAN'T TELL THE BOTTOM FROM THE TOP

✅ **@DexysOfficial**
This is really moving. So glad to see people appreciating it.

**9.** LABELLED WITH LOVE (I'LL STAY WITH MY DREAMS)

✅ **@DexysOfficial**
Thanks Chris Difford for allowing me to change some lyrics.

**10.** REFLECTIONS OF MY LIFE

✅ **@JamesMPaterson1**
Reflections of My Life, it's my favourite song. I love the video, not cause I'm in it of course. It's serene, beautiful, brings me peace. The whole record does.

✅ **@DexysOfficial**
This is amazing. It sounds completely different when I hear it with you guys. I'm hearing the Beauty in it again!

**11.** YOU'LL NEVER WALK ALONE

✅ **@DexysOfficial**
It's so odd. I hear these songs so differently when we listen collectively. When I listen alone, all I hear is criticisms, but now, I hear the passion and the overall effect of everything combining together to make it what it is. Thanks Tim. Perspective changing!

✅ **@wichitarecs**
(Mark Bowen, Creation/Wichita Records)
Some of the best memories of my life are from the making of this record from Kevin just singing 3 feet away from me in the office. To be so close to my heroes was amazing.

↓
You'll never walk alone. Kevin Rowland at the Reading Festival in 1999.

# Faded Seaside Glamour
## Delays
Rough Trade, 2004

Just before Delays were due to stage their second Listening Party, for their second album *You See Colour*, frontman Greg Gilbert (**@GregDelays**) was taken ill and could not join in. Having been diagnosed with bowel cancer in 2016, he passed away aged 44 just a month later. At the time his brother and Delays bandmate Aaron (**@AaronDelays**) went on with the playback explaining: "I think the most wonderful thing we could do right this now would be to just listen to Greg's voice…" It is in a similar spirit that we can revisit the Listening Party the whole band – bassist Colin Fox (**@Colindelays**) and drummer Rowly (**@Delays_**) joined in too – held for their debut album *Faded Seaside Glamour* a year beforehand. A swirl of indie, synths and Greg's soaring, impassioned vocals, the record exists in a timeless world of its own, as often from melancholic impulses it rises to moments of pure, smile-inducing euphoria. *Faded Seaside Glamour* is a record filled with beauty, but as the title suggests they are not idolised or unattainable ideals, but instead are moments of real, sometimes flawed, beauty that stir the heart and enliven the soul. When this Listening Party took place, it proved a great celebration of a unique record. Now it stands as a tribute to Greg Gilbert and the lives he touched.

**ARTWORK:**
Jeff Teader

Stay Where You Are.
Delays' Greg Gilbert
onstage at the
V2004 festival.

### 1. WANDERLUST

**@GregDelays**

So here we are – Wanderlust – the first song Aaron and I wrote together, remember hearing the steel drums coming from his room and I started writing along with it. From the second it was finished it was going to open the album.

**@AaronDelays**

The steel drum melody was the first thing I ever really wrote. I wasn't part of the band at the time. Mine and Greg's bedrooms were next to each other and he just started jamming along to it one night. It was a happy accident...

### 2. NEARER THAN HEAVEN

**@GregDelays**

When I first wrote this I thought it was about Catholic guilt, now I think it's about finding the transcendent in everyday life – I much prefer that.

### 3. LONG TIME COMING

**@GregDelays**

We wrote it in my folks' garage – Aaron had the riff and it was immediately special. It feels like it was written in about 3 minutes. The lyrics are about a friend of ours who was killed in a car crash in 2003 – love you Steve.

**@AaronDelays**

I dreamt the synth to Long Time Coming. I was having a dream where there was a creaking door, except the creak sounded like the synth I wrote. I woke up at 3am and tried to recreate it, except the sound didn't exist so I had to make that first... I was so fucking excited to play it to Greg the next day.

### 4. BEDROOM SCENE

**@GregDelays**

I remember writing the lyrics in the field next to my parents' house, the melody I think references a Smiths track I can't place at the moment – became a live favourite, ample space for Rowly to flex on the outro :)

**@AaronDelays**

I used to play this piano part to myself when we were getting ready to rehearse. I didn't know how it would work in a song, but everyone just started to play along one day and it just seemed to work.

### 5. NO ENDING

**@AaronDelays**

No Ending was our waltz... I've always loved how this track just lilts and sways like a tide... Aux etoiles mon coeur...

**@Colindelays**

One of my favourite songs Greg has ever written. Along with a never recorded song which I think was called Farraday.

### 6. YOU WEAR THE SUN

**@GregDelays**

Another track originally meant for a b-side, I think it was on the first promos we ever sent out? After Wanderlust this might be my favourite vocal on the album, completed at some ungodly hour at Rockfield. My wife has just confirmed that this is her favourite vocal of mine on the album.

**@AaronDelays**

In the early days I used to just climb on stage to play this and Wanderlust and then leave... I was terrified. I'm not crying again... I've always loved the ending on this, it makes me feel sad and hopeful all at the same once. I'm definitely feeling a bit emotional right now...

### 7. HEY GIRL

**@AaronDelays**

We first recorded this acoustically on an 8 track, it always worked like that. I'd never really sang before this song, and the next minute we were all figuring out 3 part harmonies...

**@GregDelays**

We'd made a 5 track acoustic demo for the label which included this, Satelite's Lost, Whenever You Fall I Die, Overlover and Hideaway. Those tracks have always belonged together.

### 8. STAY WHERE YOU ARE

**@AaronDelays**

This was another synth line that woke me up in the night and kept me awake for hours. I sat up with the dawn chorus trying to make the sound. I don't ever remember the crowd getting the kick in right, we did that just to fuck with you. I remember Robbie Williams ripping this off for his song Bodies. It was all kinds of flattering, probably.

# delays

## ON TOUR WITH CLEARLAKE IN MAY:

7th Zodiac **Oxford**
8th Mamba Café **Taunton**
9th The Mill **Mansfield**
10th The Empire **Middlesborough**
12th Roadhouse **Manchester**
13th Sugarmill **Stoke**
14th Chinnery's **Southend**
15th Brass Monkey **Hastings**
16th Met Lounge **Peterborough**
17th The Square **Harlow**

18th Barfly **York**
19th Barfly **Cardiff**
20th The Garage **London**
21st Charlotte **Leicester**
23rd Louisianna **Bristol**
24th Rock City **Nottingham**
25th Reading Rooms **Dundee**
27th Boatrace **Cambridge**
29th Soundhaus **Northampton**
30th Forum **Tunbridge Wells**

## NEARER THAN HEAVEN
## Debut single – out now

www.thedelays.co.uk     www.roughtraderecords.com     ROUGH TRADE

Long time coming. The poster for Delays first ever support tour and one of their musical foundations. "I can't believe I even found this. This is the original CD I made of the Wanderlust loop and strings to give to Greg to take away and play with," tweeted Aaron of the CDR. "It still has original 2003 dust on it, look."

DELAYS

...uss Ruff

**@Delays_**

Rowly: I loved recording this at Bath Moles. Sounded extra phenomenal in that amazing, scarf-filled winter.

## 9. THERE'S WATER HERE

 **@GregDelays**

Our first appearance on the main stage at IOW fest and the equipment wasn't working so I had to open up with a solo rendition of this. The trauma hit me about a week later. I think it's a companion piece to Wanderlust, the riff and lyric are certainly related…

 **@Delays_**

Rowly: Every single time Greg played There's Water Here – absolute silence from the crowd during the gaps. Incredible.

## 10. SATELLITES LOST

 **@GregDelays**

I was nervous of touring, had a lot of anxiety around travelling, and I think this track is the most direct expression of that. But I think it's a theme that runs through the whole record, the push & pull of leaving.

## 11. ONE NIGHT AWAY

 **@GregDelays**

Written in Edinburgh under an almost exclusive diet of Big Star. If I recall, Geoff Travis [label boss] contacted Jim Dickinson [producer] re the Big Star guitar sound. How long were we at Rockfield? At one point I think we were the second longest residents after The Stone Roses, in my head it was months and months. Second home – big love to everyone there.

 **@Colindelays**

I'm pretty sure I learned how to track deer during the faded sessions.

## 12. ON

 **@GregDelays**

We needed a perfect complement to Wanderlust's opening and Aaron nailed it with this, the sound of ships leaving the harbour, filling out the album concept.

 **@AaronDelays**

I remember writing this pounding synth over an 808 kick drum. I started singing over it in sound checks & asking for loads of reverb on my voice. Later on I realised the synth was the exact same key as the ships I could hear from the docks growing up.

 Forever delays. Colin Fox, Aaron Gilbert, Rowly and Greg Gilbert.

# *Brothers In Arms*
## Dire Straits
Vertigo, 1985

Released just on the cusp of CD's growing popularity, for a long time the floating steel guitar on the cover of *Brothers In Arms* was visible on the racks in every record shop the world over. Its ubiquity is understandable just for the epic intro of *Money For Nothing* – let alone the rest of the '80s-defining tracks – as Mark Knopfler (guitars/vocals), John Illsley (bass), Alan Clark (keyboards), Guy Fletcher (keyboards) Omar Hakim (drums) and Terry Williams (drums) created an album that blended rock atmospheres, guitar pyrotechnics and warm synths. If there was a downside to creating a global soundtrack, it is perhaps in the wake of such success many listeners often now know the London band's songs without realising they are by Dire Straits.

The *Brothers In Arms*' Listening Party – led by Illsley (**@John_Illsley**) – proved a great opportunity to refocus on what made that pale blue album cover travel so far in the first place. "I think [title track] Brothers In Arms is one of Mark's finest compositions and it means so much to so many people because it deals with the futility of war in a simple and poignant manner," the bassist explained as old fans and new listeners were given a unique guide to one of the defining albums of the 1980s.

ARTWORK:
Thomas Steyer

---

LISTENING
PARTY
**7 OCTOBER
2020**

### 1. SO FAR AWAY

✓ **@John_Illsley**
Right now you're listening to So Far Away which is about being on the road and missing the people you love.

### 2. MONEY FOR NOTHING

✓ **@John_Illsley**
Money for nothing was written in an appliance store in New York City, a couple of guys working there were saying this stuff about Michael Jackson... Did Sting really get a writing credit and royalties for his four words on Money for Nothing sounding like Don't stand so close to me? Yes he did and I was amazed at how calmly mark handled it. Sting was on holiday in Montserrat where we recorded the album and came up for supper – just a lucky coincidence that he happened to be there.

### 3. WALK OF LIFE

✓ **@John_Illsley**
People often ask if we had a rockstar life – sex and drugs and rock'n'roll etc – we didn't throw many TV out the window – it was much more than all that, a real pleasure to have so many people enjoying what we created.

### 4. YOUR LATEST TRICK

✓ **@John_Illsley**
I love the sound of Michael Brecker's sax on this track. He put this part on when we got to The Record Plant in New York, where we mixed the album.

### 5. WHY WORRY

◉ **@John_Illsley**

Why Worry was a kind of lovely duet Mark had with himself. This song went through a few different versions before we settled on this one, I just kept taking bass lines out until it was really trimmed down, it demanded a unique approach.

◉ **@Tim_Burgess**

Whoa. I don't think I've ever heard Why Worry? by Dire Straits before – what a song. Discovering a gem like this on an album I don't really know, is what the listening parties are all about. Glad to be sharing the experience with you all.

◉ **@John_Illsley**

Tim – even I listened to the record today with fresh ears, it's been some time since I've heard it.

### 6. RIDE ACROSS THE RIVER

◉ **@John_Illsley**

Ride Across the River was about the murky mercenary business. I liked the courage in the writing of this song, a difficult subject.

### 7. THE MAN'S TOO STRONG

◉ **@John_Illsley**

The Man's too Strong was another example of Mark's writing working on so many levels, you can read into it whatever you like.

### 8. ONE WORLD

◉ **@John_Illsley**

We had a great production team on this, Neil Dorfman had engineered Local hero and Love over gold and I think Mark felt that Neil should share production duties on Brothers, he is a great engineer and producer. We heard that Montserrat was a very good studio owned by George Martin who also owned Air Studios in London, The Police, The Stones, Phil Collins had all used it. Beautiful island, but not many distractions apart from the local disco on a Saturday night.

### 9. BROTHERS IN ARMS

◉ **@John_Illsley**

Being in Dire Straits was a little like being in a bubble, recording & touring took up most of our time, there was a huge response globally to the band, which was a humbling and unique experience.

Brothers in arms. John Illsley (left) and Mark Knopfler onstage in Rotterdam in 1985.

# Faster Than The Speed Of Night
## Bonnie Tyler
Columbia, 1983

From Skewen in Wales to the world's radios, via recording sessions with Meat Loaf's long-term collaborator Jim Steinman, Bonnie Tyler's story is as remarkable and enduring as her mega hit Total Eclipse Of The Heart. The enduring appeal of that track, and the album that brought it to the world, is no accident. Steinman was approaching his peak as a writer and producer (although there's a bit of a very famous lyric on this album that he would recycle a few years later... see right), and members of Bruce Springsteen's E-Street were among those who played on the sessions, though the primary reason for *Faster Than The Speed Of Night*'s success is Gaynor Hopkins, AKA Bonnie Tyler (**@BonnieTOfficial**). And the strength, theatricality and emotions of her vocals have chimes with audiences ever since.

**PHOTOGRAPHY:**
Robert Elsdale

←

Total Tyler. Bonnie
onstage in Paris
in 1983.

## 1. HAVE YOU EVER SEEN THE RAIN?

✔ @BonnieTOfficial

The album was produced by Jim Steinman. When we first met he played me 'Have You Ever Seen the Rain' by Creedence Clearwater Revival. He was trying to see if our music tastes were compatible. It felt right that this track should be first on the album. I met Jim for the first time in 1982. My manager and I went to his penthouse overlooking Central Park. We stepped out of the lift and we were met with a trail of M&Ms leading up to his front door... I knew we were in for a surreal experience. When the record label asked who I wanted to work with, I asked who produced Meat Loaf's Bat Out of Hell. CBS's A&R guy said there's no way he would agree to it. But you don't get anything in life if you don't ask!

## 2. FASTER THAN THE SPEED OF NIGHT

✔ @BonnieTOfficial

The title track was a showcase for the brilliant backing band. Jim picked the players – members of Bruce Springsteen's E-Street Band, Rick Derringer on guitars, and incredible backing vocals from Rory Dodd, Eric Troyer & Holly Sherwood. The incredible high notes you hear at the end are from Holly Sherwood. The sleeve notes call it "vocal wail". Don't know if that really does her justice. Takes a lot of skill to sing like that!

## 3. GETTING SO EXCITED

✔ @BonnieTOfficial

We must have gone through thousands of songs when I was between record contracts in 81-82. My manager at the time, David Aspden, discovered Getting So Excited. With every song we covered, Jim made sure that we gave it our own sound. "I'd do anything for love... but I won't do that!" The beginnings of a song that would become a huge hit for Meat Loaf 10 years later.

## 4. TOTAL ECLIPSE OF THE HEART

✔ @BonnieTOfficial

Jim never did any demos – I learned all the songs beside him at the piano. I'll never forget the feeling when he played me Total Eclipse for the first time. Rory Dodd sang the vocals. I couldn't believe he was offering it to me. We filmed the music video over two days at an old psychiatric hospital near London. The whole place had an eerie feel to it. They used to do electroshock treatment in the cellars, and the security dogs wouldn't go near. It was like they sensed something. The place was called Holloway Sanatorium. Think it's all apartments now.

## 5. IT'S A JUNGLE OUT THERE

✔ @BonnieTOfficial

For 'It's a Jungle Out There' Jim wanted to capture a kind of reggae feel, so he brought in a new band of jazz players to record with us.

## 6. GOIN' THROUGH THE MOTIONS

✔ @BonnieTOfficial

You think you've heard everything the album has to offer and then he throws in a children's choir. Jim uses everything but the kitchen sink in his production. Blue Öyster Cult did the original in 1977. This was the other song that Jim played to me the first time we met in 82.

## 7. TEARS

✔ @BonnieTOfficial

Duet coming up next with Frankie Miller. Frankie Miller was the first artist I ever saw live on stage. I have been lucky enough to record so many of his songs over the years, and Tears was the very first. I think this was my first ever duet. Frankie wrote Tears as a goodbye love letter. It works well as a duet – you get both sides of the story.

## 8. TAKE ME BACK

✔ @BonnieTOfficial

Take Me Back has the longest note on the album. You'll know when you hear it. If I could go back in time, I'd probably have asked for the E Street Band's autographs.

## 9. STRAIGHT FROM THE HEART

✔ @BonnieTOfficial

It was an incredible experience recording Faster Than The Speed of Night. What topped it off for mc was having the chance to record something by Bryan Adams. He came into the studio to watch me record Straight From The Heart. That was nerve wracking!

# *Anthem*
## Toyah
Safari, 1981

A coming together of Tim's Twitter Listening Party and one of the artists who understood the need to engage, entertain and connect people during the Covid-19 lockdowns just had to happen. In response to people's isolation, pop icon Toyah Willcox reached out via YouTube, creating a new weekly tradition for us all to keep. Her Sunday Lunch sessions with husband Robert Fripp, yes him of prog rock pioneers King Crimson, became appointment viewing as the pair, sporting appropriate fancy dress, blasted their way through a cover each week before everyone tucked in to their roasts. Renditions of The Prodigy's Firestarter, The Who's My Generation and Guns N Roses' Welcome To The Jungle, along with agony aunt sessions and, of course, Toyah's outfits became must see online TV. Like a Traveling Wilburys of the lockdown entertainment, Tim's Listening Party and Willcox finally came together, as taking a break from leaping around by her Aga to other people's songs, Willcox (**@toyahofficial**) gave us a playback of her… *Anthem*.

**ARTWORK:**
John Gordon

Anthemic. Toyah, and the Hammersmith Odeon all set for her 1981 tour.

---

**LISTENING PARTY**
**10 OCTOBER 2020**

### 1. I WANT TO BE FREE

**@toyahofficial**
A young person's guide to Anarchy. I deeply needed to express my belief we're all utterly unique. When it comes to personal preferences in life we have the right of choice. My background was authoritarian!

### 2. OBSOLETE

**@toyahofficial**
In 40yrs only one person has clicked it's about the Flat Earth Theory. A theory that fascinated me as a child, especially once I discovered JRR Tolkien. Tolkien allowed me escapism form the interminable boredom of school.

### 3. POP STAR

**@toyahofficial**
… during the vocal recording I had to pop out for tea at St. James Palace with the Queen Mother & Princess Margaret. It's A Mystery was No.4 in the charts and so called respectability was beckoning. Pop Star is about this sudden change in my life brought on by mainstream fame.

### 4. ELOCUTION LESSON

**@toyahofficial**
An autobiographical nightmare song, a collage of my school experiences. My speech impediment caused a big stir all my life, as a child I was chastised, as an adult loved for it. The vocal scope mimics my voice teacher's inflections.

### 5. JUNGLES OF JUPITER

**@toyahofficial**
Joel Bogen and Phil Spalding wrote the backing track to Jungles… when I was away filming [TV drama] Tales Of The Unexpected. When I received the cassette it was love at first hearing.

### 6. I AM

○ @toyahofficial

Ok, I am incapable of writing a straightforward life song. This is about otherness, my favourite subject. Cleopatra transported to 80s London and stuck in a bedsit.

○ @phil_marriott (podcaster)

I once submitted the lyrics of I Am to my art teacher as an example of something that conjured up vivid imagery. He was blown away by the words and bought a copy Anthem as a result.

### 7. IT'S A MYSTERY

○ @toyahofficial

[Hawkwind member and Ginger Baker collaborator] Keith Hale's incredible band Blood Donor performed this song mainly as an instrumental. John Craig [co-founder and CEO] of Safari recognised its commercial potential. A while after I'd cut a demo of it with Blood Donor myself, Joel Bogen and Nick Tauber rearranged it, I wrote a second verse and we recorded it.

### 8. MASAI BOY

○ @toyahofficial

I was growing up in Birmingham, in a conventional Western house, eating Western food, ordered to be demure/ladylike when I first discovered Masai and their ritualistic life, centred around community, hunting and gathering. I was blown away. I literally exploded with rebellion and joy.

### 9. MARIONETTE

○ @toyahofficial

I was heavily into the poems of Wilfred Owen. My all female teachers in school had all lost loved ones in World War II and where melancholic about them, which made me empathetic. We were taught that thanks to World War II there would never be another war. How wrong time has proved this...

### 10. DEMOLITION MEN

○ @toyahofficial

Total fantasy with sense of premonition about the world today. In my head I see various corrupted world leaders on the run from half-humanoid military, decaying shopping malls and big black Cadillacs.

### 11. WE ARE

○ @toyahofficial

This song is so right for Toyah audiences, the idea of group identity, shared experiences. The lyric idea is of an underclass developing a strong self-identity. Many of our fans at the time were having troubled times at home/school. For some it was near impossible to come out as gay without leaving home first, for others they simply felt they didn't fit the system.

# Blossoms
## Blossoms
Virgin EMI, 2016

If ever there was a band with a clear mission in life, it is Blossoms. Hailing from Stockport, the birthplace of Fred Perry, Tom Ogden (vocals/guitar – **@BlossomsBand**), Charlie Salt (bass – **@Chaz_Salt**), Josh Dewhurst (guitar – tweeting via **@Chaz_Salt**), Joe Donovan (drums – **@JoeDonovan92**) and Myles Kellock (keyboards – **@MylesKellock**) have set themselves the target of eventually earning a hometown plaque to match the one celebrating the British tennis legend turned polo shirt icon. Their debut album certainly set them on the right path towards that goal. Inspired by the heart-swelling anthems of their heroes Oasis, Blossoms certainly put their own spin on the kinds of songs that get crowds singing along. Not only are their impassioned tracks augmented by delicate keyboards and swooning synth that add a future pop element to their indie sounds, but with their big song from this record they weaved a dancefloor classic out of the story of first Holy Roman Emperor, Charlemagne. Blossoms served up a guide to their eponymous debut which truly aced it.

PHOTOGRAPHY:
Danny North

⊕

In bloom. Tim with Tom Ogden.

⊕

King of the Franks. Blossoms onstage in Paris in 2016.

## 1. CHARLEMAGNE

### @BlossomsBand (Tom Ogden)

It had to be the opening track. I remember writing this on my Casio keyboard I'd had since i was 12 at home. originally called 'Made Of Lead' my brother suggested the name Charlemagne after hearing the 'kingdom reigned' lyrics. It was also the first time I'd put lyrics to the main hook of the song and made that the chorus. I heard Arctic Monkeys do it on Knee Socks so I thought I'd give it a go, thank fuck i did…showed it the band next day I'm pretty sure Myles was like 'I'm not sure about this one'. We had no record deal at this point but Virgin had got involved on previous single Blown Rose as a tester so to speak, we sent Charlemagne as the follow up single and they called back an hour later offering us an album deal…

### @Chaz_Salt (Charlie Salt)

To get the outro guitar sound, I played the part then reversed it, learned it in reverse, recorded it and reversed that again! Confusing but cool (if you're into that sort of shit). Fun fact: the first time we played Charlemagne live was in a library [in] St Helens…

## 2. AT MOST A KISS

### @BlossomsBand

Wrote this immediately after my Dad showed me Harvest Moon by Neil Young, sounds nothing like it now but funny how a song can initially inspire you and then take on a life of it's own. [producer and member of The Coral] James Skelly wanted me to write a song that had the octave bass thing you hear, but I just couldn't seem to get one, however when I showed the lads this tune Chaz suggested doing the octave bass thing on this one and there we go! I got At Most A Kiss' from a line in a poem book I was reading at the time, just sounded good. Melody on the verses was inspired by Sweet Escape by Gwen Stefani, haha.

### @JoeDonovan92

This drum beat was purely me! I remember doing the demo and @MylesKellock saying 'you're actually alright on drums aren't you'. Nice one Myles.

## 3. GETAWAY

### @BlossomsBand

Last song I wrote for the album, we'd pretty much finished recording the album in November 15'. I wrote this that month and we went back in and recorded it January 16'. Lyrics were 100% personal, raw heartbreak emotions, also it's not 'GET under me' it's 'YOU'RE under me'.. but it does sound like 'get' now listening back haha

### @Chaz_Salt

This was the first time I recognised Tom's songwriting become more direct and sincere. If you listen to it, it's almost as if the song has written itself it's that good. It ends with the hook being repeated over and over and you can hear Skelly's dulcet tones accompanying Tom.

## 4. HONEY SWEET

### @BlossomsBand

Probably my favourite of this album. I remember [when] recording the album James Skelly said you needed a song that sounded like Taylor Swift could sing it, me and Myles had done a quick demo of Honey Sweet the month before… Heartbreak lyrics all over this album, got Honey Sweet from an Oscar Wilde poem, thought it looked good written down. One of my favourite melodies I've ever written on this track.

### @Chaz_Salt (Josh Dewhurst)

One of our most euphoric tracks, in my humble opinion. Tom's writing is so honest and you can really feel this tune. It always takes me straight back to 2016 when I hear it. Probably the most frantic year of our lives, thus far… - J

## 5. ONTO HER BED

### @BlossomsBand (Tom Ogden)

Remember writing this after learning the chords to Rock With You by MJ. Originally wanted to try the disco thing on the tune but James Skelly suggested doing it just me on the piano and making it all weird with reverse reverbs… Someone needs to remix it and do the disco thing with it, i always wanted to hear it how i originally wrote it in my head.

## 6. TEXIA

### @MylesKellock

Went through this one a lot to get it right. James Skelly said it sounded too Irish Jig so we took away some notes off the riff.

#### @BlossomsBand (Tom Ogden)
I asked the lads if they could think of anything and Chaz had the name Texia from something he'd read, he knows the story better than me!

#### @Chaz_Salt
Tom was struggling for a title on this one so I suggested using the name Texia, taken from Rosalie Texier, mistress of Pianist Claude Debussy. Was reading about this turbulent relationship at the time and the name sounded pretty cool. Ripped the groove off Love Is In The Air!

### 7. BLOWN ROSE

#### @BlossomsBand (Tom Ogden)
James Skelly gave me an acoustic guitar of his and I took it home and wrote this on it. Almost as if the song was hiding in the guitar and maybe he'd have written it if [he] didn't give it to me haha. Very proud of this song. It just has that timeless quality to it, could have been written in any decade... loads of the lyrics were inspired from a book of quotations I had, 'full blown-rose' was the original quote. I just took Blown Rose.

#### @MylesKellock
Ye mint tune. I remember when Tom first played it and I was well onto it, just sounded boss straight away even stripped down.

### 8 SMASHED PIANOS

#### @BlossomsBand
The only song I didn't write at my mum and dad's house. We were demo'ing in Charlie's uncle's studio and wrote it there one night. We did a demo the same night with Josh on drums Joe wasn't there. Demo sounded more like Tame Impala. It's really cool actually, will have to dig it out.

#### @Chaz_Salt
It's almost got a hip-hop feel this track. I think we subconsciously cribbed the groove off Stylo by Gorillaz!

### 9. CUT ME AND I'LL BLEED

#### @BlossomsBand
One of the oldest songs on the album written in 2013. I woke up one morning with the phrase in my head and had to google it cos i thought I must have seen it somewhere... but there was nothing, it was mine. Was listening to a lot of the Doors around writing this, can hear it on the chorus to me. Lyrics were about meeting someone new and being hesitant about opening yourself up again to somebody... Cut Me And I'll Bleed just means don't fuck me over, haha.

← Some flare.
Blossoms touring their self-titled debut.

## 10. MY FAVOURITE ROOM

⊘ **@BlossomsBand**
Originally written as a kind of Charlatans tune funnily enough, Tim. And that version exists somewhere on a rare Japanese release (that we had no involvement in but that's a whole other story…ha)

⊘ **@MylesKellock**
Nice and stripped down this one. We played it live at a uni leaving ball once and I went on drums for a laugh and played the ending like 60bpm slower.

Slide into my DMs. Blossoms' Joe Donovan shares a screen grab of their first chats with The Coral's James Skelly, who would go on to produce their debut album.

**The Coral**

09 SEP 2013, 13:42

Alright, Im in a band called blossoms from Manchester just started out and released a demo we recorded ourselves called blow. you guys ever need a support act we would love to fill the spot and wont be asking for money or out we just wanna get our name out and about here a link to the video! hope you like it!

**Blossoms - Blow (Official Video)**

09 SEP 2013, 14:47

sounds good mate…like it. Not touring at the mo but will bear it in mind when we are

## 11. BLOW

⊘ **@BlossomsBand**
I remember it coming together in the scaffolding yard [where the group used to rehearse] and thinking this band has something different to anything we'd done before. Everyone's parts just completed the song so well, Joe's drum intro, Chaz bassline and Josh's riff. We had this tune before Myles joined the band, so when he did eventually join his first song to play on was this and he came up with the Doors inspired great keyboard line. He always says he peaked there on his first rehearsal haha.

⊘ **@MylesKellock**
Fucking hell I remember when I first joined the band shitting myself at the first rehearsal not being able to play an E chord. Luckily Tom's nice and came to mine and went through the songs with me. I basically just ripped off When The Music's Over for the synth part on it.

## 12. DEEP GRASS

⊘ **@Chaz_Salt**
Probably one of my favourite tracks of ours this one. Still waiting for Dr Dre to sample it.

⊘ **@BlossomsBand (Tom Ogden)**
Was always going to be the last track on the album when we did this one. We had the singles covered and we did a few different things on this track, big long outro, some weird synth sounds etc. Love the lyrics too, again straight to the point heartbreak. Very different sounding to the rest of the album, could feel my songwriting pushing itself into different corners when i was writing it. Little bit darker…

⊘ **@JoeDonovan92**
What a tune, still love playing this live! Liam Gallagher once said he loved the bit we went into the Beatles after this tune! So I'm taking that as he loved the tune…

# How To Be A Human Being
## Glass Animals
Wolf Tone, 2016

Glass Animals have quietly come to own the internet. With their songs increasingly the choice of the discerning TikTok creators, the Oxford band's music has found its way to millions around the globe as Glass Animals routinely occupy chart places, for weeks on end, usually reserved for massively marketed streaming hits. However, it's no accident that Dave Bayley (vocals/guitar – **@GlassAnimals**), Drew MacFarlane (keyboards – **@feelinlokki**), Edmund Irwin-Singer (keyboards – **@edmundi_s**) and Joe Seaward (drums – **@JoeSeaward**) have made this enduring connection with people. First and foremost they have the songs, but the group have also created a world to go with them: "Each song on this record is a different story about a different character, some based on real-life people, some made up," Bayley told the Listening Party. "Each song's character was cast at a casting we did, and we photographed them for the album cover, and they feature in the videos. Some of them have fake personal websites…"

**PHOTOGRAPHY:**
Neil Krug

LISTENING PARTY
13 OCTOBER 2020

### 1. LIFE ITSELF

**@GlassAnimals (Dave Bayley)**
I think the character in this track is based a bit on myself… He lives in his mum's basement and invents electronic devices. The character likes old sci fi and comics…so the sounds and chords were inspired by old sci-fi films/series.

**@edmundi_s (Edmund Irwin-Singer)**
Opening sample is from a 1960s Pakistani soundtrack – Life Is Dance. It's Tafo feat. Afshan – Wey Titly Non Par.

**@JoeSeaward**
Started off life as a small angry ball in my memory, it was a really dark demo called TAFO, and then blossomed. It changed the most of any of the songs in HTBAHB. Went from nothing to lead single in a few days at The Church [studios].

### 2. YOUTH

**@GlassAnimals**
This one is a bit sad…about someone I met who told me a story about how her child had passed away. She was crying… but at the same time the memories that they had from that previous life made her so happy… so she was also smiling. She had found a way to see happiness in this awful thing that had happened to her. That combination of emotions is what this song is getting.

### 3. SEASON 2 EPISODE 3

**@GlassAnimals**
Everyone knows someone like the character from this song. If you don't then it's you. But there are lots of references to different psychedelic cartoons in this one. Sonically and lyrically. Including adventure time. That show is crazy.

### 4. PORK SODA

**@JoeSeaward**
Some of the talking at the beginning was a recording of a man I met in Denver before a show one day. I met him outside a post office, sitting in the shade in a parking lot. We got talking, and he told me about his life. I'll never forget him. His name was Forrest 'like Forrest Gump', the first thing you hear on the track.

### 5. MAMA'S GUN

✔ **@GlassAnimals**

This song is mainly about mental health and I remembered this song by The Carpenters called Mr Guder. Fit the atmosphere musically while the song Mr Guder itself was about an odd character, and then on top of that Karen Carpenter's story added another dimension to the lyrics.

### 6. CANE SHUGA

✔ **@GlassAnimals**

Wrote stream of consciousness lyrics for this one to try to capture a certain mentality you might have when you're a bit f***ed up. when you start speaking what seems like gibberish... but maybe that gibberish is actually quite revealing.

### 7. PREMADE SANDWICHES

✔ **@GlassAnimals**

Well... I forgot about this one. I mean... What the fuck was I thinking. My favourite word in the album is in this song. 'McFuck.' It's something that someone's gotten at McDonalds. Here it is used in a sentence: 'what the mcfuck are you eating?'

✔ **@feelinlokki (Drew MacFarlane)**

It was the first and last time anyone asked me to play the sitar.

### 8. THE OTHER SIDE OF PARADISE

✔ **@JoeSeaward**

This song was always a hidden gem imo, it's a real odyssey. But it really had its moment and cemented it's self as a GA fav at Red Rocks – where Dave summoned thunder in the driving rain.

### 9. TAKE A SLICE

✔ **@GlassAnimals**

Umm my secret fave off the record maybe. It is about someone with a lot of lust. It's as sleazy as I'll ever get in lyrics. But everyone has that inside them somewhere. Even if it's only a tiny bit.

### 10. POPLAR ST

✔ **@GlassAnimals**

This song is meant to open with a kind of musical/lyrical image of a place. A little guitar hook and a floating vocal line that all seems quite peaceful. but things get more and more twisted as the song goes on. The guitar starts doing weirder things, the music builds tension, and then the whole thing flips on its head at the end. And you find that maybe that place isn't what you first expected it was.

### 11. AGNES

✔ **@GlassAnimals**

As soon as i started writing it I knew it would be the album closer. This is my favourite song on the record and the saddest song I will ever write. It started with the first verse. Secret: I know it's a girl's name, but Agnes is about a boy.

Out on a limb. Glass Animals' Dave Bayley onstage in London in 2016.

# Working Men's Club
## Working Men's Club
Heavenly, 2020

⚑ Dancefloor rebels manning the bleep barricades, there is something wonderfully confrontational yet irresistibly feet-moving about Working Men's Club. A storm of angled synths, angry sonics and insisting beats, the Yorkshire collective featuring Sydney Minsky-Sargeant (vocals/guitar/drum machine/synth), Liam Ogburn (bass), Rob Graham (guitar) Mairead O'Connor (guitar/keyboards/vocals) and the mysterious Craig (just 'Craig' according to the band's official site) happily recall some of electronic music and post punk's pioneers, yet on this, their eponymous debut, are propelled forwarded into their own space with an attitude and vision that belongs only to them. Giving everyone honorary membership for the night, Minsky-Sargeant (**@work1ngmensclub**) showed us around Working Men's Club.

ARTWORK:
Steve Hockett

Clubbers. The band onstage in Oslo in 2020.

## 1. VALLEYS

☑ **@work1ngmensclub** (Sydney Minsky-Sargeant)

One of the last tunes I wrote for the record, thank fuck I wrote this one, wouldn't have had a first tune otherwise haha. I wrote the first 3:30mins of the tune and then realised it needed one more element. It had to be a 303, I had a little bit of money spare so I rushed to Manchester to buy a reissue and the first [drum machine] Bassline I wrote on it went straight on Valleys haha. Acid till I die!

## 2. A.A.A.A.

☑ **@work1ngmensclub**

Funny fucking tune man ahaha. [Producer] Ross Orton says this is pure Sheffield. I remember hating this tune but Jeff Barrett [boss of label Heavenly] said it should be on the album, @ross_orton made all the drum sounds on a Korg MS20 and it totally blew me away and transformed the track. I'm very pleased Jeff reassured me it should be on the album. Written from a place of pure bleakness and destruction, aha.

## 3. JOHN COOPER CLARKE

☑ **@work1ngmensclub**

I remember it taking about 12 hours to record the beat and then Liam tracking the bassline at about 2am as I fell asleep on the couch next to him. I was awoken to a finished rhythm track to JCC. I finished writing the instrumental but then needed some lyrics. I had a book of John Cooper Clarke poems in my room and thought it would be funny to write a song about him dying. Please don't die John. It was just a morbid joke.

## 4. WHITE ROOMS & PEOPLE

☑ **@work1ngmensclub**

My least favourite track on the album but it was always a single. Wrote the guitar line in my room then Liam added his sexy bass and we wrote the chorus together in a practice space in Hebden Bridge. We added the Jupiter 6 synth parts in Ross' studio and it transformed the track.

## 5. OUTSIDE

☑ **@work1ngmensclub**

A song I wrote when I first got into smoking Weed ahahahahaha. The oldest song on the record.

## 6. BE MY GUEST

☑ **@work1ngmensclub**

The start of the much darker side of the album. When we went into the studio the screaming guitar tones was one of the things I really wanted to get right. We barely used any distortion and just layered piercingly high end guitars on top of each other to make it sound more white noisy and clear.

## 7. TOMORROW

☑ **@work1ngmensclub**

A dark as fuck song with jolly as fuck music. We recorded the most part of this and Be My Guest in one day. Just me and Ross. Right productive day that aha. Can't sing the chorus for fuck. I've got asthma and it makes me weeze. As wimpy as that sounds, it's true.

## 8. COOK A COFFEE

☑ **@work1ngmensclub**

Not much to say. Really love Mairead's BVs in this tune and Tomorrow they really made the choruses. This was one of the hardest tunes to record. Had to redo the guitars because they weren't brutal enough, we got there in the end though.

## 9. TEETH

☑ **@work1ngmensclub**

Not much to be said other than I'm so glad we got to come back and do an Album mix, fuck that single mix. One of the darkest recording and writing experiences I ever had making this tune. We got there in the end though. All you need is a 909, 505, Volca FM and a Jupiter 6. Vocoder too. Would love to play this with a live orchestra one day...

## 10. ANGEL

☑ **@work1ngmensclub**

Another sad song lol. The last song we recorded, and never stopped adding parts too. Think there arc well over 100 guitars on this tune ahaha. Remember leaving Ross Orton to bounce the stems and thinking he wouldn't make it out alive. Julia Bardo used to sing the "Angel" vocal line but when she wasn't there I had to step up to the challenge and the vocoder was my vice. The end is just me and Ross thrashing it out live Man to man ahaha. A memory I'll never forget.

# Little Black Numbers
## Kathryn Williams
Caw Records, 2000

With folk music flourishing among a new generation of songwriters, the dark days when the genre was almost frozen out of contemporary music seem far off. The wider access to audiences and the ability of would-be listeners to dip into new sounds that digital services offer has helped this most enduring of music make new connections, proving in the process that simple arrangements wedded to the most tangled of emotions not only has a place in the modern world but can actually document and articulate our experience of it in the most perceptive of ways. However, it is not technology alone that has reignited the passion for folk music, as we need to pay tribute also to the artists who kept the flame alive in the media wilderness that existed before streaming. Chief among those is Liverpudlian Kathryn Williams (**@kathwilliamsuk**), who having sold homemade CDs at early gigs was forced to start her own label, Caw Records, to release her music. It was a worthwhile enterprise though as her second album, *Little Black Numbers*, illuminated many minds, with its bright songs that seem to arrive on a gentle breeze yet linger long in the imagination. Among those heads charmed by Williams' compelling melodies and beautifully hushed vocals were the 2000 Mercury Prize judges who nominated *Little Black Numbers* bringing it, its creator and folk as a whole to a new, wider audience keen to explore some truly stirring sounds.

PHOTOGRAPHY:
Mark Winkley & Dean Bowen

(↓)

Numbers game. Kathryn Williams up on the roof.

## 1. WE DUG A HOLE

**@kathwilliamsuk**

I wrote these lyrics on the North Shields ferry with [singer-songwriter] Nev Clay. Got the whole family in for backing vocals. My sister and her husband mike takes of us laughing "warmer than Safeway". Growling cello going mental.

## 2. SOUL TO FEET

**@kathwilliamsuk**

I remember playing this at the Mercury Prize award ceremony. I could hardly sing for the beating of my heart in my throat.

**@magpiesdaughter [fan]**

How gorgeous is Soul to Feet. Breaks my heart a bit each time...in a good way...

## 3. STOOD

**@kathwilliamsuk**

I always introduced this live by saying "with two o's not a u". I sound like my sister singing which is weird cause she's sing the backing! Laura's [Reid] cello playing always distinctive and recognisable it's like her voice.

## 4. JASMINE HOOP

**@kathwilliamsuk**

I love Alex's [Tustin] laid back drumming like he's driving a Cary across a desert. Aw Davey's [Scott] backing vocals. I love that man. He's the best human. Understated guitar solo and Laura playing. The band really melted together, the heady giddy way this makes me feel.

## 5. FELL DOWN FAST

**@kathwilliamsuk**

This song still feels raw all these years later. [Mike] Tunner, our friend, who died "Became a saint from just a friend". I always argued with him, he would do everyone's head by discussing things. See his face every time I sing this song.

## 6. FLICKER

**@kathwilliamsuk**

I wrote this while working in a cafe at the rising sun country park. I had it in my head like a radio playing and I had to go write it down on toilet roll, then hum it until I got home and could record it. Warm melancholy like a duvet.

## 7. INTERMISSION

**@kathwilliamsuk**

This was made as a turnover the record moment. I love the weird chords that are wrong/right. French horns. Muted trumpets. Ahhhh, I love that.

## 8. TELL THE TRUTH AS IF IT WERE LIES

**@kathwilliamsuk**

That's a great bass solo intro, it's like it's talking. I heard double vocals a lot writing then, like I had two people in my head. Wonder what happened to that guy?

## 9. MORNING SONG

**@kathwilliamsuk**

This track takes me right back to my bedroom in Sidney Grove, Fenham. Bare floorboards, big windows and a four track. I keep seeing the band playing in my mind.

## 10. TOOCAN

**@kathwilliamsuk**

Wow Laura's [Mundy, flautist] sister playing saxophone. I totally forgot about that. Cello and sax sisters playing together. A bird flew into my window last week...

## 11. EACH STAR WE SEE

**@kathwilliamsuk**

Jeez that scared the jam out of me. I have a funny relationship with this song as it reminds me of Danilo [Moscardini, instrumentalist/collaborator]. It's a bit melodramatic lol.

## 12. WE CAME DOWN FROM THE TREES

**@kathwilliamsuk**

I really like the heavy melancholy of this slime a weighted blanket. The Leslie amp whir, that organ in the studio. The last track! It's gone so quick. I feel really emotional, but then music has to mean stuff doesn't it?

# April/月音
## Emmy The Great
Bella Union, 2020

⚓ Sometimes albums are directly shaped by big life experiences. Events or relationships emerge in songs years after they happened as their writers find ways to make sense of them. Few records, though, are created in the middle of that major change, which makes Emmy The Great's fourth solo album a unique document, written and recorded after a trip that inspired the singer-songwriter to move from New York to Hong Kong. *April/月音* was recorded in two weeks in New York, just before Emma-Lee Moss (**@emmy_the_great**) relocated to the city of her birth where she would eventually start her own family. Capturing the hope and the nerves, the restlessness and the excitement, the record evokes a unique moment in its creator's life, while also capturing aspects of Hong Kong itself. "All my records have led me somewhere, and this one sent me on my life path, all the way home," she told the Listening Party. "I'm not in Hong Kong anymore, but I am so immensely proud of the life foundations I built there with my family."

**PHOTOGRAPHY:**
Alex Whittaker

⬇
Emmy winner. The great
Emma-Lee Moss onstage.

## 1. MID-AUTUMN / 月音

⊘ **@emmy_the_great**

This song is supposed to set the scene. It's about the night I woke up in a small apartment in Sheung Wan and saw the mid-autumn moon. I wrote this in Cantonese because it was entirely true, and felt so personal, I wanted to use my 'secret' language.

## 2. WRITER

⊘ **@emmy_the_great**

When deciding the track-listing, Bea [Artola, co-producer] suggested I make sure it told a story I was happy with. I wanted Writer to head up the songs, as a sort of announcement that there was a bit of fiction in each story, though it was also my life.

## 3. DANDELIONS / LIMINAL

⊘ **@emmy_the_great**

When I was writing this song...I was thinking about the fragmented ways that my friends and I were living, touring, travelling, being between places. Texting always to say, "Are you back in town? I'll be back soon."

## 4. CHANG-E

⊘ **@emmy_the_great**

When I arrived in Hong Kong during in October 2017, I fell under the protection of the mid-autumn moon. I stayed in Hong Kong for a further three moons, which is why the album was original called 'Four Moons' (this is synonymous with April in Chinese).

## 5. A WINDOW / O'KEEFFE

⊘ **@emmy_the_great**

Like Dandelions/Liminal, this song began its life in my last summer in Brooklyn. The world was changing. On the grass outside my apartment, people documented their lives on their phones.

## 6. OKINAWA / UBUD

⊘ **@emmy_the_great**

This song features field recordings made in Bali, when Ash Gardner [from band Emperor Yes] and his wife Jackie drove me to Mt Agung in search of gamelan music. Ash told me how the gamelan scale is the Okinawa scale, and I recorded snippets of our trip on my field recorder.

## 7. YOUR HALLUCINATIONS

⊘ **@emmy_the_great**

My friend Sarah asked me if this album was the 'baby album'. Even though we didn't know we were having one when I wrote it, it's very much a record of inheriting the world from my parents.

## 8. MARY

⊘ **@emmy_the_great**

Jo Lampert is 'Mary' on this. I met her when I was put in a group with her for a gig, we also met Margot, who plays violin on the record, through that. These women taught me so much about performance and collaboration, I love them so much.

## 9. HOLLYWOOD ROAD / APRIL

⊘ **@emmy_the_great**

January 2018. The four moons had gone by, and the album was almost written. Hong Kong was cold, and as wintery as it gets, and everyone was in a tailspin because Anthony Bourdain was filming around the city and kept being spotted in the street. It turned out he was filming an episode of Parts Unknown in Hong Kong. I got invited to sit in the background of the restaurant he was filming in, on Hollywood Road, and eat dumplings. All I had to do was eat. When the filming was finished, I remember skipping down Hollywood Road to my boyfriend's flat in Sheung Wan, and seeing flashes of light from signs and doorways, and the headlights of red taxis. I knew then that I was coming back here to live.

## 10. HEART SUTRA

⊘ **@emmy_the_great**

This song is about letting everything go and having a clean heart. In the credits of the record I've thanked all the people I loved in NYC for putting their stories into the album.

# Little Dominiques Nosebleed
## The Koreatown Oddity
Stones Throw, 2020

To get in one childhood car accident might be considered bad luck. Two is downright depressing. However, for Dominique Purdy (@KoreatownOddity), these brushes with other cars have, eventually, proved somewhat fortunate. *Little Dominiques Nosebleed* is a semi-narrative record stretching from the rapper and actor's first life-changing accident – a car U-turned into his mother's vehicle breaking The Koreatown Oddity's nose landing which landed "Little Dominique" with constant childhood nosebleeds – through a second which broke his leg, before sprawling out into the eponymous Los Angeles neighbourhood where he grew up. A former stand-up, The Koreatown Oddity's rhymes and flows are vivid and tinged with humour, yet there's a seriousness to the delivery backed-up by the kaleidoscopic production which features fierce beats, disembodied voices and a sprawling atmosphere that truly captures the seemingly endless urban mass of LA. Part trip down memory lane (including all those painful bumps), part vision for the future, *The Koreatown Oddity* gave the Listening Party a guided tour around his sonic 'hood.

ARTWORK:
Mark Bijasa

LISTENING PARTY
21 NOVEMBER 2020

### 1. LOOKING BACK FROM THE FUTURE

⊘ @KoreatownOddity
First joint wit Baby Rose singing people thought she was a sample. The homey CS Armstrong brought her to the session. He's singing on this track too.

### 2. LITTLE DOMINIQUES NOSEBLEED PART 1

⊘ @KoreatownOddity
This 2nd joint has Sudan Archives on it. And is the title track introducing you to where Little Dominiques Nosebleed comes from. My mom is featuring on the 2nd half of the track recalling the experiencing of the [car] accident off top of her head. Moms did that in one take too.

### 3. KOREATOWN ODDITY

⊘ @KoreatownOddity
"Ridin round in the riots wit my momma to loot..." not salute, as some people quotin the line said. I was out lootin wit moms at 8 years old.

### 4. CHASE THE SPIRIT

⊘ @KoreatownOddity
Chase The Spirit opening wit angelic singing of Jimetta Rose. I was like we need tht opera level shit. This track also features my dad and is inspired by a conversation we had.

### 5. DARKNESSES INTERLUDE

⊘ @KoreatownOddity
Darknessess is a transition into the next moods of the album.

### 6. GINKABILOBA

⊘ @KoreatownOddity
Ginkabiloba track was inspired by when my mom was stealing cable and inviting err body to the crib to watch the Tyson fight. And all the things that can happen just in tht day round then. Featuring Taz Arnold as one of the party goers.

### 7. WEED IN LA

✓ @KoreatownOddity

Weed in LA is about the ever changing blocks and things I'm used to growing up in a certain area all my life and being affected by it.

### 8. LITTLE DOMINIQUES NOSEBLEED PART 2

✓ @KoreatownOddity

The 2nd accident I was struck by car and the second half of the track is when I was layin in the street having an outer body experience. I prolly was 6 or 7.

### 9. A BITCH ONCE TOLD ME

✓ @KoreatownOddity

A Bitch once told has a sample at the beginning of me and Ras G talking about my album when I was playing it for him in 2019 January. J. Rocc on the cuts! Song features Ahwlee tellin me about Napoleon and his fetish.

### 10. NO LLORES

✓ @KoreatownOddity

No Llores features Trenttruce on the hook and Emmanuel Coto on bass also doing vocals with a singer named Edule. I remember when I first played Trent this beat and we he said the hook I knew tht was it. Also this was RAS G fav joint.

### 11. ATTENTION CHALLENGE

✓ @KoreatownOddity

Attention Challenge is the phrase of the year for me. Featuring Skyler Duf. Everything is such an Attention Challenge I don't even know what's real. Hook part wit the homey Swift. Black Google the track behind Attention Challenge is like an infomercial.

### 12. KIMCHI

✓ @KoreatownOddity

I remember one time I told this black chick that I lived in Koreatown and she said ewwwww it be smelling like kimchi all the time huh. And tht made me laugh cuz my experience there kimchi is the last thing I think of. So thts where it came from.

### 13. THE WORLD'S SMALLEST VIOLIN

✓ @KoreatownOddity

There's a lot of buildings tht I have lived in in Ktown that have been torn down after I left or we had to get out of cuz they were gonna tear it down. This joint is for the people tht experienced this constant shifting featuring Jimetta Rose.

### 14. WE ALL WANT SOMETHING

✓ @KoreatownOddity

We All Want Something is just J Rocc on cuts and the only vocals by the great Anna Wise. I told her what the album was about she wrote a few things down and then went in. Aaron Shaw on flute. I was like man this track don't need no rap.

### 15. LAP OF LUXURY

✓ @KoreatownOddity

Featuring the singing of Qur'an Shaheed and my man Kintaro introducing my rap. Lap Of Luxury is the reminder of what actual luxury is and how just your gratitude can make u luxurious.

### 16. LITTLE DOMINIQUES NOSEBLEED OUTRO

✓ @KoreatownOddity

Last track is what I like to call the Little Dominiques Nosebleed Theme Song. Like it's a TV or and end of the play. All the voices are me and then the last person you hear on the album is my mom talkin shit.

↓

Odd one out. Dominique Purdy has captured the essence of his Los Angeles neighbourhood on this record.

# Sex Dreams And Denim Jeans
## Uffie
Ed Banger/Because, 2010

There is a hyper reality to Uffie (**@UffieUfficial**), which is breathtaking. The French-American rapper, producer and songwriter is an icon for the digital age, able to consume, process and understand a stream of constant influences and stimuli before producing her own, insightful takes on this fast-paced culture. Her debut album includes a guest spot from Pharrell, meditations about modern car culture, a duet with a member of post-punk disco faves The Rapture… and sees her adapt The Velvet Underground's Rock & Roll into her title tack. And yet for all his head-spinning inputs, *Sex Dreams And Denim Jeans* is a coherent, envelope-pushing synth-hop cavalcade. Naturally, for a rapper so at home in the digital space, staging a Listening Party was a must…

**PHOTOGRAPHY:**
Ysa Pérez

**@AlanLorwhen**
Fun fact: there's a wall in Berlin with UFFIE graffiti. Fans are said to still kneel in front of it.

## 1. POP THE GLOCK

✓ @UffieUfficial

This is the first song I wrote and originally released with a little label called Arcade Mode in January 2006. We pressed 100 blue 7" vinyls. The music video for Pop The Glock was filmed in the house from Boogie Nights.

## 2. ART OF UFF

✓ @UffieUfficial

I'm a strong believer in the art of backing vocals. Art of Uff may be my favorite [producer] Oizo collaboration.

## 3. ADD SUV

✓ @UffieUfficial

I was reading Valley of the Dolls before writing this, and it was a big inspiration along with upbringing memories. My car in this video was covered entirely in denim… I didn't have a license so my friend Alex had to drive for me. [Featured vocalist] Pharrell's Porsche customized by Kaws is still my dream car.

## 4. GIVE IT AWAY

✓ @UffieUfficial
Young love and heartbreak…

## 5. MCS CAN KISS

✓ @UffieUfficial
[Beastie Boys'] Mike D Remix. Straight mooood.

## 6. DIFFICULT

✓ @UffieUfficial
I could be a bit difficult at times I suppose…

## 7. FIRST LOVE

✓ @UffieUfficial

When I got home from a big night out, I started writing this about someone I very much fancied as the sun came up. Firsts are magical… I hope to always experience these feels.

## 8. SEX DREAMS AND DENIM JEANS

✓ @UffieUfficial

Lou Reed sample. This title really encompassed the adventures of youth… and the journey that the record followed.

## 9. OUR SONG

✓ @UffieUfficial
Bittersweet.

## 10. ILLUSION OF LOVE

✓ @UffieUfficial

Is living with the illusion of love better than having none at all? Discussions from [French producer and electronic artist] Mirwais' kitchen table. I met [featured vocalist] Mattie Safer on tour when he was playing with [New York band] The Rapture. I've always been a fan of the souls his voice captures, and he's such a sweetheart.

✓ @Tim_Burgess
Illusion Of Love – it's a masterpiece

## 11. NEUNEU

✓ @UffieUfficial

This one always reminds me of an epic Ed Banger night at Zouk in Singapore!

## 12. BRAND NEW CAR

✓ @UffieUfficial

My go-to soundcheck song… I always found it so comforting when nerves would hit even then… Beep beep.

## 13. HONG KONG GARDEN

✓ @UffieUfficial
Siouxsie and the Banshees forever!!!!!!!!!!!!!!

## 14. RICKY

✓ @UffieUfficial

4 minute 12 second pure flex. Used to write these lyrics on the inside blank vinyl sleeves before recording.

# *Raintown*
## Deacon Blue
Columbia, 1987

⚐ "When my mum heard When Will You (Make My Telephone Ring) she said, 'This song will be Number 1 all over the world!'" A bold prediction by Dougie Vipond's mother but perhaps she should have got into the A&R game, because parental love aside it was a bold call... but a pretty good one. Named after a Steely Dan song, the Glasgow band's tender pop rock was not necessarily the pushiest of sounds, particularly at the tail end of the 1980s when some acts were getting a little carried away as studio technology evolved... forever dating the music they were working on. Instead, there is an authenticity and charm to Ricky Ross (vocals), Lorraine McIntosh (vocals), James Prime (keyboards) and Vipond's (drums) (all **@deaconbluemusic**) approach that eschewed production pyrotechnics in favour of melody and heart... which as their drummer's mother predicted resonated strongly with audiences.

**PHOTOGRAPHY:**
Oscar Marzaroli

The Very Thing.
Deacon Blue live in
London in 1988.

## 1. BORN IN A STORM

⊘ @deaconbluemusic

Ricky Ross: Born in a Storm isn't an obvious choice for an album opener but I'll never forget the speech our A&R made on why we should open with it. It was along the lines of: 'Everyone starts with an up track. You won't… that's what will make this album make an impact'.

## 2. RAINTOWN

⊘ @deaconbluemusic

Lorraine McIntosh: The first song I sang on was #Raintown, I was blown away when the sound the band were making came through my headphones.

## 3. RAGMAN

⊘ @deaconbluemusic

Dougie Vipond: I've always loved Graeme's [Kelling] guitar lines that he plays in the space between piano the chords of the intro & verse.

## 4. HE LOOKS LIKE SPENCER TRACY NOW

⊘ @deaconbluemusic

Dougie Vipond: There's a real beauty to this song, even though the subject matter is pretty harrowing.

## 5. LOADED

⊘ @deaconbluemusic

Dougie Vipond: I seem to remember that we knew this was good but when we recorded it initially it didn't soar away at the end. A decision was made to add a key change and it gave us the freedom to take it somewhere else.

## 6. WHEN WILL YOU (MAKE MY TELEPHONE RING)

⊘ @deaconbluemusic

Ricky Ross: This song was on [our] very first DB demo. Only Dougie Vipond and I survived that lineup. At one point Janice Long's brother Jeff loved it so much he nearly signed us.

## 7. CHOCOLATE GIRL

⊘ @deaconbluemusic

Dougie Vipond: This has become one of our strongest live songs. We wanted to create a cool country vibe on this and Graeme's guitar sounds so in the groove.

## 8. DIGNITY

⊘ @deaconbluemusic

Dougie Vipond: The studio was on the top floor of the Top Shop building right above Oxford Circus in London. It was an amazing if slightly terrifying place. Air was owned by Beatles producer #GeorgeMartin and everywhere you went there were photographs of the Fab Four.

## 9. THE VERY THING

⊘ @deaconbluemusic

Dougie Vipond: "One day, all of us will work", a bold prediction.

## 10. LOVE'S GREAT FEARS

⊘ @deaconbluemusic

James Prime: We recorded the piano part at night in Studio 2 at AIR studios in Oxford Circus. Lights were all dimmed, I was sat at the Bosendorfer, headphones on. "Ready, Jim? Relaxed?" came Jon Kelly, our producer's soft, smooth voice.

"Yeah, I'm good to go to Jon."

"OK", says he, "Stevie Wonder wrote Superstition on that piano. Tense up. Tape's rolling."

Several takes later, my hands were still shaking.

## 11. TOWN TO BE BLAMED

⊘ @deaconbluemusic

Dougie Vipond: Something really magical happened when we [were] recording this. Encouraged by producer Jon Kelly, Ricky took us to places we'd never been before as a band. Listening to him as he went through this extraordinary improvised performance, was amazing. We followed and ended up with something special.

⊘ @deaconbluemusic

Ricky Ross: The songs on #Raintown were the songs from all of my life and the lyrics are songs which had gathered for a number of years.

# Kings Of The Wild Frontier
## Adam And The Ants
CBS, 1980

If the New Romantic scene that began to blossom after punk echoed all the pomp and creative energy of a Renaissance court, in Adam Ant it found its prince. A showman ready to parade new looks and styles in the spotlight, he was also a consummate frontman with his own vision. Though nurtured in the punk rock crucible of Malcolm McLaren and Vivian Westwood's SEX clothes boutique on London's Kings Road, he followed his own path. With The Ants – Marco Pirroni (guitars), Kevin Mooney (bass), Chris "Merrick" Hughes (drums/production) Terry Lee Miall (drums) – he not only moved the New Romantics and the New Wave scene out of punk's shadow, but with *Kings Of The Wild Frontier*, released on the cusp of the 1980s, they created one of the records that would lay the artistic foundations for the decade ahead, making an impact across a spectrum of musical genres, fashion and beyond. With the influence of *Kings Of The Wild Frontier* still being felt today, particularly its bold, unrelenting rhythms (Kanye West and Daft Punk certainly adopted the feel on their 2013 collaboration Black Skinhead), the heart beat behind Antmusic, Chris Hughes (**@C_M_Hughes**) took us to the wild frontier and beyond…

(←)
Frontier community.
Adam and his Ants
(Chris Hughes, far left).

## 1. DOG EAT DOG

**@C_M_Hughes**

I remember me and Terry Lee hitting the crap out of our bass drum fibre cases. Adam thought the sound of Zulu Warrior Shields being hit with spears would be just the thing.

It was a very exciting overdub to do and a very exciting sound to have on the track.

## 2. ANTMUSIC

**@C_M_Hughes**

I love Marco's guitaring on this track. What a mad guitar solo. How Great! We were at Rockfield Studios in Wales. We dragged a huge wooden gate post into the studio to hit with sticks for the intro. Kevin Mooney joined in on sticks too.

**@Tim_Burgess**

Antmusic was big at The Morg in Northwich x

## 3. FEED ME TO THE LIONS

**@C_M_Hughes**

Always enjoyed playing this live. Fun Tympani overdub. Great Adam vocal. Crazy Kettle drums.

## 4. LOS RANCHEROS

**@C_M_Hughes**

I love Cowboy tunes. It's such a great tune… CLINT EASTWOOD. We used to clown around a bit playing this.

## 5. ANTS INVASION

**@C_M_Hughes**

One of my all time faves. I always remember laughing at Terry Lee when we played it live.

He always looked totally committed and solid gone into this tune. I loved it. Great dual Adam and Marco Guitars. Horror Movie Stuff!

## 6. KILLER IN THE HOME

**@C_M_Hughes**

What a vocal ! So emotional. They cut you in half with a gun!!! We got an endless feedback tone for Marco. He is a distortion and feedback god.

## 7. KINGS OF THE WILD FRONTIER

**@C_M_Hughes**

Quite a lot of drums on this one. Repeated overdubbing of tom toms for hours on end. For me that was bliss. It is the title track of the album for all the right reasons. My absolute top AATA tune. You'll find the DNA of the whole thing in this epic track.

## 8. THE MAGNIFICENT FIVE

**@C_M_Hughes**

More Cowboy mayhem. He who writes in blood…

## 9. DON'T BE SQUARE (BE THERE)

**@C_M_Hughes**

We are told Dirk Wears White Socks. We are told this is Ant Music for SEX People. And why not? You may not like it now, but you will. Punk Funk for Sure.

## 10. JOLLY ROGER

**@C_M_Hughes**

Pirate insanity. Great fun. I remember hiring tympani drums for this track but we couldn't get them through the studio door. I played them with headphones in the corridor. Hilarious for passers by.

## 11. MAKING HISTORY

**@C_M_Hughes**

Very underrated track in my opinion. Would be great in a musical I always thought. Wonderful rhythm gtrs. Really enjoying listening to this track. After such a longtime.

## 12. THE HUMAN BEINGS

**@C_M_Hughes**

Love this track. Very inventive bass gtr work. Great track to play live, always seemed to get the crowd going. Great lyrics.

## 13. PRESS DARLINGS (KINGS OF THE WILD FRONTIER'S B-SIDE)

**@C_M_Hughes**

Oh my word Press Darlings. Loved playing this live! Might just listen to a few more…

## 14. PHYSICAL (YOU'RE SO) (LOS RANCHEROS' B-SIDE)

**@C_M_Hughes**

Oh I see "Physical" is up next. Hang on for dear life. One of my favourite Adam performances on record!

# Forever Changes
## Love
Elektra, 1967

⚱ As apt album titles go, few can compete with *Forever Changes*. Inspired and recorded during a unique moment of cultural history – 1960s West Coast America – the album not only offered a creative prism refracting a deeper glimpse of its times than the surface-deep caricatures that have followed it, but the record's vision and inventiveness has left its mark on so many musicians who have experienced it. Created as flower power swelled towards its high tide, Arthur Lee (vocals/guitar), Bryan MacLean (guitar/vocals), Johnny Echols (guitar), Ken Forssi (bass) and Michael Stuart-Ware (drums) understood and experienced hippy culture yet were also able to make sense of. While chart success was modest at the time, the record has the higher honour of subsequently inspiring even more glorious music, with the likes of The Stone Roses, Jesus And Mary Chain, Primal Scream (bassist Simone Marie Butler joined in the Listening Party) and more all heralding the enduring freshness of Forever Changes. Offering a guide to this most influential of albums, the band's co-founder Echols (**@johnnysecho**) hosted a Listening Party for *Forever Changes* which really showed us the Love.

ARTWORK:
Bob Pepper

Primal Scream's Simone Marie Butler shared "A serendipitous find on my phone today" featuring Arthur Lee with her band's Bobby Gillespie (right) and Andrew Innes.

---

**LISTENING PARTY**
**3 JANUARY 2021**

### 1. ALONE AGAIN OR

✅ **@johnnysecho**
Alone Again Or, was meant to have a banjo intro with a kind of bluegrass feel, but after trying to play one, it turned out that neither Bryan nor I played Banjo worth a damn, so the song was about to be axed. David Angel (the arranger) heard me sitting in the corner warming up, noodling Spanish riffs, and he suggested that I play that kind of thing on Bryan's song. After a bit of friendly cajoling, Bryan agreed and because neither of us played the banjo, serendipity morphed a rather pedestrian bluegrass tune into the Spanish-flavoured masterpiece called Alone Again Or, and a shitload of money for his estate.

### 2. A HOUSE IS NOT A MOTEL

✅ **@johnnysecho**
The title came about due to Arthur coming home and finding a couple (Bryan had invited over) getting busy on the living room floor of the Castle. Arthur yelled out "BRYAN, my house ain't no fucking motel." The incident became an inside joke among members of the group. We thought it would be a great song title, the record company abridged it.

### 3. ANDMOREAGAIN

✅ **@johnnysecho**
Andmoreagain is a beautiful bit of poetry, everyone thought the song would sound better if Arthur's voice was slightly higher, so the track was sped up a tiny bit in order to change the pitch of Arthur's voice.

### 4. THE DAILY PLANET

✅ **@johnnysecho**
The title comes from Superman comics, it's the newspaper where Clark Kent worked. This is the only song Love ever recorded that I used a distortion pedal [on].

### 5. OLD MAN

#### ✓ @johnnysecho
Old Man by Bryan Maclean is about our dear friend David Biali, rest in peace, my friend.

#### ✓ @sunstackjones [band]
Forever Changes nerd fact you may not know (sure many do). Neil Young initially agreed to produce the album, but it didn't happen in the end. Be interested to know how close it was to happening

#### ✓ @johnnysecho
Not a chance, when we got to the studio and saw Neil, we all started laughing... Arthur couldn't stand him, neither could I.

Love me do. Michael Stuart, Johnny Echols, Ken Forssi, Bryan MacLean and Arthur Lee backstage in Los Angeles in 1967.

### 6. THE RED TELEPHONE

#### ✓ @johnnysecho
The Red Telephone was and is one of my favourite songs, Arthur's vocal delivery is just superb. The man's mind was always working, even while relaxing at a Movie Theatre. We had gone to one of the local art cinemas to see a movie called Marat Sade. A phrase in the movie stuck in his mind "we're all normal, and we want our freedom." That beautiful, poignant, prescient song had its beginnings with that simple phrase.

### 7. MAYBE THE PEOPLE WOULD BE THE TIMES OR BETWEEN CLARK AND HILLDALE

#### ✓ @johnnysecho
Between Clark and Hilldale was about a small café on the corner of Sunset and Hilldale, called The Eating Affair that was often frequented by patrons of the Whisky and located on Sunset and Clark street. Arthur dubbed the place The Slop Affair.

### 8. LIVE AND LET LIVE

#### ✓ @johnnysecho
Live And Let Live opens with the line "Oh the snot has caked against my pants, it has turned into crystal" and goes on to paint a picture of a dystopian society marked by violence, mistrust, and tribalism, much like the times in which we were living.

### 9. THE GOOD HUMOR MAN HE SEES EVERYTHING LIKE THIS

#### ✓ @johnnysecho
This song was a beautifully written Homage to James Moody and King pleasure, If you're at all familiar with the song Moody's Mood For Love you will recognise the influence.

### 10. BUMMER IN THE SUMMER

#### ✓ @johnnysecho
This has a very interesting rhythmic structure, it starts out as an upbeat countryish tune with some really cool finger picking by Bryan that soon morphs into a kind of Bo Diddly influenced R&B beat.

### 11. YOU SET THE SCENE

#### ✓ @johnnysecho
This was actually three different songs, that were never finished. Kenny Forssi put those unfinished songs together into one song that became You Set The Scene, he did a fantastic job.

# The Performance
## Dame Shirley Bassey
Geffen, 2009

**PHOTOGRAPHY:**
Mary McCartney

✦ Shirley Bassey is the only Listening Party artist who has a damehood. She is also one of the few around to have one who remains so effortlessly cool. It is only right the nation has honoured the singer, as from Bond films to big ballads she's made her mark on music. Yet while beauty, style and sophistication might inform the arrangements of her songs, the soul of the "girl from Tiger Bay" in Cardiff is always there to give a gritty, real quality to her performances. And this celebration of her music was all about *The Performance*, the 2009 album Dame Shirley made with composer David Arnold (**@DavidGArnold** – also see page 148), which proved – as she tackled songs written by the likes of the Manic Street Preachers, Pet Shop Boys and Richard Hawley – the singer was as vivid and as relevant as ever. "I wanted to make this album because I wanted people to take her seriously as a singer," Arnold explained as he took us through his collaboration with Dame Shirley Bassey (or DSB to him). "A proper record with proper songs, not covers of hits. DSB was keen to make that record but I talked her out of it and felt we could make a 'proper record'. I think overall we managed to make a record which felt real…" So please, sit back and enjoy *The Performance*…

LISTENING PARTY
11 JANUARY 2021

### 1. ALMOST THERE

☑ @DavidGArnold
People love a big voice...real control, real power, real emotion....like watching an elite athlete do something incredible right in front of you. No tricks, no mic technique get outs... just raw talent. Tom Baxter's Almost There gave her the platform to fly and she really took advantage of it.

### 2. APARTMENT

☑ @DavidGArnold
The Apartment by Rufus Wainwright was slinky and fun and pointed and arch and wonderful. Shirley loved it... It was a bit rude... I tried to keep a bit of filth in it.

### 3. THIS TIME

☑ @DavidGArnold
This Time by Gary Barlow was Gary trying to write what we as writers would call a standard. Timeless and tuneful. He was very excited by his use of 9th chords in this song... its a throwback to Shirleys earlier song choices... very melodic... I took it to a Bacharachy kind of vibe.

### 4. I LOVE YOU NOW

☑ @DavidGArnold
I'd worked with Kaiser Chiefs a few times and wed always had a blast. Nick Hodgson was a great songwriter and I asked if if he'd want to write for DSB (Dame Shirley Bassey!) Not a combination you'd expect but the juxtaposition of these styles really work.

### 5. OUR TIME IS NOW

☑ @DavidGArnold
Our Time Is Now is a John Barry/Don Black song.... the first they'd written for Shirley since Diamonds Are Forever, I think. It's a timeless Barry melody and I was thrilled when John and Don agreed to write.

### 6. AS GOD IS MY WITNESS

🔗 **@DavidGArnold**

As God Is My Witness was a song I'd written for DSB with David Mcalmont. A hugely underrated writer I feel. I love his voice and he's been a good friend for many years. I love the lyric David wrote for this. I love a bit of tragedy in a song.

### 7. NO GOOD ABOUT GOODBYE

🔗 **@DavidGArnold**

No Good About Goodbye was a song I'd written with Don Black. I'd sketched an idea after Quantum of Solace came out as I liked a string line I'd written for that film and asked Don to put a lyric to it when

I knew Shirley was going to sing it. Shirley struggled a little with the recording, took a while to connect. That was when having her long serving (at that point) Musical Director Mike Dixon with me for the vocal sessions [was so] valuable. Mike knew what it took to negotiate these twists and turns and I was very happy that he could come with us to Dublin to record the vocals and smooth the way.

### 8. THE GIRL FROM TIGER BAY

🔗 **@DavidGArnold**

The Girl from Tiger Bay written by the Manic Street Preachers was a thing of wonder. They're such great melodists, they so completely understood what we were trying to do and being Welsh and so aware of the history of Wales and Shirley that they were an authority. It's a poetic song and feels like a homecoming musically. I threw a few ideas in as a producer and the band insisted I have a writing credit despite me saying I didn't want it. I love the song and I love the band.

### 9. NICE MEN

🔗 **@DavidGArnold**

Kt Tunstall's Nice Men was a song that appealed to Shirley's sense of naughtiness. It was provocative, slinky and a bit rude. Right up her street.

### 10. AFTER THE RAIN

🔗 **@DavidGArnold**

Richard Hawley had something very special with After The Rain. Richard is another of those writers who understand the bones of a song, the anatomy of it, he knows where the secrets are musically and lyrically. It's my favourite vocal from her on the album... delicate, exposed, truthful.

### 11. THE PERFORMANCE OF MY LIFE

🔗 **@DavidGArnold**

To a certain extent there was always going to be a couple of 'BIG' songs on this record, she wouldn't have it any other way. I bookended the record with Tom Baxter's Almost There and this Pet Shop Boys song The Performance Of My Life. This was so in DSB's wheelhouse a song, both musically and lyrically.

The Dame from Tiger Bay. Shirley Bassey mid-Performance.

# *Anna Calvi*
## Anna Calvi
Domino, 2011

There was something truly thrilling, unlikely yet so, so satisfying about Anna Calvi's early shows. Arriving onstage in a vividly crisp red shirt and trouser suit with her hair neatly drawn back, the singer-songwriter cut an immediately stylish presence. Yet sometimes among crowds who did not know her – from dingy indie venues to supporting labelmates Arctic Monkeys solo before she'd released many records – the suspicion that this sophisticated presence was somehow in the wrong place. How could this petite figure, wielding her beloved sunburst Fender Telecaster, hope to silence the pre-show chatter and demand the attention with a batch of relatively unknown songs?

PHOTOGRAPHY:
Emma Nathan

It is always a mistake to underestimate Anna Calvi (**@annacalvi**). Subsequent records, candidly confronting sexuality and gender, have sat alongside acclaimed soundtracks for the likes of *Peaky Blinders*, proving the South Londoner can pretty much do anything she sets her mind to. And it was the same with those early shows. With her force-of-nature presence, stunning vocals and probably the best guitar-playing of her generation, Calvi soon had even the most raucous audiences eating out of her hand. Her self-titled debut album, which provided the material for those gigs, was the fuel behind the emergence of this most extraordinary of musicians. Noir atmospheres and swirling sonic textures gave Calvi the perfect base from which release blasts of pure passion both from her heart and her fretboard. With *Anna Calvi*, the record not the person, marking its 10th birthday exactly, this Listening Party truly was a cause for celebration.

⊕

*La grande bellezza.*
Anna Calvi's self-titled debut ripples with light and shade.

## 1. RIDER TO THE SEA

✓ @annacalvi

I wrote rider to the sea on the morning of my first gig because I realised I only had 4 songs!

## 2. NO MORE WORDS

✓ @annacalvi

The great Dave Okumu [from the band The Invisible] came to the studio during the recording of No More Words and as well as his singing I recorded a whole 4 minutes of Dave just breathing, which if you listen carefully you can hear all over this song! The choir vocals at the end were improvised – I wanted it to echo the final lyric "my prayer".

## 3. DESIRE

✓ @annacalvi

There was once a version of desire which had trumpets at the beginning of the song instead of harmonium! Brian Eno came to the studio when we were mixing Desire and sang backing vocals whilst reading a magazine, which he said was the best way to get a great take.

## 4. SUZANNE & I

✓ @annacalvi

Brian Eno is also singing backing vocals on Suzanne and I drew a picture of Elvis for him, and he showed me some moon dust. When I did the vocals for Suzanne and I it was the first time I felt I had confidence in my voice. Suzanne and I was inspired by the [2007 "docu-fantasia"] film My Winnipeg. Who is Suzanne? Answers below...

*Fans replied suggesting everyone from "a girl I fancied at university", Leonard Cohen's Suzanne, The Bangles' Susanna Hoff and themselves. Calvi, naturally, won't be drawn.*

## 5. FIRST WE KISS

✓ @annacalvi

First we kiss used to be called "as the wind blows". First we kiss was the first song I used harmonium on, and I completely fell in love with this instrument. I played the strings on this song, and they were a nightmare to record! Because I was so out of practice at playing the violin. Have you noticed that First We Kiss sounds a lot like the theme tune for the cartoon Banana Man? This wasn't intentional.

## 6. THE DEVIL

✓ @annacalvi

I wore dark red lipstick when doing the vocals of the Devil, to get in the mood. It's the scariest song to play live! Because it's very technical.

## 7. BLACKOUT

✓ @annacalvi

For about a year, all I had of blackout was the intro. This song was written after experiencing a blackout in my house whilst in the bath. I tried to channel Chrissie Hynde in Blackout.

## 8. I'LL BE YOUR MAN

✓ @annacalvi

I'll be your man was inspired by hearing Grinderman for the first time. The lyrics of I'll be your man were written on the spot – very unusual for me! The backing vocals are from my original home demo.

## 9. MORNING LIGHT

✓ @annacalvi

Morning light was written in the studio in an hour. It was based on a dream I had. Mally Harpaz's harmonium playing on morning light is one of my favourite moments on the record.

## 10. LOVE WON'T BE LEAVING

✓ @annacalvi

Love Won't be leaving was the first song I recorded for the album. Mally Harpaz is playing drums on love won't be leaving, but she was having an asthma attack during the recording, which was scary – she's wheezing as she's playing. She recovered but we decided to keep her breathing on the song! I wanted the middle section to sound like someone treking through the wilderness, so I recorded my footsteps on lots of different surfaces, but this didn't make the final version! When I heard the final mix, I was so elated that I remember thinking I could die happy right at that moment, because I had created something I was really proud of. Thanks so much everyone, what a 10 years it's been!

# *Different Light*
## The Bangles
Columbia, 1986

You can be assured that your record is a hit when you change the way people walk. Such was the popularity of The Bangles' single Walk Like An Egyptian, that in 1986 the gawky dance-aping figures depicted in ancient hieroglyphs escaped clubs and could be seen in bedrooms, parks and pavements all over the globe. However, like the pyramids themselves that only slowly revealed their secrets, that shuffle was not *Different Light*'s greatest treasure: that was Prince. A fan of the band featuring Susanna Hoffs (vocals/guitars), Vicki Peterson (vocals/guitars), Michael Steele (vocals/bass) and Debbi Peterson (vocals/drums), he had given the band a song written under the pseudonym "Christopher". The group's leader, Hoffs (**@SusannaHoffs**), offered to decode more of *Different Light*'s gems for us, so get ready to do that funny walk… and pay tribute to Prince!

PHOTOGRAPHY:
Raul Vega

(left) Susanna Hoffs onstage; (below) Vicki Peterson, Michael Steele, Hoffs and Debbi Peterson; (bottom) @CraigatCoF's 1986 ticket.

EVENT CODE    SECTION/AISLE    ROW/BOX    SEAT    ADMISSION
MC0417    SEC A    G    1    $14.00
$14.00    ADULT
ADMISSION
1.00
SEC A
SECTION/AISLE
OMOX    4
G    1
ROW/BOX    SEAT
ADH1444
32986

SOUTHERN STAR & TUCP PRES
THE BANGLES
SPECIAL GUESTS
HOODOO GURUS
TULANE'S MCALISTER AUD.
THU APRIL 17 1986 8:00 PM

## 1. MANIC MONDAY

**@SusannaHoffs**

I am forever grateful to Prince for the gift of this song. I vividly remember driving down Sunset Blvd to pick up the cassette from Prince which had Manic Monday on it. The thrill of us Bangles hovered around a cassette player listening to it. The SUPREME pleasure of singing it.

## 2. IN A DIFFERENT LIGHT

**@SusannaHoffs**

Vicki [Peterson] and I co-wrote In A Different Light. The Bangles love for psychedelic rock is evident in this song, from the opening riff and driving beat.

## 3. WALKING DOWN YOUR STREET

**@SusannaHoffs**

I wrote this with Louis Gutierrez and [Different light producer] David Kahne. I've loved The Supremes my entire life and I remember wanting to write a song about yearning – about being in the throes of a mad crush and I wanted to write a song with a driving bass line and Girl Group harmonies... I give you Walking Down Your Street!

## 4. WALK LIKE AN EGYPTIAN

**@SusannaHoffs**

I can still remember David Kahne playing me this cool demo at the Columbia Records offices in LA. It was Marti Jones singing Walk Like an Egyptian. My memory is, the record company released Walk Like an Egyptian to radio on a lark, not expecting much. But then kids started demanding their local radio stations play it, and it took off!

## 5. STANDING IN THE HALLWAY

**@SusannaHoffs**

Debbi sings lead on this. Fun doing the call and response vocals! There is joyousness in singing together as a group.

## 6. RETURN POST

**@SusannaHoffs**

Return Post has a cool swagger to the groove, like it's begging for some choreography to go with it. Now there's a thought.

## 7. IF SHE KNEW WHAT SHE WANTS

**@SusannaHoffs**

The brilliant Jules Shear wrote this gorgeous song! I love how the bridge takes you by surprise–how the melody soars. I played 12 string electric on it!

## 8. LET IT GO

**@SusannaHoffs**

A rare song written by the four of us! My memory is that one of the inspirations for this song was from a film I was obsessed with called Beyond the Valley of the Dolls, directed by Russ Meyer, co-written by Roger Ebert. The film revolves around an all girl band called the Carrie Nations.

## 9. SEPTEMBER GURLS

**@SusannaHoffs**

Big Star! One of my favorite bands, ever and always! This song is gorgeous & delicious & plaintive. Naturally it wanted some Byrds-esque 12 string guitar, as well as a psychedelic solo... and of course loads of caressing harmonies.

## 10. ANGELS DON'T FALL IN LOVE

**@SusannaHoffs**

Vic & I wrote this one. Turns out she and I were both obsessed with the film The Trouble with Angels, when we were young girls. This song sprung to life from our conversation about that.

## 11. FOLLOWING

**@SusannaHoffs**

This is a gorgeous Michael Steele composition, haunting and beautifully performed. A gem.

## 12. NOT LIKE YOU

**@SusannaHoffs**

Debbi and I wrote this with David Kahne. I love the harmonies, the call and response vocals and chiming guitars... I learned so much from David Kahne. We are still good friends to this day. Much gratitude to him for making Different Light what it was!

# SUCKAPUNCH
## You Me At Six
Underdog, 2021

⚓ As current leading torch bearers of British rock, this most brash but emotive of music traditions is in safe hands with You Me At Six. The Weybridge five-piece trade in the sort of enduring anthems that when released among a large crowd of people, whether at gigs or festivals, inspire a communal urge to move your neck – and the rest of you – in time with the chunky beat.

Yet while Josh Franceschi (vocals – **@joshmeatsix**), Max Helyer (guitars – **@Maxmeatsix**), Chris Miller (lead guitar – **@youmeatsix**), Matt Barnes (bass – **@mattmeatsix**) and Dan Flint (drums/sampling – **@DanMEATSIX**) might represent the best of rock, they are not looking to recreate anything that has gone before, and it is precisely their desire to innovate that makes them such a good thing for moshpits everywhere. Their seventh album, the caps-lock loving SUCKAPUNCH, is a great demonstration of this outlook as it marries heavy riffs and smouldering, throat-shredding vocals with electronic samples and studio experimentation that saw them record in locations as diverse as Thailand, Los Angeles and good old Cookhill, just down the road from Royal Leamington Spa.

**ARTWORK:**
Giles Smith

Beach house. Writing WYDRN in Thailand.

## 1. NICE TO ME

**@Maxmeatsix**

Nice to me was a last-minute gem that came out of nowhere, when I had the demo of this I didn't expect it to come out as good as this!!! Last week magic happening in the studio!!

## 2. MAKE ME FEEL ALIVE

**@youmeatsix (Chris Miller)**

This was probably one of the funnest times making a record, we all knew exactly what we were doing with that song and came alive super quickly. We recorded the drums and guitar in variable speed which allowed us to make those instruments sound like they've been sampled.

## 3. BEAUTIFUL WAY

**@youmeatsix**

When we wrote Beautiful Way we knew that our fans would love this song, we were talking about how we needed a big anthemic jump up and down song and then a few days later we created this song with Nick Hodgson who used to be the drummer of Kaiser Chiefs.

## 4. WYDRN

**@youmeatsix**

WYDRN was a Thailand creation, Josh and Dan one day had a few beers and worked on 2 songs they both had and mashed them together to make this. They both loved it so much they showed the rest of us and said we would love to record this, we put faith in their direction and it's one of the songs that really pushes the sounds of this band by taking influences from hip hop and RnB.

## 5. SUCKAPUNCH

**@mattmeatsix**

This one gives me club feels. Probably my favourite lyrics josh has done on this record, constantly resonate with them!

## 6. KILL THE MOOD

**@youmeatsix**

Kill The Mood was a song that we created when we were on tour in America, we did a writing session and 4 hours later we came out with this song. Being in LA we wanted to try and bring some of the West Coast vibe to the song hence why the vocal is sung super lazy and how some of the instrumentation is being played here.

## 7. GLASGOW

**@youmeatsix**

Glasgow was actually one of the only songs we had played all together before we recorded it.

**@mattmeatsix**

Glasgow might be my favourite song we've ever written.

**@joshmeatsix**

Found a lot of joy in this song coming to life while recording.

## 8. ADRENALINE

**@youmeatsix**

We wrote the bridge in 45 minutes of us all jamming out in the main room of the studio capturing the energy of just really arriving in Thailand.

## 9. VOICENOTES

**@youmeatsix**

Voicenotes again was another really difficult song to finesse, everything was sitting really good but the guitars felt a bit dated at first. It was just like a wall of sound but not in the right way, it didn't allow the drum and bass groove to really take lead so we approached the guitar tracks more like a call and response DJ scratch battle. After a few weeks we finally got there and was worth all the late nights working on this, otherwise it might of not made the record.

## 10. FINISH WHAT I STARTED

**@youmeatsix**

Finish What I Started was a song we have been sitting on for a long time, we started work on this when we were recording our last album VI and kept coming back to it because we kept being told it was a fantastic song.

## 11. WHAT'S IT LIKE

**@DanMEATSIX**

Such a fun one to play live the final couple of shows last year. Everyone went mental.

# Inside In/Inside Out
## The Kooks
Virgin, 2006

In perhaps a demonstration of what a fertile time it was, The Kooks narrowly missed out on having the biggest-selling British debut album of 2006 because Arctic Monkeys released their first record in the same year. Still, there was no lack of exuberance and youthful energy behind Luke Pritchard (vocals/guitar), Hugh Harris (guitars), Max Rafferty (bass) and Paul Garred's (drums) first foray into the studio, and *Inside In/Inside Out* brims skims from jaunty anthems to heartfelt break-up songs with an assured, natural ease. Celebrating the record's birthday, 15 years to the day of its release, Pritchard and Harris (both **@thekooksmusic**) cut the cake, popped the streamers and gave us the Inside info of The Kooks' debut.

PHOTOGRAPHY:
Ben Parks

LISTENING
PARTY
**23 JANUARY
2021**

### 1. SEASIDE

☑ **@thekooksmusic**
Luke: Funny this started out as a piano ballad, Paul had the idea and I helped a bit. We moved studio from Konk to Strongrooms in Shoreditch to do the finishing touches and last overdubs for the album. The final day recording all the guys were out at the pub and [producer] Tony (Hoffer) asked if there was anything last minute I wanted to try so I just did a few takes of Seaside on the acoustic, sounded way better on the guitar than piano...

### 2. SEE THE WORLD

☑ **@thekooksmusic**
Hugh: The opening guitar riff was inspired by the Daleks from Doctor Who. Before the TV show made its big comeback, I was a fan of the original re-runs and requested (from Hoffer) that his riff imitate the piercing sound that their voices made!

### 3. SOFA SONG

☑ **@thekooksmusic**
Hugh: The melodica line at the outro took Max around twenty takes and three melodicas to get. He smashed (literally, not figuratively) the first two in fury, so Dave McCabe from @ZutonsThe had to pop round to lend us his.

### 4. EDDIE'S GUN

☑ **@thekooksmusic**
Luke: You'd think it would be embarrassing for an 18-year-old to write a song about erectile dysfunction. Well, it was... Haha.

### 5. OOH LA

☑ **@thekooksmusic**
Hugh: The post chorus organ line was taking a long time to get and after a lot of frustration and direction, I said to Hoffer, "why don't you just do it?". Hoffer said, "okay," and they switched places. The producer became the produced!

### 6. YOU DON'T LOVE ME

☑ **@thekooksmusic**
Hugh: The guitar solo sound came predominantly from a Culture Vulture [a valve-produced harmonic distortion studio unit]. The inventor of the unit stopped by the studio to deliver a new model and I suggested that he make a pedal version as it would sell really well for guitar players. The answer was a flat "no."

### 7. SHE MOVES IN HER OWN WAY

☑ **@thekooksmusic**
Hugh: The video for this song was a debauched

road trip from LA to Tijuana which resulted in Max losing his passport and armed border police holding us at gunpoint.

Luke: Yeah that video was a trip! The plan was: get the band as pissed on tequila as possible and keep rolling the camera… haha.

### 8. MATCHBOX

⊘ @thekooksmusic

Luke: This is like four songs we spliced together, somehow it works. Reminds me so much of nights out in Brighton…

### 9. NAÏVE

⊘ @thekooksmusic

Luke: Still can't believe the life of this song. I can't really remember that time too well but I know we recorded Naive so many times with various producers, was a real tough one to get in the studio.

### 10. I WANT YOU

⊘ @thekooksmusic

Luke: I wrote this after breaking up with my girlfriend and I listened to Bob Dylan's 'I Want You' on repeat for the rest of the night. I wanted to write something with the same feeling, but I ended up with something completely different. It's almost emo or grunge.

### 11. IF ONLY

⊘ @thekooksmusic

Hugh: The song refers to the behaviour of reckless, powerful leaders being attributed to childhood loneliness and neglect.

### 12. JACKIE BIG TITS

⊘ @thekooksmusic

Hugh: Jackie Big Tits is a character in the film Sexy Beast played by the wife of Mike Batt [Julianne White], who Luke had a big altercation with whilst watching a concert in Amsterdam.

### 13. TIME AWAITS

⊘ @thekooksmusic

Luke: I seem to remember Paul talking about Fleetwood Mac's 'The Chain' a lot when we recorded it. We were definitely trying to go a bit prog rock on it. Was always one of my favourites from the album.

### 14. GOT NO LOVE

⊘ @thekooksmusic

Luke: Max's voice is so cool on this record, I sound so fucking sleepy haha! I love Paul's drum sound on this; really special. Great way to finish the album this.

Inside track. The Kooks perform in Newcastle in 2006.

# *If I Was*
## The Staves
Atlantic, 2015

⚓ Watford to Wisconsin is not a well-trodden path, so it is testament to the brilliance of The Staves that they forged their own way. Having started off at open mic nights in their Hertfordshire hometown, the Staveley-Taylor sisters' – Emily, Jess and Millie (Camilla) – harmony-driven, folk has charmed and beguiled many along the way with its earthy heart and acoustic beauty. Among those impressed by The Staves was Bon Iver's Justin Vernon, and after the trio supported his group in 2012 he offered to produce their second record, *If I Was*. Revisiting the album they made together in Wisconsin's bucolic countryside, Jess and Millie (both **@thestaves** – Emily was looking after her baby on the night of the Listening Party "so can't join the madness!") retraced the steps of their unique, musical journey.

**PHOTOGRAPHY:**
Justin Vernon

LISTENING
PARTY
**26 JANUARY
2021**

### 1. BLOOD I BLED

⊘ **@thestaves**
I remember when Rob Moose and CJ Camerieri played the string and horn parts for this song our minds were blown. It took it to such new heights. Listening to it in the studio in Wisconsin looking out the window at a glorious sunset as the outro hit – all of us looked at each other and knew it was one of those moments we wouldn't forget.

### 2. STEADY

⊘ **@thestaves**
Themes include: Self loathing. Laying awake at night. Anxiety. Being tangled up. Fallen out of love but stiiiiiiiiiillllll randy.

### 3. NO ME, NO YOU, NO MORE

⊘ **@thestaves**
This started out on acoustic and banjo and had a country feel. It was one we kept coming back to but felt it was lacking something. We ended up scrapping the demo and did an a cappella version instead and the song was completely transformed.

### 4. LET ME DOWN

⊘ **@thestaves**
This record marked a change where could make production decisions that we didn't have to be able to re-produce live. It was all about inspiration. (Jess sings the highest note at the very end of the song and our Mum always used to laugh and say 'which one of you was that again?!')

### 5. BLACK & WHITE

⊘ **@thestaves**
Black & White is about the feeling of not being good enough for the people around you. All you do reduced to cold words on a page.

### 6. DAMN IT ALL

⊘ **@thestaves**
This song is written like a stream of consciousness, almost a dreamlike narrative. We watched Twin Peaks every night at the studio in Eau Claire and were so inspired by the soundtrack. It's so brooding and mystical.

Shining. Emily, Camilla and Jessica Staveley-Taylor onstage in Manchester in 2015.

### 7. THE SHINING

◎ @thestaves

The Shining is a nod to the creepy hotel image in the song, inspired by a hotel in LA we stayed in (where our drummer Ollie did try and climb the fire escape).

### 8. DON'T YOU CALL ME ANYMORE

◎ @thestaves

A drunken lament. We wanted it to sound dreamlike and channel that specific sore haze of fresh heartbreak. The sharp intake of breath through the teeth in the chorus was an homage to The Beatles' Girl.

### 9. HORIZONS

◎ @thestaves

We wanted Horizons to feel like a new beginning. Hopeful.

### 10. TEETH WHITE

◎ @thestaves

Teeth White is about feeling nothing you do is good enough. Jumping through hoops set out by the label or the industry yet still not pleasing anyone. We wanted it to be a "band" song. Bass, drums, guitar and vocals. Simple. It's a fave to play live.

### 11. MAKE IT HOLY

◎ @thestaves

There was a guitar lying around in a weird tuning D#G#CG#A#D# (possibly created by Chris Rosenau of Volcano Choir ?? They had just finished their record there) and Jess wrote this song one evening once we'd finished recording for the day.

### 12. SADNESS DON'T OWN ME

◎ @thestaves

This goes between being a request for sadness to no longer be so enveloping, and a statement/declaration that sadness no longer owns this person. Used a great upright piano in the main room in the studio (April Base, Eau Claire, Wisconsin). We recorded it at night wrapped up warm inside while everything was frozen in the depths of Winter all around.

# *Red*
## The Communards
London, 1987

This was a Listening Party of firsts. It was the first to be led by a vicar (**@RevRichardColes**). It was classicist Professor Dame Mary Beard's debut party, and it marked the first time the Listening Party was discussed on BBC2 when Mary, Tim and the Rev Richard Coles got together on a video call afterwards for the *Inside Culture* TV programme.

ARTWORK:
DKB

Fittingly, though, The Communards were a band of firsts too. With lead singer Jimmy Somerville they seemed to be one of the first pop groups to really hit the high notes, while with Richard Coles they were the first '80s synth group to have a member who joined the Church Of England and became a regular on Radio 4. The Communards were also one of the first artists to not only openly embrace their sexuality and gay culture within their songs, but also reflected the realities of AIDS on their community in the 1980s. "It surprised me how emotional it was. That record was made at a tough time for us, the AIDS pandemic was at its full strength then and our lives were completely overshadowed by that," Richard Coles explained on TV after the party. "It was really powerful to engage with those memories and doing it together intensifies it. It was something really good." Yet The Communards were also a group full of joy and dancing, and Coles' Listening Party reflected the different sides of this record: the highs and the lows, the reflection and the hedonism. It certainly impressed one Listening Party attendee. "Great stuff rev," tweeted Mary Beard and everyone listening wholeheartedly concurred.

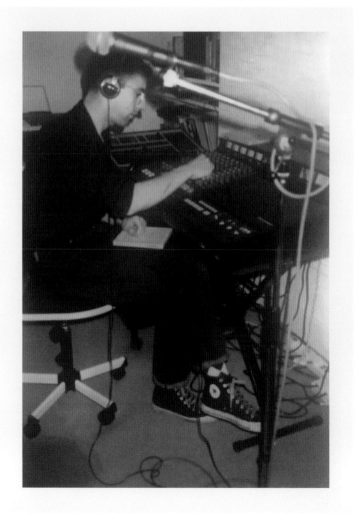

## 1. TOMORROW

☑ @RevRichardColes

This was, typically for us, a synth pop song about domestic violence, and – amazingly! – failed to do very well. I pinched a figure in the string arrangement from Mozart's Magic Flute.

## 2. THERE'S MORE TO LOVE THAN BOY MEETS GIRL

☑ @RevRichardColes

I really like this song. The Italian voice over was by Zita Wadwa who was a secretary at our record company. Somebody on a ship years later told me that this song had changed his life. I think he meant for it the better.

## 3. MATTER OF OPINION

☑ @RevRichardColes

I didn't realise until later that Jimmy might as well have been singing it to me, because we were fighting so much at that time. I like the jolliness and the string arrangement, which was my department. I thought of myself then as the next Burt Bacharach, which was perhaps a tiny overestimation of my powers.

## 4. VICTIMS

☑ @RevRichardColes

Sounds like a not very good pastiche of someone else to me. The keyboard figure sounds amphetamine-driven, which it may well have been. Judd Lander played harmonica, who played on Do You Really Want to Hurt Me. He twas noted for taking his trousers off when he played, I don't know why.

## 5. FOR A FRIEND

☑ @RevRichardColes

Written in memory of our friend Mark Ashton, the first of our circle to die of AIDS, in 1987. He was 26, and a wonderful, exciting, inspiring man – the central character in the film Pride which came out a few years ago.

## 6. NEVER CAN SAY GOODBYE

☑ @RevRichardColes

Another of our reworkings of a disco classic. It was a big hit, like our first attempt, Don't Leave Me This Way. Both expose the shortcomings of our songwriting, and reveal Jimmy's miraculous voice.

## 7. LOVERS AND FRIENDS

☑ @RevRichardColes

I wrote music and lyrics for this. It was written after another friend died, thirty years ago. I can't listen to it now because it reminds me of David, my husband, who died a year ago.

## 8. HOLD ON TIGHT

☑ @RevRichardColes

You can tell we'd been on tour with the Style Council.

## 9. IF I COULD TELL YOU

☑ @RevRichardColes

Music by Jimmy words by WH Auden. It sounds again like a lament. I can see now we were overwhelmed by grief making this album. The jolly numbers have something a bit manic about them.

## 10. C MINOR

☑ @RevRichardColes

Not the most imaginative title. I originally called the track London Wall, I can't remember why. I really like it. You can tell we'd toured it for a year before recording it. Great performance by Jimmy.

⬈

Pre-ordination. Richard Coles shared this photo of him making his contribution to the track Victims.

⬇

In tune. Jimmy Somerville and Richard Coles.

# Collapsed In Sunbeams
## Arlo Parks
Transgressive, 2021

**PHOTOGRAPHY:**
Fraser Taylor

Debut albums can be tortuous affairs. An introductory work inviting the outside world to understand and connect with ideas and music that have lived inside someone's head for years. Misfires and misunderstandings are common as artists don't quite make the right first impression. There are, of course, the incendiary debuts that seem to reflect and then define their times, records that often represent a catalogue peak as that initial energy is never quite recaptured. Then there are debut albums that don't need to worry about chiming with the outside world, because they establish an entire universe of their own, one that an artist is going to grow to fill in the coming years. *Collapsed In Sunbeams* by West Londoner Arlo Parks (**@arloparks**) is one of these debuts. From its dreamy opening atmosphere and hazy spoken words, it's clear the singer-songwriter is about to take you on a journey, something the grooves, melodies, breathy vocals and evocative lyrics confirm over the 12 snapshots that make up the record's tracks. "I would say it's quite introspective. It's based around a kind of nostalgia and healing, and the experiences that have shaped me as I grew up," Parks has said of the world she has created. "I take influences from everything: from indie music, to pop, to R&B, to trip hop. So it's kind of almost like a melting pot of a lot of different influences and a lot of different sonic palettes – and I hope people like it." People did. Parks' debut took the 2021 Mercury Prize in a very competitive field, while audiences have swooned for *Collapsed In Sunbeams*' languid atmospheres, an experience the artist seem certain to repeat thanks to this beautiful introduction.

LISTENING PARTY
3 FEBRUARY 2021

### 1. COLLAPSED IN SUNBEAMS

**@arloparks**
Collapsed in sunbeams was written in my bedroom staring out of my skylight one afternoon.

### 2. HURT

**@arloparks**
Hurt is based off a quote by Audre Lorde – "pain will either change or end". It's the first song I wrote in 2020, after a few months of writers block :)

### 3. TOO GOOD

**@arloparks**
With Too Good I wanted to channel my inner 90s popstar. I barely remember writing this song – it was a blur of excitement.

### 4. HOPE

**@arloparks**
Hope was inspired by DJ Shadow, Sufjan Stevens and Sneaker Pimps. I wrote the spoken word part all in one go – it came flooding out of me.

### 5. CAROLINE

**@arloparks**

With Caroline I really did witness a couple having a scrap by the bus stop. It's inspired by my favourite album on the planet – In Rainbows by Radiohead.

### 6. BLACK DOG

**@arloparks**

Black Dog was written in the same 24 hours as Eugene. It's for and about a person who was and still is my best friend.

**@Tim_Burgess**

"You do your eyes like Robert Smith"

### 7. GREEN EYES

**@arloparks**

Kaia from Green Eyes is a real girl but her name isn't Kaia. This song is kind of an homage to Frank Ocean.

### 8. JUST GO

**@arloparks**

Just go feels so distinctly French to me and I love it. This is the one song on the album that took an ETERNITY to get right.

### 9. FOR VIOLET

**@arloparks**

In my notes this song is called For Viole(nce). I was listening to Angel by Massive Attack on repeat when we made this.

### 10. EUGENE

**@arloparks**

Eugene is the oldest song on the record and has a special spot in my heart. It was written sitting on the floor of an apartment in Victoria.

### 11. BLUISH

**@arloparks**

Bluish started off as a lil demo in my bedroom. The sample at the beginning is my favourite moment on the record.

### 12. PORTRA 400

**@arloparks**

The sample on Portra 400 makes me think of the last scene in the Breakfast Club. The spoken word verse took me the longest to write out of anything on the album.

Arlo Parks onstage at the End Of The Road Festival in 2021.

# Greenfields: The Gibb Brothers Songbook, Vol. 1
## Barry Gibb
EMI, 2021

꜡ Many songwriters believe that the mark of a good song is one that you can play acoustically, no matter how it was originally written or recorded. To celebrate his immense catalogue, Bee Gee Barry Gibb (**@GibbBarry**) went one further: he took his and his brothers' songbook country. Despite now being forever linked with dazzling white suits, lit-up dance floors and shimmering glitter balls, Barry Gibb was also a life-long country and bluegrass fan and so for his third solo album he decamped to Nashville's RCA studios (scene of iconic recordings by the likes of Elvis Presley and the Everly Brothers) to create a series of duets with some of country music's most interesting names. The result was no disco goes dixie, but a genuinely earthy uncovering of the hearts of songs you may well have spun around a club to before. Gibb's final duet on this project was to link up the Listening Party to introduce us to his collaborators… and to reintroduce us to some true classics.

**PHOTOGRAPHY:**
Zsolt Zsigmond

(←) Top of the pyramid. Barry Gibb live at Glastonbury in 2017.

(↑) Jive Talkin'. Barry Gibb with (producer) Dave Cobb and Jason Isbell. "I miss this my friends," Barry tweeted.

## 1. I'VE GOTTA GET A MESSAGE TO YOU

**@GibbBarry**

I love Keith Urban and the fact that [he] said yes to singing this song. I'm very proud to have him on this album. The song was Robin's idea. The message is a little bizarre but that's rob for you.

## 2. WORDS OF A FOOL

**@GibbBarry**

How do you discover a song you have written in the distant past that always should've been featured? I don't know but here it is. A song I've always been truly proud of. I salute you Jason Isbell! You brought this song to life!

## 3. RUN TO ME

**@GibbBarry**

On the horizon is one of the greatest female artists of all time. Her name is Brandi Carlile and her light will shine forever. I love you Brandi. Thank you for bringing your gift to me.

## 4. TOO MUCH HEAVEN

**@GibbBarry**

This beautiful angelic voice has haunted me for years. She is above and beyond spiritual. She is the one and only Alison Krauss. I'm so blessed she went to bat for me. Thank you Alison!

## 5. LONELY DAYS

**@GibbBarry**

What an absolute pleasure it is to work with Little Big Town. The harmonies are superb. They are like a rare painting and the sweetest people I've ever met.

## 6. WORDS

**@GibbBarry**

Dolly Parton is the greatest artist of her kind on earth. What else can I say? Dolly has made so many dreams come true for me. I hope we're not done yet. Isn't that Dolly? She has made so many people's dreams come true. That's Dolly.

## 7. JIVE TALKIN'

**@GibbBarry**

Miranda Lambert and Jay Buchanan gave to me a version of Jive Talkin' that I've always wanted to hear but could have never imagined. Thank you Miranda and Jay! It's truly inspiring every time I hear it.

## 8. HOW DEEP IS YOUR LOVE

**@GibbBarry**

We managed to talk Little Big Town into doing the vocals on How Deep Is Your Love. I love them and I couldn't get enough. The timeless musicianship of Tommy Emmanuel is an immediate connection me and Australia. Love you Tommy!

## 9. HOW CAN YOU MEND A BROKEN HEART

**@GibbBarry**

Sheryl Crow is to me one of the greatest artists in music period. What a joy it was to be on the microphone with her. There is no limit to what she can do. A consummate professional and one of the best all around musicians I've ever met.

## 10. TO LOVE SOMEBODY

**@GibbBarry**

I always thought this was a great soul song. Appropriate for Otis and some other brilliant singers but to have Jay Buchanan sing this song rises beyond anyone's expectations. I love you Jay! I can't wait to do more stuff with you. What a voice!

## 11. REST YOUR LOVE ON ME

**@GibbBarry**

I grew up in Australia and got to know Olivia Newton-John as we were all immigrant families and we crossed many paths over the years. She has always been my favourite female artist who just happens to be one of my oldest and dearest friends. Sending love always.

## 12. BUTTERFLY

**@GibbBarry**

I saw [the Cohen Brothers' country music documentary] Down From The Mountain and fell in love with David Rawlings and Gillian Welch. There are still artists that will move you. I told them I loved them when I met them. Listen to Dave play like a "butterfly". I love you both very much.

# *Powerslave*
## Iron Maiden
EMI/Capital Records 1984

Alongside their work as airline pilots, word class fencers, video directors, radio presenters and the creator of one of Britain's most enduring icons – Eddie! – the members of Iron Maiden are also in a band… In many other groups, the extra-curricular activities of the Brits would have long ago eclipsed their music, but not so 'Maiden. Few bands can say they have played such a role in pioneering a sound that spread all over the world, but Iron Maiden's place in the Heavy Metal Hall Of Fame was never in doubt. Yet Bruce Dickinson (vocals), Steve Harris (bass), Dave Murray (guitar), Nicko McBrain (drums) and Adrian Smith (guitar), joined since 1999 by Janick Gers (a legendary rock guitarist already in his own right), are not resting on their flaming laurels, remaining a festival-filling, theatrically driven live act who play to pan-generational crowds the world over. With heavy metal's affection for all things devilish and skeletal – band mascot, the aforementioned Eddie, being the prime example – who better then to host the six hundredth and sixty-sixth Tim's Twitter Listening Party, or Listening Party: 666 for short? With Iron Maiden opting to celebrate their acclaimed and influential 1984 album *Powerslave* in honour of the Number Of The Beast, Dickinson, the band's guide through the intricate riffs and throat-bursting vocals ensured they added yet another skill to their embarrassment of talents. Meet Iron Maiden (all **@IronMaiden**): social media influencers.

**ARTWORK:**
Derek Riggs

Come to mummy. Bruce Dickinson and Iron Maiden mascot Eddie wrap things up Ljubljana (now in Slovenia) in 1984.

Iron Maiden frontman Bruce Dickinson onstage in Nottingham in 1984.

## 1. ACES HIGH

☑ **@IronMaiden (Steve Harris)**
Hearing it without the Churchill's Speech intro now is a bit odd, it should almost be there. People have heard it so many times live now that that's the deal!

☑ **@IronMaiden (Janick Gers)**
It's always been thrilling to come onstage playing Aces High, just an explosion of power at the beginning of any Maiden set. Short and to the point, with all the power of Maiden live in a short, concise song with a great theme.

## 2. 2 MINUTES TO MIDNIGHT

☑ **@IronMaiden (Dave Murray)**
A great place. We hired a hotel to play and stay in. It was a quiet little island until we showed up!

☑ **@IronMaiden (Bruce Dickinson)**
We wrote this on Jersey, where we were holed up in January and February, freezing cold, Atlantic gales lashing the whole place. We were in a hotel, 'locked down' ourselves pretty much, except the bar was open and it was free which was worrying… There was one TV, there was no internet, all there was to do was drink, go play some football, get very, very cold and windy outside and play music and write music all night long and all day long.

☑ **@IronMaiden (Adrian Smith)**
Think "The Shining" but with amps and guitars.

☑ **@IronMaiden (Steve Harris)**
We were supposed to be there writing. I say supposed to, because mainly the first week or so we ended up getting pissed! We had the whole hotel to ourselves and it had a 24 hour bar… You've got to get into the vibe of things I suppose.

☑ **@IronMaiden (Bruce Dickinson)**
I read this book, Dispatches by Michael Herr. It is a Steve Harris sort of book but it is absolutely incredible. And there's a line in here which is straight in the song: "Blood is freedom's stain." It was a US General who said that. The song is about the glory of war and the despair and futility of war. It displays the best of humankind and also the worst of humankind in sharp focus.

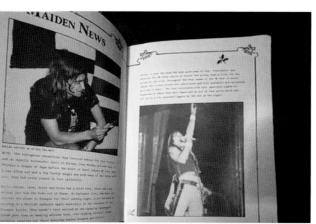

←

@alexandermilas [fan]
A glimpse of the
@IronMaiden FC mag
issue 11 – Christmas
1984 – it had been a
very good year.

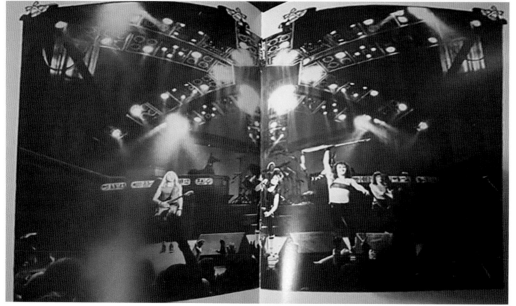

⊘ @IronMaiden (Adrian Smith)

I started work on this in Jersey. I pretty much had the music written already & Bruce finished off the lyrics in Nassau. I remember AC/DC arriving at the studio just as we were leaving. Bruce collared Brian Johnson and we played him a rough mix.

### 3. LOSFER WORDS (BIG 'ORRA)

⊘ @IronMaiden (Steve Harris)

Well, that was just a bit of a joke... That we couldn't come up with any words for it because we were Losfer Words...

### 4. FLASH OF THE BLADE

⊘ @IronMaiden (Adrian Smith)

A bit overlooked this one. I went a bit mad on the guitar overdubs! We pretty much did one backing track a day as a band, then went in individually to record overdubs. Martin [Birch, producer] had a great work ethic, and would be in the studio non-stop for weeks. Then he'd go out for an evening to "let off steam" and he'd go missing for a few days...

⊘ @IronMaiden (Steve Harris):

He had a way of getting what he needed or getting what he wanted from you in a performance without you realising that he'd done it. There's quite a knack to that, I think. He was such a character on days off. There weren't many of them as he'd be working all hours concentrating and that takes it out of you. I was in there a lot of that time as well but I could nip off. So when he did get a day off, if we were out by the pool or whatever, he'd just walk past and push everyone in, things like that. So that's where the "Pool Bully" nickname in the credits came from.

### 5. THE DUELLISTS

**@IronMaiden (Bruce Dickinson)**

The guy who choreographed the fights in [Ridley Scott's 1977] film The Duellists was Bill Hobbs. He founded a fencing club called the Swash and Buckle where I fenced. A lovely guy who wrote a definitive book on stage fighting. He made The Duellists savage and brutal.

### 6. BACK IN THE VILLAGE

**@IronMaiden (Bruce Dickinson)**

A throwback to the track The Prisoner. A kind of psychedelic fall through time, in a world in which somebody is suddenly transported back in time from the present day, and he's The Prisoner again, back in the village…

*Talking of villages the band recorded the album at residential studio Compass Point in the Bahamas…*

**@IronMaiden (Dave Murray)**

It was our second time there. I loved the studio, the vibe and the whole tropical paradise.

**@IronMaiden (Steve Harris)**

It was just a great vibe really. I mean, I loved it so much I ended up living there! I always thought one day I'd like to come back and live here… I just liked it. Island life's not for everyone, but I think we all enjoyed our time there.

**@IronMaiden (Nicko McBrain)**

There was a bar that did a splendid banana daiquiri and great food like conch fritters. It was after about 5 of these drinks that I decided that I was going to jump in the sea and have a swim. It was a very rough ocean with some very big waves!

### 7. POWERSLAVE

**@IronMaiden (Bruce Dickinson)**

There was an ironic message to Powerslave. When you had amplifiers powering a big PA system, you had ones just generating power and nothing else and they were called slave amplifiers because they were just slaves to the big amplifier… Powerslaves! The irony was not lost on me because we'd been going through this crazy touring schedule and I thought that maybe we were that too as musicians… Maybe we were slaves to the power of death!

**@IronMaiden (Steve Harris)**

I just don't think we realised what we were taking on at the time [with the tour]! It was the first tour we headlined America & this just cemented it. We played so many places that we've never been able to do again. We spent months in the US alone &

Gainfully employed. The full, 1984 Iron Maiden line-up.

played places people just don't play. We were really pushing boundaries. A highlight of the tour was an appearance in front of over 250,000 fans at Rock in Rio in 1985. As far as we knew we were just on a festival bill. We didn't really think much more of it. We weren't headlining it. It was with Queen, which was fantastic anyway. I love their early albums, so to be on the same bill as them was an honour.

**@IronMaiden (Adrian Smith)**
We had a dressing room next to them. I heard them doing Bohemian Rhapsody acapella before they went on.

**@IronMaiden (Dave Murray)**
Nicko and I climbed up the ladder to the top of the lighting truss. You still couldn't see the back row of the audience... astounding.

**@IronMaiden (Steve Harris)**
I think Bruce had two or three bits which ended up being the Powerslave song and I just said "Why don't you put it all into one and make one great song out of it?" I don't know if he remembers it like that but it's how I remember it!

**@IronMaiden (Bruce Dickinson)**
I didn't want to be obvious and Egypt seemed to be an interesting place to go because despite all the power you have as a Pharaoh you are still going to die. It's almost like the regime was so pissed off at that thought that everybody had to die too.

**@IronMaiden (Adrian Smith)**
When I recorded my guitar solo for this track, Robert Palmer was in the studio. Robert lived next door and he and Martin had been up drinking together all night.

**@IronMaiden (Janick Gers)**
A beast of a song. Very powerful live, especially with the three guitars making it even heavier. The harmony guitar interplay works really well and the live rendition always creates an amazing atmosphere at gigs wherever we play it.

**@IronMaiden (Steve Harris)**
Powerslave was such a powerful title and powerful subject that it just felt right to use as the album title. It conjures all kinds of imagery. You're also thinking what you're going to do in the stage set and all that stuff too.

Walk like an Egyptian. Iron Maiden's mascot Eddie gets in on Powerslave's hieroglyphic vibes.

↑

Slaves to the rhythm.
Iron Maiden's Dave
Murray, Bruce
Dickinson and Steve
Harris onstage in
Ljubljana in 1984.

## 8. RIME OF THE ANCIENT MARINER

### @IronMaiden (Steve Harris)

Mariner was written in the Bahamas. I had just an inkling of an idea but it wasn't worked up in any way. I hadn't got it done by the time we left Jersey so it felt like I was cramming for exams because I'd have had Master Birch on me!

### @IronMaiden (Bruce Dickinson)

Steve was locked in his room for ages and ages and then turned up one day and said "I've got this song called Rime Of The Ancient Mariner." My jaw hit the floor and bounced off again and I went, "Huh? Samuel Taylor Coleridge? The epic poem?!"

### @IronMaiden (Steve Harris)

It was a poem I'd done at school, mountains of verses going on, and we had to do a synopsis and try to cut it down and that's what I had to do with the song. So many people said it helped them get through their exams on that poem which is nice! On an album you can have loads of different diverse subjects going on. But if you've got an overall vibe and a feel of something... that's what we always try and work for. That's why a lot of people think our albums could be concept albums.

### @IronMaiden (Bruce Dickinson)

On the Maiden pinball, where I have a top score of 368 million by the way, The Mariner multiball is where you shoot into the Pharaoh's tomb and then shoot the albatross. A lady's voice comes on and says "No, I said shoo the bird, shoo the bird!" As I used to say on stage, this is what not to do if a bird shits on you!

# Stage Fright
## The Band
Capitol, 1970

⚐ Opting to call yourself simply The Band might imply a lack of vision. However, the creative energy that Rick Danko (bass), Levon Helm (drums/vocals), Garth Hudson (keyboards), Richard Manuel (keyboards/vocals) and Robbie Robertson (guitar/autoharp) did not expend on naming their group more than went into their music. Bob Dylan certainly appreciated The Band's talents. After a stint playing together for rockabilly singer Ronnie Hawkins, the "voice of a generation" snapped up the American-Canadians to back him up when he "went electric". Yet this being present for this moment of musical history did not eclipse The Band's own reputation and with their famous instrument-swapping, singing drummer and euphoric songs, they went on to become one of the bedrocks for the now flourishing Americana scene. Their 1970 album, *Stage Fright* possessed a harder, rockier edge then some of The Band's other works, mixing bright sounds with lyrics that charted disenchantment and change as the 1960s just came to an end. Demonstrating none of the nerves associated with Stage Fright, Robbie Robertson (@r0bbier0berts0n) gave us a backstage tour of the making of this classic.

ARTWORK:
Bob Cato

(←)

I'm with The Band. Garth Hudson, Levon Helm, Richard Manuel, Robbie Robertson and Rick Danko in 1969.

## 1. THE W.S. WALCOTT MEDICINE SHOW

### ● @r0bbier0berts0n (Robbie Robertson)

Our renowned mixing engineer, Bob Clearmountain, commented that this track was like The Band's version of The Beatles song Sgt. Pepper Lonely Hearts Club Band. It's really about a piece of Americana. The traveling music and medicine shows, that inspired a lot of early rock and roll artists.

## 2. THE SHAPE I'M IN

### ● @r0bbier0berts0n

The song features Garth's brilliant organ solos, and Richard's vocal telling it like it is. The subject matter addresses remnants of the 1960s, and a weariness in the aftermath.

## 3. DANIEL AND THE SACRED HARP

### ● @r0bbier0berts0n

It's like a small movie, on the theme of Dr. Faust selling his soul to Mephisto for worldly knowledge and pleasure, mixed with the tale of Robert Johnson, father of the Delta Blues, selling his soul at the crossroads. Of course, nothing is for free. Another classic case where The Band members switch instruments.

## 4. STAGE FRIGHT

### ● @r0bbier0berts0n

I was inspired in the writing first of all by Alfred Hitchcock's movie Stage Fright. This an acknowledgment of a bad dream many performers have had, where you go out there and can't remember your lines or what song you're playing. Rick's amazing vocal while playing fretless bass — don't know how he did it. On this, Garth plays a style of organ, like nobody else.

## 5. THE RUMOR

### ● @r0bbier0berts0n

Here, The Band's performing and singing in our most comfortable set up – to each other in a circle. While living in Woodstock NY, we experienced some "small town talk". How an unfounded rumour can scar a person, even if it's untrue.

## 6. TIME TO KILL

### ● @r0bbier0berts0n

When I wrote this song it reminded me of a new type of modern mountain music. Living up in the Catskills, the days can run into one another like a river going by. In fact, they said the song written in 1908, Down By The Old Mill Stream was written in Woodstock. But that too, may have been a rumour.

## 7. JUST ANOTHER WHISTLE STOP

### ● @r0bbier0berts0n

Here's an unusual performance and a wicked shuffle! Always liked that old Americana image of crowds gathering as a train pulls into their town with a famous personality or politician.

## 8. ALL LA GLORY

### ● @r0bbier0berts0n

This is a lullaby, and I wasn't sure Levon could pull off this kind of vocal, but it turned out so touching. My first daughter was born, and this is a celebration of the heart...

## 9. STRAWBERRY WINE

### ● @r0bbier0berts0n

Levon had just returned from Arkansas with half of a blues-style tune written. I loved helping him finish it. This song is a throwback to early Rockabilly. Richard's drumming is so funky, with Garth's raunchy accordion, and Levon returning to his roots.

## 10. SLEEPING

### ● @r0bbier0berts0n

The movie's over, and now you can dream on it. There's a picture of Levon taking a nap on the floor between recording songs. Our recording engineer, Todd Rundgren, thought that was strange. Richard's gorgeous vocal. Coming back to it, this an exceptional kind of playing on this track. Unusual for The Band or maybe anybody...

# *Invisible Cities*
## A Winged Victory For The Sullen
Artificial Pinearch/Ninja Tune, 2021

As collaborative works go, ambient classical duo A Winged Victory For The Sullen are no strangers to creating ideas in tandem with other creators. Dustin O'Halloran and Adam Wiltzie (**@AWVFTS**) have scored acclaimed soundtracks for films, yet *Invisible Cities* represented a unique interaction with other artists.

In the first instance, the music was commissioned to accompany a 90-minute video being directed by Leo Warner. Yet this would then be embedded into a dance production and shown onstage live. Added to that, the work was inspired by Italian writer Italo Calvino's 1972 experimental novel of the same name, which retells the journeys of explorer and merchant Marco Polo. This meant A Winged Victory For The Sullen had to not only take into account the practicality of the production but also reflect the ideas of the late novelist. Sadly after the show's 2019 premiere, the pandemic prevented it from touring, yet the duo's album of their work has emerged ensuring the creative energy was not in vain. O'Halloran and Wiltzie guided us through *Invisible Cities'* brooding musical allies and impressive string-swept streets, with a listening party that in many ways embodied the record's illusive scope, with one of them tweeting from Reykjavík and the other "somewhere near the border of Mexico". "Come hither broken-hearted," they invited us, "and press play…"

ARTWORK:
Davy Evans

---

LISTENING
PARTY

**1 MARCH
2021**

### 1. SO THAT THE CITY CAN BEGIN TO EXIST

**@AWVFTS (Adam Wiltzie)**
We try all things; & achieve what we can. This is our pitched piano. We have been working on this patch since we first experimented with it on Atomos. It's layers of different pianos played simply via a Native Instruments Kontact sampler patch. We would love to release a sample library of these sort of things.

**@AWVFTS (Dustin O'Halloran)**
Thought I would start it off where things began – our first mixing sesh for the first album in an old villa near Ferrara Italy.

### 2. THE CELESTIAL CITY

**@AWVFTS (Adam Wiltzie)**
Leo [Warner, director of the multimedia production the music was iniitally commissioned for] really had a hand on helping this one evolve emotionally, I had read the book previously before meeting Leo, but his interpretation has left me with a better understanding of its importance

### 3. THE DEAD OUTNUMBER THE LIVING

**@AWVFTS (Dustin O'Halloran)**
This is the positive dance hit of the soundtrack.

### 4. EVERY SOLSTICE & EQUINOX

✅ @AWVFTS (Adam Wiltzie)
Listen closely – that guitar drone was run through this Italian rotating speaker @ 35 sec it creeps in. Dustin always felt this sounded a bit too much like Atomos VII.

### 5. NOTHING OF THE CITY TOUCHES THE EARTH

✅ @AWVFTS (Adam Wiltzie)
This is Meg Hermant of @echo_collective on the harp, she plays violin if you have seen us live. This track is one of the intermission pieces. 59 Productions designed a theatrical world in which the (seated) audience are fragmented into four corners of a wide, long, low space, and so it required set changes that were extremely difficult to pull off in under 2 minutes.

### 6. THIRTEENTH CENTURY TRAVELOGUE

✅ @AWVFTS (Dustin O'Halloran)
Our other partner in crime Francesco Donadello on his custom CADAC mixing console.

### 7. THE DIVIDED CITY

✅ @AWVFTS (Adam Wiltzie)
One of the simplest tracks on the recording, just piano + guitar drones. For the piano we used Dustin's August Förster. Pure softness.

### 8. ONLY STRINGS AND THEIR SUPPORTS REMAIN

✅ @AWVFTS (Dustin O'Halloran)
We recorded a lot in Budapest with their wonderful orchestra, been a pleasure working with them.

### 9. THERE IS ONE OF WHICH YOU NEVER SPEAK

✅ @AWVFTS (Dustin O'Halloran)
One of our long term collaborator cellist Clarice Jensen once said we were like the Odd Couple. guess who is who?

### 10. DESPAIR DIALOGUE

✅ @AWVFTS (Adam Wiltzie)
This is my favourite piece on the record for some reason.

✅ @AWVFTS (Dustin O'Halloran)
Our violist Neil Leiter taking the new album for a test listen.

### 11. THE MERCHANTS OF SEVEN NATIONS

✅ @AWVFTS (Adam Wiltzie)
A little backstory for the song titles: They are all taken directly from Calvino's novel and are directly connected to the different cities that are visited over the course of the piece.

### 12. DESIRES ARE ALREADY MEMORIES

✅ @AWVFTS (Adam Wiltzie)
This is the continuation of the choir that leads to the climax of Invisible Cities.

### 13. TOTAL PERSPECTIVE VORTEX

✅ @AWVFTS (Adam Wiltzie)
Here we are at the end, this is Hildur Gudnadottir about to eat enchiladas in Berlin after we made the vox sample you are hearing now, one octave lower…

⊕
Dustin O'Halloran
@AWVFTS
We recorded a lot in Budapest with their wonderful orchestra, been a pleasure working with them.

# *Star*
## Belly
4AD, 1993

⚑ A member of Throwing Muses and The Breeders, Tanya Donelly (**@TanyaDonelly**) was already a key figure within alternative American rock before she formed Belly. With that band though, the singer-songwriter added to her already considerable reputation as she found greater room for self-expression. The Rhode Island group's first album *Star* landed fearsome lyrics and vocals among a dreamy soundscape, inviting listeners into an intriguing otherworld of strange but beautiful imagery and compelling guitars. Joined by bandmates Tom Gorman (guitar – **@disappearingdrs**), Chris Gorman (drums – **@bellytheband**) and bassist Gail Greenwood (who replaced founding member Fred Abong just after *Star*'s release, also using **@bellytheband**), Donelly and co gave us plenty to digest as they revisited Belly's much-loved and highly influential debut.

**ARTWORK:**
Chris Bigg

**@bellytheband**
Feed the Tree opened the world up for the band with so many opportunities to play great places like THE ARSENIO HALL SHOW. [See also page 155]

## 1. SOMEONE TO DIE FOR

**@TanyaDonelly**
As delicate as it is, I was *mad* when I wrote this pretty ditty. I think we set the tone leading off with this one...

**@disappearingdrs (Thomas Gorman)**
Tanya had a Gibson endorsement when we made Star, & we got borrow some guitars from the Nashville showroom to record with. I remember the one we used on this was a weird 12-str sorta 'fake' acoustic thing, but it sounded cool. One guitar was weird semi-hollow 'prototype' the Gibs guys said was junk, but I thought it was kinda cool and ended-up using a lot. At end of recordng I convinced them to sell it to me ($300 I think). Was my main guitar four a long time.

## 2. ANGEL

**@bellytheband (Chris Gorman)**
At the time I was listening to a lot of Echo And The Bunnymen when we were tweaking the drum parts, I always thought this song had a nice dose of that influence.

**@bellytheband (Gail Greenwood)**
I'm listening along firstly as a fan of the record (the amazing Fred Abong played on the record!) and subsequently as a band member who won the lottery when they asked me to join.

## 3. DUSTED

**@TanyaDonelly**
A live favourite of mine. Gail's and Chris's (extended) intro interactions, Tom's waves of feedback, and then everyone slams in. Love the harmonies on this one too. Deeply sad song, but a joy to play.

**@disappearingdrs (Thomas Gorman)**
First of the four recorded with [producer] Gil Norton in Liverpool. We did a week of pre-prod in London before going in the studio, playing songs over and over, from 9-5 in a rehearsal space (then spending the eve in the pub...)

## 4. EVERY WORD

**@TanyaDonelly**
This one is a weirdo! Said with love. Proud of the sequencing – we sure weren't trying to trick anyone into sticking around. The thereminy vocal that doubles the lead was spontaneous. I could see [producer] Tracey Chisholm laughing in the control room.

## 5. GEPETTO

**@bellytheband (Chris Gorman)**
At first I hated working with Gil, it was soul crushing, he was used to working with far more experienced studio drummers. This session really taught me so much, I will always recall those lessons when I'm playing. GIL ALWAYS RANTED ABOUT DAVE LOVERING... "why can't you play more like Dave Lovering!" trust me if I could play more like Dave Lovering I would!

**@TanyaDonelly**
The stage shakes when we do this one live, from audience and me and Gail jumping. Never fails to make me a little giddy, tbh. Also, now's as good a time as any to acknowledge my misspelling of Geppetto. It's two P's.

## 6. WITCH

**@disappearingdrs**
I think we were workng on this when Shania Twain and Garth Brooks came in to record vocals for a duet in the next room (the 'fancy' one)... They were both really nice.

**@TanyaDonelly**
Witch (She is me).

## 7. SLOW DOG

**@TanyaDonelly**
My kids' favourite when they were little. I don't think they were listening very closely.

**@bellytheband (Chris Gorman)**
Stopped counting at 100 takes on this song. Most didn't make it past the 1 min mark.we put ice buckets next to my throne. Gil would tip his head back to look at the ceiling, I knew I blew it. ITS TOO LUMPY!

## 8. LOW RED MOON

**@TanyaDonelly**
A happy recording memory. Tom playing this organ part. He wasn't wearing a cloak, but I choose to remember it that way. One of the Nashville batch, and it was a blistering hot day, which you can almost hear.

144

(far left)
**@bellytheband**
Here's a super handsome pic of Tom [Gorman] on stage of venue Cargo 92 – a ship in Nantes, France made to look like a city street. Just because (sorry Tom).

(left) OK! Parts of the Feed The Tree Tour saw Belly join "a little band called Radiohead" on the road. The band shared this backstage shot of both groups together.

**@bellytheband**
We were so fortunate to tour with another little band called the Cranberries and Delores joined us one night.

### 9. FEED THE TREE

**@disappearingdrs**
The HIT! Kinda ironic that a tune about fidelity & death might be the 'sunniest' sounding track on the record! The one thing I don't like about Feed The Tree, it's the only song I use a wah pedal on, but it's the 'hit' so I always have to drag this big pedal around for that one part live.

**@bellytheband (Chris Gorman)**
As it was considered to be the single front runner from the get go, surprisingly this was a really fun and easy song to record. We finished the drums in very few takes. Gil was pleased, it felt like a triumph.

**@TanyaDonelly**
The tree song. Probably the one that changed the most in the studio with Gil, and it came in under the wire. I sang the third verse minutes after writing it.

### 10. FULL MOON, EMPTY HEART

**@TanyaDonelly**
Full Moon, Empty Heart became a dark horse singalong live, and it still slays me when everyone joins on the long high note. Gives me goosebumps. This one was almost [Throwing] Muses, then almost Breeders, before landing.

### 11. WHITE BELLY

**@disappearingdrs**
I have a vague recollection that this might have been the first song we every tried to play together as a band, rehearsing in the basement of the Trader's Cove guitar shop in Newport, RI.

**@TanyaDonelly**
Co-written with Fred while we were both in Throwing Muses. Kim Deal played some guitar on the original demo. Another live favourite of mine.

### 12. UNTOGETHER

**@TanyaDonelly**
Three true stories with one common ending.

**@bellytheband (Chris Gorman)**
Makes me cry every night. We toured with a little band called Radiohead and sometimes Thom came out and sang with Tanya. Swoon. xo (with Velocity Girl!)

### 13. STAR

**@disappearingdrs**
Can't remember why we didn't do this as a band originally [on the album] – maybe just didn't have time? but eventually we did as a b-side.

### 14. SAD DRESS

**@TanyaDonelly**
I love this one, and loved playing it in our practice space (still do, at home) but it always seemed to get away from us live. A hard one to recover once the wheels start coming off.

### 15. STAY

**@bellytheband (Chris Gorman)**
One of the all time great set closers. There were nights when we would drag this one out for what seemed like days...

**@TanyaDonelly**
My album favourite, maybe? Came out fast and whole-cloth when written, but it changes every time we play it. It's always at the end of the set and I love looking down and seeing it waiting there at the bottom of the list. Good old friend.

# *Tin Drum*
## Japan
Virgin, 1981

Part Listening Party, part the secret diary, there have been few playbacks with such thorough chronologies as Japan's. Amazingly, when Steve Jansen (drums/keyboards – **@istevejansen**) decided to take us through his, David Sylvian (vocals), Mick Karn (bass) and Richard Barbieri (keyboards) fifth and final album, he was able to consult his notes made during the recordings. "I decided to check diary entries for this period to discover any interesting facts or timelines," he explained of the precise dating as he revealed the timeline of the Catford band's kaleidoscopic new wave masterpiece. Bang on!

**PHOTOGRAPHY:**
Fin Costello

Hold on. David Sylvian onstage in London in February 1981.

Japan in Japan. The band pictured in a rainy Kyoto in 1981.

### 1. THE ART OF PARTIES

☑ @istevejansen

We mixed TAOP at Air studios on 27th March 1981 & LWB on 30st. Cut the single on 31st and released a month later on 01st May – fast tracked. On 12th May with the single was at 48 we got the call for our first Top Of The Pops. Headed straight to Air studios to 're-record' the track (union rules, always flouted). We had a show in Edinburgh that night so hire equipment was brought in. John Punter was at the desk ready to give the illusion of re-recording the track when we got a call …. due to a football match being rescheduled TOTP was cancelled, and we lost out.

### 2. TALKING DRUM

☑ @istevejansen

This was intended to be the next single & B-side (Canton). We'd been rehearsing the tracks bringing the arrangements together. Diary says we recorded reference versions in rehearsals.

### 3. GHOSTS

☑ @istevejansen

What to say about this…an outstanding composition. Highest chart position despite being musically stripped to its essence. Best vocal performance-found that comfort zone. Only Japan track Mick doesn't play on. Only Japan track I play a solo on.

### 4. CANTON

☑ @istevejansen

This was one of those rare occasions where Mick and I nailed it in the same take. Drums have priority as the bass can always be overdubbed, (unlike the drums) however in this case Take-4 was the one for both of us.

### 5. STILL LIFE IN MOBILE HOMES

☑ @istevejansen

I decided to use the Linn drum machine bass drum for this track. It was a new bit of tech allowing sync to tape. I believe it was the first drum machine to do so. Studied manual overnight!

### 6. VISIONS OF CHINA

☑ @istevejansen

Despite many approaches the track wasn't working. Just before finishing I happened to kick in with a more useful drum pattern and everything flowed from there. At around 1am I had to stop as the neighbours complained about the noise the drums were making.

### 7. SONS OF PIONEERS

☑ @istevejansen

This was the opening track on our final tour which provided good drama as we were able to build up the mood and anticipation for the staggered vocal entry. And Mick got to glide around the stage as frontman for a few minutes.

### 8. CANTONESE BOY

☑ @istevejansen

I did the single sleeve photo shoot of the 'boy' in my flat in Kensington. Upon return to the studio we got pulled up by the cops (which was a regular theme for us). Mick managed to conceal his stash despite a search.

# Shaken And Stirred:
# The David Arnold James Bond Project
## David Arnold
East West, 1997

⚘ Cue the famous riff and the camera shot peering down a rifle's barrels… but instead of an armed secret again it's a composer, baton in hand: Arnold, David Arnold. While James Bond himself was delayed as the pandemic stopped the latest film reaching cinema screens on time, the prolific soundtrack scorer (with plenty of actual Bond films among his credits) arrived on Twitter right on time to deliver the intelligence on his 1997 album, a celebration some of the spy franchise's best-loved songs with a series of fizzing covers.

ARTWORK:
Stylorouge

"I wanted to make this record because I loved songs and I loved radio and they don't play film scores on the radio very much," Arnold (**@DavidGArnold**) briefed the Listening Party. "I'd done a couple of movies so people I called started picking up the phone. Before there was nothing . I loved the Bond songs and so decided to do a covers album. No writing, so could get straight into the studio." With Chrissie Hynde, Aimee Mann, Propellerheads, Pulp and Iggy Pop among his agents, Arnold's musical Secret Service not only paid tribute to 007, but challenged some of the most interesting artists around to step outside their comfort zones as they tackled the older material. Now Mr Arnold, we expect you to tweet…

LISTENING
PARTY
**7 MARCH
2021**

### 1. DIAMONDS ARE FOREVER

☑ **@DavidGArnold**
Diamonds was the first track I did. Started in 1995! David Mcalmont was my only choice as he is everything you want in a song like diamonds who isn't Shirley Bassey.

### 2. NOBODY DOES IT BETTER

☑ **@DavidGArnold**
So next up The spy Who Loved Me. Aimee Mann is a brilliant writer and I love her voice. Jon Brion was working on Aimee's record so he popped in too and ended-up playing harmonium and some brilliant guitar on it.

### 3. SPACE MARCH

☑ **@DavidGArnold**
Space March with Leftfield came about after I'd heard their debut album. I was sharing a flat at the time with Danny Cannon who was shooting Judge Dredd and I was recording Stargate. Leftfield lived opposite. We didn't know until I asked their record company where they were. I popped over and they showed me their brand-new massive synth and we talked about the track.

### 4. ALL TIME HIGH

☑ **@DavidGArnold**
I loved this version. It was a song that didn't get as much love as other Bond songs. I think [writer] Sir Tim Rice gave us the thumbs up for putting a different spin on it. Pulp were magnificent and an orchestra sat very comfortably with their sound.

### 5. MOONRAKER

◉ @DavidGArnold

Moonraker was a reasonably faithful cover of the original. Everyone loved Shara Nelson's voice since we heard the work she did with Massive Attack. I was happy she agreed and made the song so unlike Shirley Bassey that you almost forget the original (I know you can't ACTUALLY forget) but it was a swoonier take.

### 6. THE JAMES BOND THEME

◉ @DavidGArnold

I was listening to a lot of drum and bass at the time and had come across LTK Bukem when I heard his stuff in pirate radio from a block of flats in Camden. The same block Goldie lives in, I later learned when I visited Goldie. Bukem's stuff was jazz influenced to my ears and I loved what he did with beats. It's true there's not much James Bond theme in this version, but it's ridiculously groovy and has the DNA in it. It reminds me of very late nights/early mornings.

⊕
Fully licensed.
Bond composer
David Arnold.

### 7. LIVE AND LET DIE

◉ @DavidGArnold

Lovely Chrissie Hynde ran in to do the vocal on this as she was in a hurry. Two takes and we had it. I also had so much fun playing bass and guitar on it. Mel Gaynor of Simple Minds on drums – he hits them REALLY hard.

### 8. THUNDERBALL

◉ @DavidGArnold

Martin Fry of ABC [see page 46] did the vocal. Tom Jones is a tough act to follow but Martin had alluded to cinematic drama with his own records so it was a great fit. Derek Watkins on trumpet on all of these songs btw. He played on every Bond score ever. A master and sadly no longer with us. It's a real thunderclap recorded outside the studio one night...

### 9. FROM RUSSIA WITH LOVE

◉ @DavidGArnold

I had been working with Natacha Atlas previously on Stargate and even though she was from Northampton she bought the unknowable to From Russia With Love. This was the first Bond theme song ever written by Lionel Bart.

### 10. ON HER MAJESTY'S SECRET SERVICE

◉ @DavidGArnold

I'd heard "Spy Break" by PropellerHeads and immediately thought they sound like they know what's what. Amazing drums and instrumentation and the spirit of John Barry.

### 11. WE HAVE ALL THE TIME IN THE WORLD

◉ @DavidGArnold

I was in New York for the Grammys *cough * I won *cough cough* and thought it a good idea to record Iggy the next day at Electric Lady studios. When I got there he asked me what I'd been doing? I said I'd been to the Grammys (my first ever time). He shouted "the Grammys suck!" Anyway. I asked Iggy to sing this beautiful song as he had the sound of a lifetime of experience in his voice and he would suit a croon. And he did. It was lovely. He was lovely.

# Smoke Ring For My Halo
## Kurt Vile
Matador, 2011

There is something truly impressive about the way Kurt Vile (**@therealkurtvile**) manages to balance the earthy roots of Americana and folk with a series of production-driven, forward-thinking atmospheres. It is particularly inspiring as Vile seems to manage this improbable blend with seemingly little effort. His songs feel so natural and organic despite the depths and shades they contain. Refreshingly, as Vile revealed with the Listening Party for his fourth album *Smoke Ring For My Halo*, he admits to working as hard as anyone. A transformative moment for Vile and his band The Violators – who featured at the time The War On Drugs' Adam Granduciel (see page 238) – *Smoke Ring For My Halo* reflected fatherhood, day jobs and hard graft in the studio, as it blew listeners away…

**PHOTOGRAPHY:**
Michael Ast

Fresh air. Kurt Ville live in Chicago in 2011.

## 1. BABY'S ARMS

@therealkurtvile

A milestone song in my life. Always thought it shoulda been a hit (not too late!) and also thought it was quite cinematic... wrote it before I had any record deals to speak of (on my couch in Philly). Rob Laakso (before he was in the band but a friend I liked to jam with)... triggered the acoustics thru a modular synth (I know which one I'm just not telling you)... they call him the doctor for that reason. Meg Baird: Philly folk legend goddess... kills it on backing vocals in the outro.

## 2. JESUS FEVER

@therealkurtvile

I actually started recording this with Jeff Zeigler circa "he's alright" era (Childish Prodigy) but we needed some more "singles" on smoke so we added to it w/ John Agnello toward the end of sessions, and it was the first SINGLE for Smoke Ring so, hey...

## 3. PUPPET TO THE MAN

@therealkurtvile

Somewhere in the process of turning in the record, Matador asked for a rocker so I gave them two. This is the first one, so... Get the play on the lyrics(?) "I bet by now you probably think I'm a puppet to the man... well I'll tell right now you best believe that I am." Full on Violators here: KV, [now War On Drugs'] Adam Granduciel, Jesse Trbovich, Mike Zanghi... we were sorta like the suburban Ramones back then (a gang) (even tho we lived in the city it was still Philly and not CBGB's)

## 4. ON TOUR

@therealkurtvile

Mary Lattimore kills it on harp here. Love those melodies. One of the first songs to be recorded for the album... [producer] John Agnello's young daughter Bella (maybe she was 6 or 5 at the time?) would sing this all the time back then, so... (hit!)

## 5. SOCIETY IS MY FRIEND

@therealkurtvile

Love Adam G's dreamy space jangle chime guitar (it's the one that sounds kinda like an 80s keyboard). John Agnello recorded Society with us first as a band up at J Mascis's Bisquiteen studios... then while we were final mixing I sang and strummed acoustic for those keepers.. good to the last second, right John?!

## 6. RUNNER UPS

@therealkurtvile

Makin me misty this sec. Love Adam's lead acoustic... locked right in with my finger picked acoustic... Mike Z's percussion, Jesse's gorgeous electric strums

## 7. IN MY TIME

@therealkurtvile

The first "dad song" I ever wrote .. few days after Awilda was born. This album was recorded for two weeks before my first daughter was born, then John came to me down in Philly where we *tried* to finish soon after I became a... DAD

## 8. PEEPING TOMBOY

@therealkurtvile

Rumor has it this song made Courtney Barnett cry when it came out. Love you. This was a live staple circa Childish Prodigy album cycle (previous album!) I remember writing it the night before I walked into my job at Philadelphia Brewing Company and got fired a couple hours later... cosmic! (A week later it was in all the local papers that I signed to Matador Records... in yo face!).

## 9. SMOKE RING FOR MY HALO

@therealkurtvile

Made this the title track cuz it was my fave tune of the sessions... deceptively simple but special, hypnotic and groovy... didn't want it to accidentally get overlooked. Got some late 70s early 80s Stones influence. Violators... a beautiful era lookin back.. nostalgic... solid album... I was 30 years old makin music... felt like a child.

## 10. GHOST TOWN

@therealkurtvile

Can't fuck with these thunderous drums by Mike Zanghi. Mary Lattimore kills it on the harp. Space blues, baby...

## 11. SHELL BLUES (HIDDEN TRACK)

@therealkurtvile

Mystery jam. "In my time I was whacked and a-wild"

"I was jus bein myself... then."

# Brain Damage
## Dennis Bovell
Fontana, 1981

**ARTWORK:**
Terry Jones

⚑ Without Dennis Bovell there would be a big hole in British music – in the world's music. Moving to London from Barbados as a child in the mid-1960s, the producer, instrumentalist and performer was ideally placed to absorb the crests of two great music cultures as they were happening, experienced firsthand the rise of Jamaican dub along with the progressive edge that was emerging from the beat group-driven pop scene of his new home. From his initial forays with his first band Matumbi in the 1970s, via his production collaborations with artists as diverse as The Slits, Jarvis Cocker, Orange Juice and Bananarama, to his own studio creations – perhaps best defined by lovers rock classic he did for Janet Kay, Silly Games – there has always a been a unique flavour to Bovell's dub-infused sounds. British reggae probably wouldn't exist without him, while he has brought new textures to disco, indie and his beloved dub. His 1981 album *Brain Damage* is a great testament to the fusion reactions Bovell triggers. Recorded in his own South London base, Studio 80, the record was not just a demonstration of Bovell's skills as a producer, but it was a proof of the depth and spectrum of reggae as a whole as he married its heavier components and his own signature lovers rock sound, with elements of pop, jazz, Afrobeat, rock, funk and more. In anyone else hands it might have been a chaotic affair, but with Bovell (**@DubMaestro1**) at the faders *Brain Damage* proved to be a coherent, enthralling work and a treasure map for further sonic exploration.

⬇
Blackbeard. Bovell started out as the guitarist for the band Matumbi.

The Professor. Bovell soon graduated to producing his own records, along with tracks for others from his Studio 80 HQ.

### 1. BRAIN DAMAGE

**@DubMaestro1 (Dennis Bovell)**

Happy Listening Y'all. After having rented a multi track dolby system from Sir George Martin's Air London Studios in order to complete my work with [Japanese composer] Ryuichi Sakamoto on his B-2 Unit album. I decided to keep them on and finish this project.

In this song I have proclaimed the coming of the Michael Jackson album thriller. Rod Temperton said so 'Rightaboutnowyouareintunetothathriller'.

### 2. BETTAH

**@DubMaestro1**

An appeal to the authority to give us better in all walks of life. I enlisted the help of Laura Logic who supplied a 'sleeky' saxophone solo that was put through a precious piece of outboard: Dimension D Phaseshifter

### 3. AFTER TONIGHT

**@DubMaestro1**

After discussions with the legendary Ian Dury we decided that the drummer Mac Pool and myself would lay down a Rock'n Roll version of this Matumbi hit. A lovers rock tune, eliciting the services of Steve Gregory on saxophone – he was a guest on one of The Rolling Stones recordings, Honky Tonk Women. To date it has the reputation of being the most covered lovers rock tune with some 23 versions by other artists

### 4. OUR TUNE

**@DubMaestro1**

Courtesy the late [live engineer] Martin Rex, my soldering iron confidant who supplied me with a pulse machine that played the kick drum that gave me confidence on the top kit, enabling me to be the drummer on this piece. Henry Tenyue supplied the trombones. [Singer] Marie Pierre heard it and insisted that she do a version. I obliged.

### 5. RUN AWAY

**@DubMaestro1**

A ska tune originally created for the Babylon movie soundtrack [1980 drama directed by Franco Rosso which Bovell scored]. A longer version reworked, for inclusion on this album. The piece is my answer to one of my favourite Jimi Hendricks song: Wait Until Tomorrow.

### 6. HEAVEN

**@DubMaestro1**

This is my Afrobeat anthem. I decided to attempt this genre after having tangoed with my hero Fela Anikulapo Kuti. Drums are supplied by Errol Melbourne, guitars John Kpiaye talking, drums Webster Johnson and horns Patrick Tenyue and Henry Matic.

### 7. BAH LE BON

**@DubMaestro1**

My observation of ghetto runnings inna London. Yes, We are living inna Babylon existing on a system furthest stone from the sun.

### 8. BERTIE

**@DubMaestro1**

Hailing from heaven on earth Barbados, I felt obliged to indulge in a soca beat. Once again I found myself behind the top kit with the pulse of Martin Rex's machine, driving the kick drum.

Attempting to emulate the style of my hero [singer] The Mighty Sparrow #doubleentendre. My grand dad Joseph Frederick Bovell was amused.

## 9. AQUA DUB

🌀 **@DubMaestro1**

This is the beginning of the Brain Damage Dub section. Drums by Drummie Zeb, keyboard Tony Gad both, members of the group Aswad. Accompanied with the clavinet of Nick Straker doust in small stone phaser, hence the water effect, Aquatic Reggae. It's all about #thebubble

## 10. FREA STOIL

🌀 **@DubMaestro1**

A late night session with the mystical Rico Rodigues. I still adore his musicality. As a youngster he supplied trombone for my 4th Street Orchestra horn section. Rico was an original Jamaican trombonist whom I produced Children of Sanchez for Island Records and I encouraged him to sing hence his vocal version of The Kinks' You Really Got Me, I think it was. Recorded at Studio 80 in the weee hours

## 11. SMOUCHE

🌀 **@DubMaestro1**

A track originally intended for Janet Kay, yet to be explored. The legendary singer Delroy Wilson took a shine to it and we recorded as Hooked On You. [Producer] Steve Taylor enhanced the lyrics on Delroy Wilson's Hooked On You. For this I had borrowed a DMX synthesiser from my friend Eddy Grant and put it to use.

## 12. EL PASSOAH

🌀 **@DubMaestro1**

Named by my beautiful cousin Brenda. Now dedicated to her memory R.I.P. The reason for this title is the Bajan pronunciation of El Paso which seemed to need a different spelling so it would be the way she pronounced it. When asked what title would most conjure a scene in a Cowboy movie, her response was El Passoah. Farewell Brenda.

## 13. CHIEF INSPECTOR

🌀 **@DubMaestro1**

Chief Inspector is the signature tune of my live dub band performances. One of the compositions featured in the Babylon film soundtrack. A Golders Green Constabulary Spy Thriller.

## 14. EHYING

🌀 **@DubMaestro1**

Ehying is the sound that the drums made when fed into the even tied harmoniser with the required amount of feedback. To be pronounced as 'Heng' omitting the H.

## 15. DUTTY

🌀 **@DubMaestro1**

Dutty is the Jamaican pronunciation of the word dirty. Here I have enlisted the drum talent of Errol Melbourne alongside the harmonica prowess of Juilo Finn. He who supplied the harmonica on [dub poet] Linton Kwesi Johnson's tracks Sonny's Lettah and Bass Culture.

## 16. CABBAGE

🌀 **@DubMaestro1**

The grande finale, a dub version of Brain Damage utilising the Melodica made famous by Augustus Pablo. Rewind and Come Again..... thanks for listening!!

fontana

6381 047
SET NO. 6627 001

33⅓

STEREO

titles:
appell Music Ltd.

6381 047.1
Made in England

1

Record Set—Side One

℗ 1981 Phonogram Ltd.

BRAIN DAMAGE
1. AQUA DUB 2. FREA STOIL 3. SMOUCHE 4. EL PASSOAH
DENNIS BOVELL
Written & Produced by Dennis Bovell
Recorded at Studio 80
Original Sound Recording made by Phonogram Ltd.

# *Immigrants*
## Nitin Sawhney
Sony Music, 2021

You'll be harder pushed to find an example of actions – or music – speaking louder than words. Conceived as a sequel to his 1999 acclaimed album *Beyond Skin*, *Immigrants* is Nitin Sawhney's examination and deconstruction of various elements underpinning British society. A timely reevaluation in the wake of headlines, debates and the very real human costs of small boat crossings that has thrust immigration and multiculturalism into the spotlight in the opening of the 21st century, Sawhney delivers his observations and makes his points in song. Assembling a globally infused, yet British collective of musicians, *Immigrants* is an exquisite record that extols the virtues of cooperation and collaboration with its creation as much as it does its message – although the latter is poignantly and clearly made via his lyrics and a series of found sound recordings. To make the album's release, Sawhney (**@thenitinsawhney**) offered us a truly "cathartic" Listening Party.

PHOTOGRAPHY:
Nina Manandhar

Music of great import.
Nitin Sawhney onstage in
London in 2015.

---

LISTENING
PARTY

**24 MARCH
2021**

### 1. DOWN THE ROAD

✔ **@thenitinsawhney**
Down the Road was originally intended as a song of hope and the Sufi lyrics of the chorus also reflect that. Hum Dekhenge is the name by which the original poem is best known, meaning, in context, "we shall see the day when tyranny ends".

### 2. IMMIGRANTS INTERLUDE I

✔ **@thenitinsawhney**
This is the first interlude from Pathe which features old news about Jamaican immigrants of the windrush generation flowing into movement variation II.

### 3. MOVEMENT - VARIATION II

✔ **@thenitinsawhney**
The album #immigrants was always intended as a sequel to my 1999 album Beyond Skin. I was so pleased to be joined by so many wonderful artists and collaborators on immigrants, as you will hear.

### 4. VAI

✔ **@thenitinsawhney**
This track is written with Brazilian singer Nina Miranda. It expresses her feelings around saying goodbye to her son.

### 5. EXILE

✔ **@thenitinsawhney**
Exile was written with wonderful friends, singer Natacha Atlas and violinist Samy Bishai.

### 6. REPLAY

✔ **@thenitinsawhney**
Replay features another old friend of mine, Aruba Red, who partially speaks this in German before Ashwin Srinivasan on indian classical flute.

### 7. IMMIGRANTS INTERLUDE II/
HEAT & DUST

✔ **@thenitinsawhney**
This song was written as a tribute to the first

generation of Asian immigrants from India and Pakistan. I incorporated flamenco inflexions to reference the Indian origins of flamenco.

### 8. BOX

⊘ @thenitinsawhney

With the amazing voice of Gina Ann Leonard who blew me away when I first heard her. There is an incredible intensity to her expression that I haven't heard before.

### 9. YOU ARE

⊘ @thenitinsawhney

You Are is the only song on the album entirely written by me, both lyrics and music. Sung beautifully by YVA I also scored an instrumental part in the middle for Anna Phoebe and Ashwin Srinivasan to perform together.

### 10. IMMIGRANTS INTERLUDE III/ DIFFERENCES

⊘ @thenitinsawhney

Differences again features Abi Sampa and Rushil who co-wrote this with me. Abi here is improvising using sargams --the indian equivalent of "do re mi".

### 11. IMMIGRANTS INTERLUDE IV/ LIFELINE

⊘ @thenitinsawhney

Lifeline features the excellent voice of Rahel along with brilliant rapper and old friend, Spek.

Spek, who rapped on Beyond Skin, wrote the rap and I wrote the chorus lyrics and melody for this.

### 12. TOKYO

⊘ @thenitinsawhney

Tokyo is about my first visit to Japan in the 90s, feeling overwhelmed. I remember standing in Akihabara (aka the electric city) and feeling like I was on the set of Blade Runner.

### 13. SAWUBONA

⊘ @thenitinsawhney

"Sawubona" is a Zulu word of greeting. I really loved writing this track with Natty who I worked with on London Undersound with Days of Fire. Natty is a fantastic lyricist and has an amazing cinematic sense of narrative in his songwriting.

### 14. IMMIGRANTS INTERLUDE V

⊘ @thenitinsawhney

This is my mum talking about the difficulties she and dad faced with a newborn baby (me) when they first arrived in the UK back in the 60s.

### 15. MOVEMENT – VARIATION I

⊘ @thenitinsawhney

This was originally written as a solo piano piece inspired by Chopin, Beethoven and Rachmaninov until Ayanna Witter-Johnson Variation II and Anna Phoebe on Variation I brought their respective brilliance to the composition...

### 16. ANOTHER SKY

⊘ @thenitinsawhney

Another sky is written with brilliant duo Ava Waves who consist of superb musicians Aisling Brouwer and Anna Phoebe. This piece feels really emotional for me to listen to... Such incredible playing from them both...

### 17. DREAM

⊘ @thenitinsawhney

Dream is about all of us. Those of the global majority unrepresented by those in power. Who feel the prejudice, bigotry and fear that screws with our sense of self esteem and identity. Immigrants is the story of our journey. Their struggle.

# *Deep England*
## Gazelle Twin & NYX
NYX Collective Recordings, 2021

✦ Gazelle Twin's 2018 album *Pastoral* was already a remarkable work. Electronic music that reached into the folk tradition, it pointed to the future while its political awareness also made a firm connection to the enduring yet corrupted soul of the artist's home, Britain. It was also an album of enticing possibilities, and a live adaptation saw Elizabeth Bernholz – the Twin's real name – and female-voiced drone choir NYX (**@nyx_edc**) radically rework the record's songs before deciding to re-record them together. Almost sacred, almost satanic, always effecting, *Deep England* is the result of that collaboration as it combines pure voices and pitch-shifting; contemporary outrage and Blakeian prophecy; and Gazelle Twin's (**@gazelletwin**) forward-thinking with NYX's communal power. They all also came together for a Listening Party to celebrate this moving, unnerving and beautiful joint record.

ARTWORK:
Barnbrook

LISTENING
PARTY
25 MARCH
2021

### 1. GLORY

✔ **@nyx_edc**
Lock the doors, lower the blinds, lie on the floor. Got your recorder ready? Got some incense? Get it on baby. We are NYX: electronic drone choir. It's pronounced "nix" for when we can meet again in person btw. We use choral music and embodied electronics to create ambient, ecstatic and noise music.

✔ **@gazelletwin**
This was one of my favourites to record with NYX like being in a field of serpents.

### 2. FOLLY

✔ **@gazelletwin**
Folly was very much about WTF is going on post 2016. I'm sure we all expected things to get even more WTF in 2020?? No we did not.

✔ **@nyx_edc**
What species IS this?? NYX Vocalist Cecilia Forssberg opens up the alien realm of Folly – every sound you hear in this piece is created by our almost human voices...

### 3. FIRE LEAP

✔ **@nyx_edc**
NYX Music Director, Sian O'Gorman, conducting the choir with her trusty recorder in hand.

You might recognise Sian from Auckland Primary Schools' Recorder Orchestra, aged 7–9 years.

✔ **@gazelletwin**
Loved Sian's arrangement of Fire Leap so much and it was one of the best things to perform live with 7 women on recorders and/or NOSE FLUTES of which Ruthie Corey is the absolute Sorceress. You should know that I NEVER got these lyrics right. Even after 50 run-throughs.

### 4. BETTER IN MY DAY

✔ **@Marta_Salogni [producer]**
We recorded the album in a U-shaped formation, all in the same room, all pretty much live with all vocal processing done while tracking. A very technically ambitious set up. Loved the challenge.

✔ **@gazelletwin**
Loved being able to see everyone, and their socks.

### 5. THRONE

**@nyx_edc**

It's almost as though when Gazelle Twin wrote Throne in 2018, she had a premonition that by the time the album was released, we'd all lose our jobs and music touring opportunities due to Brexit and Covid-19.

**@gazelletwin**

Throne was one of my absolute favourites to perform live – solo, but even MORE so with NYX – when the choir starts to sing in unison in an upwards drive, it made me feel like I was levitating on stage.

### 6. JERUSALEM

**@gazelletwin**

How scared are you right now? A lot of people have thought I'm singing the solo on Jerusalem. Nope. It's not me. It's the INCREDIBLE Ruthie Corey. I can't think of a more fitting version of Jerusalem for the state of things right now, tbh.

**@nyx_edc**

Here comes NYX's no. 1 Celtic siren (+ jungle / drum & bass head), Ruthie Corey. Singing forward, then on reverse loop. *Party Trick* Ruth has now learned how to sing that verse backwards without using the loop pedal.

### 7. DEEP ENGLAND

**@nyx_edc**

Deep England ft. NYX's Parisian songstress Dayla's cosmic wail floating out from the roof of a crumbling cathedral.... We thought the lyrics where "my Visa card" instead of "my retail park" until the day of the first show. Apologies.

**@gazelletwin**

I remember attending the very first rehearsal with NYX and hearing this come to life around me. I choked up a bit and found it really hard to sing. I was speechless. Deep England is really about HOPE for a broken place. If you can imagine such a thing.

### 8. GOLDEN DAWN

**@nyx_edc**

Golden Dawn, composed by Sian O'Gorman. The title refs to The Hermetic Order of the Golden Dawn, a secret society devoted to the practice of the occult, metaphysics & paranormal activities during the late 19th and early 20th centuries.

**@gazelletwin**

Loved singing in unison with NYX for this; Sian's amazing lead vocal and the perfection of the falling voices of the choir. And it was SO GOOD to lay down whilst performing this at the South Bank. OOoh that bass. That was such a joy.

Droning on. Gazelle Twin and NYX choir drone on stage.

# Orchestral Manoeuvres In The Dark
## Orchestral Manoeuvres In The Dark
Dindisc, 1980

⚓ If there is something grandiose about the name Orchestral Manoeuvres In The Dark, there is also a sense of overcoming obstacles too – Andy McCluskey and Paul Humphreys certainly had to clear a few hurdles to create their first synth symphony. "This album comprises songs that Paul and I mostly wrote between the ages of 16-19 years old in the backroom at his mother's house when she was at work. The complete instrument list was Bass, Vox organ, Pianotron, Korg Micro preset and MS20 synths and CR78 drum machine and Paul's homemade electro kit," McCluskey (**@OfficialOMD**) told the Listening Party of the basic set-up behind the Wirral duo's debut, before adding that DIY of a non-music kind was required to finish the record. "[It was] recorded and mixed in three weeks in our studio that also took three weeks to build from scratch on the first floor of a derelict printing warehouse in Liverpool."

ARTWORK:
Peter Saville & Ben Kelly

LISTENING
PARTY
**27 MARCH
2021**

### 1. BUNKER SOLDIERS

✅ @OfficialOMD
Everyone will be aware of my fascination over the morality issues in warfare. I grew up on a diet of Vietnam on the evening TV news. Viet Cong offsetting the might of the US forces through guerrilla tactics. The chorus is the letters to the title shouted by me in random order, and Paul shouting numbers of the letters in position of the alphabet reduced to decimal.

### 2. ALMOST

✅ @OfficialOMD
The B-side to Electricity. [Producer] Martin Hannett had taken our bouncy little song and created a swirling atmospheric beauty. The drums are Paul's homemade drum electro kit. Vince Clarke [Erasure/ Depeche Mode] says that learning the synth riff to this was instrumental in making him want to do electronic music. The opening lyric is inspired by Teardrop Explodes' Camera Camera song.

### 3. MYSTEREALITY

✅ @OfficialOMD
Originally created by Martin [Cooper, saxophone] and I in his attic. Hence the heavy use of saxophone. I have absolutely no idea what the lyrics are about. I just created the title and off I went randomly.

### 4. ELECTRICITY

✅ @OfficialOMD
It was created from an earlier song called Pulsar Energy. The bass run in the chord change section is a survivor. The synth melody on that section was the last thing written as we didn't own a synth until we had played six OMD gigs. You can really tell that it is all about the only things we had.

### 5. THE MESSERSCHMITT TWINS

✅ @OfficialOMD
This title was the name that I gave to Paul and myself because we were both Airfix plane-building geeks, and inspired by all things German. The

OMG it's OMD. Paul Humphreys, Malcolm Holmes, Martin Cooper and Andy McCluskey up on Primrose Hill in London in 1981.

backward synth parts are some of the synth lines from Electricity slowed down and reversed. "If in doubt.. fuck with something you've already got" was a useful songwriting mantra!

## 6. MESSAGES

### @OfficialOMD
Originally in the key of G until we spent 3 hours trying to get a mistake free hand selected octave alteration using the Micro preset. When we realised that we'd recorded the bloody thing in G# because the pitch wheel had been knocked right up, we just did the song in that key. Listen out for the bum chord that Paul plays on the organ change at 2.39!!!!

## 7. JULIA'S SONG

### @OfficialOMD
Paul and I wrote the music when we were in The Id and Julia was my girlfriend. She would come to the rehearsals above the library in Greasby. I couldn't get any lyrics so she demanded that I let her have a go. I'm still sure that they are about me but she swears not! Quite weird singing a song about you written by your ex! Maybe that's why I sound so pained!

## 8. RED FRAME/WHITE LIGHT

### @OfficialOMD
You all know that this is about the telephone box in Meols where Paul and I grew up. Our office as neither of us had a home phone. It's such a strange song. It has its place in time. We love that people love it. But it stuck out like a sore thumb when we had it in the set in Belfast, Dublin and Nottingham on the last tour.

## 9. DANCING

### @OfficialOMD
Intro samples of Strauss and Glenn Miller fade away to leave a totally bonkers MS20 melody that we could never ever get the sound again for! The lyrics are me reading from a book.. can't remember which.

## 10. PRETENDING TO SEE THE FUTURE

### @OfficialOMD
The last song written for the album about how weird we found it to now be signed professional musicians. I was such a moaning bastard when I was 20!

# New Long Leg
## Dry Cleaning
4AD, 2021

⚑  It's probably an experience common to most musicians. You've made some exciting new music and then you bump into an old friend so you want to play it for them. The friend is into it, but… as they've not seen you for a while, they forget themselves and start talking over your new creation. In a lot of circumstances this might cause offence, but when Lewis Maynard, Tom Dowse and Nick Buxton played some freshly written instrumentals for artist friend Florence Shaw, Dry Cleaning was inadvertently born. Her spoken words proved the perfect companion to the music. Since then, the sounds and the words have evolved, with Shaw collecting words and phrases, thoughts and feelings that have been spilled across the South London band's debut album *New Long Leg*. To mark its release, there were even more new words, as the band (not on Twitter) borrowed their record label's account (**@4AD_Official**) to talk us through all the indie-infused, er, talking.

**ARTWORK:**
Dry Cleaning

**@4AD_Official**
(below left) Here's Florence standing next to Noel Gallagher's infamous 'Wonderwall'; (below right) Here's the drum machine you can hear being put to work.

## 1. SCRATCHCARD LANYARD

**⊘ @4AD_Official**
The original title for this track was Jam Jar, being born, as it was, from a particularly inspired jam sesh!

## 2. UNSMART LADY

**⊘ @4AD_Official**
Unsmart Lady was the first song we wrote after our touring finished and was informed by the plethora of music we'd been sharing in the tour van – not least Snowblind by Black Sabbath, a rendition of which Lewis air bass'ed for us, topless at 5am. Kerry Bog Ponies [as referenced on the track] are a breed of long haired, tough pony that can survive well in harsh conditions.

## 3. STRONG FEELINGS

**⊘ @4AD_Official**
A version of this song exists from the sessions that produced Boundary Road Snacks and Drinks. Crucially, that version didn't have the amazing Optigan organ on it that John Parish laid down.

## 4. LEAFY

**⊘ @4AD_Official**
A few people have asked why this wasn't a single. For sure, it has the credentials. Why is this song not a single? Future disco classic.

## 5. HER HIPPO

**⊘ @4AD_Official**
The lyrics are made up of someone's private fantasies, secret resentments and texts.

We recorded this album at Rockfield Studios, Wales. It has an illustrious history in the world of rock music but really it's a very un-intimidating and homely place.

## 6. NEW LONG LEG

**⊘ @4AD_Official**
We wrote this song in the basement of 4AD's offices over Christmas 2019 surrounded by such artefacts as the rock that adorns the cover of Death To The Pixies and Gary Barlow's old studio door. 'Sometimes like this, sometimes like this' was a note about how to perform the original, now discarded lyrics to this song.

## 7. JOHN WICK

**⊘ @4AD_Official**
Sometimes the working titles for our songs end up sticking. Listen to this over the opening credits of any of the John Wick films and tell us it doesn't fit like a glove?!?!

We wrote this on a particularly fecund day which also brought about New Long Leg. This recording sounds very different from the song we took into Rockfield and we spent a while working through different arrangements. Rockfield founder and owner Kingsley found a wasps nest in the grass at the back of the studio. Here's Joe and John recording the sound of the nest, the result of which you can hear on this song!

## 8. MORE BIG BIRDS

**⊘ @4AD_Official**
Florence sometimes sings from drawings of recently written melodies. They're helpful as visual reminders. Part of the attraction of the title for us came from it sounding like the second instalment in a children's book series on big birds.

## 9. A.L.C.

**⊘ @4AD_Official**
We went to town on the spesh fx for this one. Engineer Joe Jones dusted off his Traynor TS50 transistor amp to use with Tom's Silvertone 1478 w/bigsby, for which Tom's only just finished repaying. The recording of that was then 're-amped' through the speaker cabinet of a Fender Rhodes. Drums and vocals were processed through an Eventide H300 harmonizer. Rhodes electric piano parts were also sent to the famous 'Rockfield Echo Chamber of Echo'.

## 10. EVERY DAY CARRY

**⊘ @4AD_Official**
The whole album was recorded to two inch tape and the end of this song is the sound of the tape machine being turned off.

**⊘ @4AD_Official**
(bottom left) No, that's not Ryuichi Sakamoto playing piano on this song, it's our very own Tom Dowse, seen here multitasking at the highest level; (bottom right) A new discovery during our time at @Rockfieldstudio, and something we would now consider essential for the recording of any album and useful in the search for extraterrestrial life are Biscoff ice creams.

# Big Science
## Laurie Anderson
Warner Bros, 1982

⚲ "The album is series of short stories about odd characters – hatcheck clerks and pilots, preachers, drifters and strangers," tweeted Laurie Anderson (**@OnlyAnExpert**) as she invited the Listening Party to study closely the equations behind her *Big Science* album.

A highlight from a much larger project, in which the avant-garde artist aimed to sketch out facets of modern-day America through a multi-media performance arts piece, *Big Science* is not just a thought-provoking record inspired by Gertrude Stein's assertion that, "The United States is the oldest country in the world because it's been in the 20th century the longest" (as Anderson tweeted), it is also an album that pushed musical boundaries as it blended new recording techniques with the organic sounds of voices and strings. "The music was a combination of homemade electronics and sophisticated processors," Anderson explained. "But we recorded much of it almost like a folk record, trying to faithfully capture the actual sounds of voices and instruments." In many ways that approach also sums up *Big Science*'s appeal. Sophisticated and considered, the album is also a heartfelt, instinctive reaction to its subject matter. As experimentation goes – scientific or artistic – few have resonated so well with hearts and minds as *Big Science*.

PHOTOGRAPHY:
Greg Shifrin

The appliance of science. Laurie Anderson onstage in the Netherlands in 1982.

## 1. FROM THE AIR

☑ **@OnlyAnExpert (Laurie Anderson)**

Did you hear [Broadway actor] Mandy Patinkin's version of this song? The Captain speaks with his tongue-in-cheek manner that he has. He says : Do you still have the same attitude towards music? In the early and mid '70s I traveled a lot. My plan was to make a portrait of the USA. Big Science was the first part of the puzzle that eventually became part 2 of the United States I–IV (Transportation, Politics, Money, Love) [a live performance art piece documented on record by 1984's United States Live extended album].

## 2. BIG SCIENCE

☑ **@OnlyAnExpert**

Big Science was about technology, size, industrialization, shifting attitudes toward authority, and individuality. It was sometimes alarmist, picturing the country as a burning building, a plane crash. Alongside the techno was the apocalyptic. The absurd. The everyday. Working on a follow up to this song called Big Pharma.

## 3. SWEATERS

☑ **@OnlyAnExpert**

Why aren't there more songs about falling out of love?

## 4. WALKING AND FALLING

☑ **@OnlyAnExpert**

And before you can fall asleep you have to get used to the sound of your name.

Walking down the street and thinking about how you've got to turn around now because if you don't turn around there'll be nothing left of you at all the same as when you were a child falling out of a tree. A song written for [choreographer] Trisha Brown.

## 5. BORN, NEVER ASKED

☑ **@OnlyAnExpert**

Died never asked either.

## 6. O SUPERMAN (FOR MASSENET)

☑ **@OnlyAnExpert**

In 1979, Iranian students stormed the US embassy in Tehran. America went blazing in with helicopters to get the hostages out. But it backfired majorly. So I thought I'd write a song about all that and the failure of technology. Inspired by the beautiful 19th-century aria by Massenet that began: "O sovereign …" A prayer to authority, which I thought was interesting, so I started writing: "O Superman" The lyrics are a one-sided conversation, like a prayer to God. The song is based around a looped "ha ha ha ha", done on a harmoniser, but I wanted it to be like a Greek chorus so I used a vocoder, which was originally developed as spy technology to disguise voices. We pressed 1,000 copies, and I'd individually mail each one. Then suddenly John Peel started playing it on his radio show and it went to #2 in the UK.

In September 2001 I was on tour and played it at Town Hall in New York City. The show was one week after 9/11. "Here come the planes / They're American planes."

## 7. EXAMPLE #22

☑ **@OnlyAnExpert**

I love slow sunshine.

Do I know you?

## 8. LET X=X

☑ **@OnlyAnExpert**

Wow this equation is timeless. How often can you be right before it gets really tiresome?

## 9. IT TANGO

☑ **@OnlyAnExpert**

That's the way it goes. Isn't it just like a woman? Still thinking of Dylan. I don't listen back to my records often but I did for this reissue and I was surprised how fresh it still sounds, 40 years later. Thanks for listening!

☑ **@Tim_Burgess**

My mind is totally blown. We are all listening to Big Science around the world and Laurie Anderson is tweeting us on a guided tour of the songs. What a time to be alive.

# Memo Rex Commander y el Corazón Atómico de la Vía Láctea
## Zoé
Noiselab, 2006

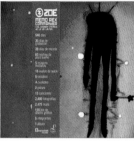

**ARTWORK:**
Ivan Krassoievitch

✦ Tim's Twitter Listening Party clearly has a global reach. Artists and fans from all over the world repeatedly sign in to listen to albums together and discuss their favourite music. Mexican band Zoé are no exception, although as one of our first global contributors, they perhaps had a little head start on joining the party. On their third album León Larregui (vocals), Sergio Acosta (guitars – **@Sergiorussek**), Jesus Baez (keyboards) Angel Mosqueda (bass – **@zoetheband**) and Rodrigo Guardiola (drums – also **@zoetheband**) managed to work with a British artist who had been a big influence on them… a certain Tim Burgess. However, don't begrudge them them their in, because being a Mexican fan of The Charlatans initially required some hard graft. In order to listen to the Brits' music in the 1990s the synth rockers needed special TV and radio receivers to listen to broadcast from the US, while obtaining Tim and co's albums required long mail order waits. Still it was worth it, as it not only helped shaped Zoé's own keyboard-driven sound, but eventually for *Memo Rex Commander y el Corazón Atómico de la Vía Láctea* they got Tim join them on record. "Tim is one of our heroes, it was a dream to have him on a song! Singing! Imagine that," declared Larregui. With The Listening Party the dream continued…

**LISTENING PARTY**
**17 APRIL 2021**

### 1. MEMO REX

☑ **@zoetheband**
Angel: The first song is Memo Rex, a fictional character who is on an introspective journey. The name comes from Memorex brand and for the album title we just used Memo Rex and added words from some other song titles.

### 2. VÍA LÁCTEA (MILKY WAY)

☑ **@zoetheband**
Rodrigo: It was one of the last songs we composed for the album, we thought we needed a "groovier" song so we took a piece of music Leon had created and we added things to it. It's one of our most played songs.

### 3. VINYL

☑ **@zoetheband**
Angel: One of the most energetic songs from the record. It has changing musical landscapes that contrast with their subtlety and musical harmony. We have great memories playing that song in our shows.

### 4. NO ME DESTRUYAS (DON'T DESTROY ME)

☑ **@zoetheband**
Rodrigo: This song had something special since the demo version. Simple and raw, yet POP. We even kept the demo drums. They were small and naive.

### 5. CORAZÓN ATÓMICO (ATOMIC HEART)

☑ **@zoetheband**

Angel: We had the privilege of having you Tim Burgess, on this song! The Charlatans have been a huge influence for the band so having you sing in the song was like a dream come true.

☑ **@Tim_Burgess**

I heard of Zoe via my friend Hector – he told me this story about one of the guys driving from Mexico to get in close enough range to listen to KROQ in LA – and the first song he heard was Weirdo by The Charlatans – it was destiny that we should together.

### 6. MRS. NITRO

☑ **@zoetheband**

Rodrigo: Mrs Nitro was always a favourite to play live. It really represents that MEMO REX era of psychedelic riffs and crunchy guitars with synth pads on top. We really had a hard time coming up with the right drum pattern for the chorus.

### 7. NUNCA (NEVER)

☑ **@zoetheband**

Rodrigo: Another sample of our "dark" side and we could experiment with the guitar and bass sounds like we had never done it before. I love recording this very slow tempo songs because it's all about the touch and feel.

### 8. THE ROOM

☑ **@zoetheband**

Rodrigo: What a crazy song. This album really explored with this ultra slow songs. It gave it a lot of its character. It was all about the contrast between the pop up beat songs and this dark ultra slow tracks.

### 9. PAULA

☑ **@zoetheband**

Rodrigo: We couldn't find a proper drum pattern simple enough for the verses to shine, so I was in our rehearsal room in Coyoacán. I grabbed a shaker with my right hand and just played bass and snare while doing it, it finally took off!

### 10. HUMAN SPACE VOLT

☑ **@zoetheband**

Rodrigo: Maybe the most upbeat track ever recorded by us. Full energy. It is just an explosion. We played a couple of shows in November 2006 at a big venue, Palacio de los Deportes and we invited Nick McCarthy from Franz Ferdinand (back then) to play with us in this song.

☑ **@Sergiorussek**

I have continued working with Nick, mixing some tracks that I produced for [singer] Andrea Franz and he invited me to compose a song for his new project The Nix.

### 11. TRISTE SISTER (SAD SISTER)

☑ **@zoetheband**

Angel: A true gem, I don't remember very well how we made this song but it's part of our musical evolution. There are hints of psychedelia and it is a more sophisticated song

### 12. SIDE EFFECTS

☑ **@zoetheband**

Rodrigo: Another one with lyrics in English and ultra slow one. We really went for the slow ones in this album!!!

### 13. PAZ (PEACE)

☑ **@zoetheband**

Paz is very experimental yet easy to listen to and dance all the way through the end. Great ending chapter for the album.

↓

Friends of mine. Mexico's leading rock band and Charlatans fans, Zoé.

# Surrounded By Time
## Tom Jones
EMI, 2021

⚲ It's not unusual, he sung… but actually having Sir Tom Jones (**@RealSirTomJones**) at the keyboard for a Listening Party was pretty unexpected. Celebrating the release of *Surrounded By Time*, an album featuring Sir Tom and his producer Ethan Johns reinterpreting songs – old and new – it was apparent from the detailed comments on each track that this was no mere collection of covers. With atmospheric production and rawness to Sir Tom's vocals not seen since some of his high times back in Vegas, the singer gave us a commentary on the record that really encapsulated the energy and authenticity he brought to the songs.

**ARTWORK:**
Oriol Massauger

→

**@RealSirTomJones**
Firstly, I want to say a huge thanks to the record's producer @ethanjohnsmusic who also played alongside this stellar band of musicians @neilcowleymusic/ @JezzaStace/ @StringTuba/ @Dansee1 who all made mine and Mark's vision possible!

LISTENING
PARTY
**23 APRIL
2021**

←

Hello sir. Tom Jones onstage in London in 2021.

## 1. I WON'T CRUMBLE WITH YOU IF YOU FALL

**✔ @RealSirTomJones**
When my wife Linda fell ill, I went to see her in hospital. I told her that I didn't think I'd be able to carry on without her. My son Mark was there too. We were cut up, but Linda was the calmest person in the room. She said, "You two are going to have to mentor each other through this." So, I see this song as the message that Linda willed me to project back on to her. [Linda Jones passed away in 2016]

## 2. THE WINDMILLS OF YOUR MIND

**✔ @RealSirTomJones**
Originally a hit for Noel Harrison, of course, but when I heard Dusty sing it, she added a bit of soul to it. Over the years, that's a song I've come back to.

## 3. POP STAR

**✔ @RealSirTomJones**
Originally a Cat Stevens song, we were quite friendly, he and I, back in the 60s. We would appear on a lot of TV shows together. With Cat Stevens, when he first arrived, they wanted him to sound more poppy than he wanted to be. I think maybe he wrote it with slightly sarcastic intent. But actually, that's not the way I choose to hear it…

## 4. NO HOLE IN MY HEAD

**✔ @RealSirTomJones**
This was originally written and recorded by a folk-singer and activist called Malvina Reynolds. Her version was great, but I felt like I could really rip the s%!t out of it. It's a song about how you should trust young people to think for themselves and not let older generations put them down – of which I think there's far too much going on. It's almost like a protest song.

## 5. TALKING REALITY TELEVISION BLUES

**✔ @RealSirTomJones**
In order to talk about this song, I first have to talk about Hank Williams. I'm a huge lifelong fan of Hank. Not just songs like Why Don't You Love Me and Jambalaya, but also the stuff he released under his Luke The Drifter alias. So Luke The Drifter re-entered my thoughts when I heard this incredible song by Todd Snider. It made more sense to speak it rather than sing it – because the song sounds to me like a modern parable anyway.

## 6. I WON'T LIE

**✔ @RealSirTomJones**
This song is written by the brilliant Michael Kiwanuka. Fun fact, Ethan produced an early (unreleased) version of this by Michael. This one is a reflection.

### 7. THIS IS THE SEA

**✓ @RealSirTomJones**

Originally recorded by The Waterboys, of course. Written by the great Mike Scott. This is a song that really resonates with me. When you start off in life, it's like you're on a river. You're on a journey. You're flowing with the current. But you don't know what's up ahead. Sooner or later though, you're going to be in the sea. So for me, the sea is the big time. It's the main event.

**✓ @MickPuck (Mike Scott from The Waterboys)**

Thank you Tom. It's a privilege to hear you sing it, and so powerfully. I am the proud recipient of a great number of goosebumps.

### 8. ONE MORE CUP OF COFFEE

**✓ @RealSirTomJones**

Bob Dylan is someone who I've come to appreciate more over the years. In the beginning, I didn't take so much notice of who wrote the songs. I was more preoccupied studying the technique of singers. Over time though, I've realised just what an incredible writer he is.

### 9. SAMSON AND DELILAH

**✓ @RealSirTomJones**

The story of the tune is one we still tell because it still resonates now. It's about temptation and straightening yourself out. I really rip the sh*t out of this one. (Even if I do say so myself) I've always loved gospel, especially hot gospel, which is what this is.

### 10. OL' MOTHER EARTH

**✓ @RealSirTomJones**

Here comes one of my favourites. One thing I hope people will take away from this album, is it will make you think! The spoken word, arrangements and the feel is very important! But even if you listen to the instrumental tracks, you know there's something happening at a deeper level. There are songs here to make you think about your inner self. And this song is a case in point.

### 11. I'M GROWING OLD

**✓ @RealSirTomJones**

The intro you can hear is an archival extract from an old episode of a BBC historical almanac, released as part of a series of vinyl albums, called Scrapbook. As you can hear, in this one, the events of my year of birth are being recounted. 1940! The song itself was first presented to me back in the early 1970s when I was singing in Vegas, by the man who wrote it, Bobby Cole. I told him I loved it – which I really did. I loved the melody of it and the chords and the mood of the whole song. But I wasn't old enough to sing it then! I was only in my 30s! But I held onto the record throughout all this time. Sometimes, you just have to be patient!

### 12. LAZARUS MAN

**✓ @RealSirTomJones**

A song by the great Terry Callier. So how do you handle knowing, and then accepting growing old? Well, you do what Lazarus did, because he had 'nothing but time'! What I wanted to explore in this song is this idea that you're both the teacher, and the student. I'm telling the story but I'm listening at the same time. You rise up again. You never die. Not really. That's why I raise my voice again at the end.

The voice. Tom Jones taking *Surrounded By Time* through its paces live in 2021.

**@RealSirTomJones**
I really rip the sh*t out of this one. (Even if I do say so myself)...

# Plastic Ono Band
## John Lennon
Apple, 1970

How do you follow up being in The Beatles? Paul McCartney had Wings and his solo albums (see the Listening Party Volume 1), while his writing partner John Lennon found an art project to guide his next endeavours courtesy of wife Yoko Ono. "Plastic Ono Band was a concept of Yoko's. A conceptual group which exists only in the mind," Lennon had said of the idea behind his first solo record. "You're in it. Everybody's in the Plastic Ono Band. We're all members of the conceptual Utopia." Indeed, Ono was a member – she released her own companion record the same year – while on John's John Lennon/Plastic Ono Band fellow Beatle Ringo Starr was present too (and George Harrison played on the single 'Instant Karma! (We All Shine On)'). For a special Listening Party, the John Lennon Estate (**@johnlennon**) dipped into the former Beatles thoughts and interviews from the time to create a commentary for the album – George Harrison's twitter account did likewise (**@GeorgeHarrison**) – while Yoko (**@yokoono**), John and Yoko's son Sean Ono Lennon (**@seanonolennon**), bassist Klaus Voormann (**@KlausVoormann**) and Ringo Star (**@ringostarrmusic**) all tweeted along live as we joined the Plastic Ono Band.

John Lennon/Plastic Ono Band album cover

LISTENING PARTY

**24 APRIL 2021**

### 1. MOTHER

**@johnlennon**
A lot of people thought 'Mother' was just about my parents, but it can apply to anyone. It doesn't have to be someone who lost them. Fathers do leave their children – not physically, but mentally. They never need the child the way the child needs the father. My mother and father split when I was four. And I lived with my Aunty Mimi and Uncle George. My mother was killed in a car accident. Run over by a off-duty policeman. I lost her twice. Once when I was moved in with my aunty and again where she physically died. I was seventeen. That was a big trauma for me.

**@ringostarrmusic**
It's so incredible, the emotion on this record, just mind blowing. The sparseness of the band, the force of John Lennon. That's why he's one of the greats.

**@KlausVoormann**
When John sings this song, you feel his hurt and his desperation. We play as little as possible to let the song unfold. When he starts screaming. . . shivers run down my spine.

**@yokoono**
With the Plastic Ono Band albums, John and I liked the idea of this really raw, basic, truthful reality that we were going to be giving to the world. We were influencing other artists, giving them courage; giving dignity to a certain style of vulnerability and strength that was not accepted in society at the time. It was a revolution for a Beatle to say, 'Listen: I'm human, I'm real.' It took a lot of courage for him to do it.

### 2. HOLD ON

**@johnlennon**
'Hold On John' was just about holding on. Even though it's not all that hot, let's hold on. It's now,

this moment. That's all right, this moment, and hold on, now. We might have a cup of tea or we might get a moment's happiness, any minute now.

🔘 **@ringostarrmusic**

John & Yoko were this incredibly close couple. And so, you know, like in the song, "Hold on Yoko, it's gonna be alright," they supported each other in that love way, musically.

🔘 **@seanonolennon**

Always found your note choice on the chorus to be surprising and cool. Of all dad's tunes that moment feels almost 'jazz' in terms of the voicing on the guitar and your bass, or whatever you call that thing you play.

### 3. I FOUND OUT

🔘 **@ringostarrmusic**

Great drums on I Found Out! They've come up a notch there. It depended on the time, on the minute. That's how it felt we should go. And so I brought in the toms a bit more there. Where the fill

is, which I always feel is my art, has to do with the surrounding atmosphere.

🔘 **@yokoono**

You have to be peaceful to get peace. If you are angry and combative, well, that is not going to help. Our heads are the source to think how to get peace. Our hearts are the source of courage to act. When you have peace in your mind, you will get peace.

🔘 **@johnlennon**

Therapy made me feel my own pain. I had to really kill off all the religious myths. You are forced to realise that your pain is yours and not the result of somebody up in the sky. It's the result of your parents and your environment. This dream of constant joy is bullshit as far as I'm concerned. If you're only feeling what you think is joy, you're not living. Life is made up of pain and pleasure. Every day is the same isn't it? There's some heaven and some hell.

⬇

John Lennon rehearsing 'Instant Karma! (We All Shine On)' for the BBC TV show Top Of The Pops at Studio 8, BBC Television Centre, London, 11 February 1970.

John & Yoko and the Plastic Ono Supergroup headline the UNICEF Peace And Love For Christmas concert, playing 'Cold Turkey' and 'Don't Worry Kyoko'; Lyceum Ballroom, London, 15 December 1969.

Alan White, Eric Clapton, Klaus Voormann and John & Yoko, the morning after the Toronto Rock 'n' Roll Revival 1969 concert at Varsity Stadium, relaxing by the swimming pool on the estate of concert promoters and department store dynasty heirs, George and Thor Eaton; Eaton Hall, King City, Ontario, 14 September 1969.

## 4. WORKING CLASS HERO

### @johnlennon
The thing about the song that nobody ever got right was that it was supposed to be sardonic. It's for people like me who are supposed to be processed into the middle-class machinery. It had nothing to do with socialism. It had to do with: if you want to go through that trip, you'll get up to where I am, and this is what you'll be – some guy whining on a record, alright? It's a warning to people. A song for the revolution.

### @ringostarrmusic
John was the best rhythm-cum-lead guitarist because his style of lead was pure. Very raw. And he was the rhythm guitar – that's what he was. George was lead, but John would throw in lead bits, and so they always had such passion.

### @KlausVoormann
If anybody has the right to talk about Working Class, then it is John.

### @yokoono
The Beatles were just saying to people, 'It's gonna be OK' and then suddenly John comes out with this Plastic Ono Band album – 'Working Class Hero' and 'God' and all that, saying, 'It's not OK. There are these problems.' People don't want to know about problems. People want somebody to always tell them it's OK. And so it's gonna be a little bit less popular, but it shouldn't be if the world gets more mature.

## 5. ISOLATION

### @johnlennon
I had to isolate, using 'being famous' as an excuse for never facing anything because I was famous. I can't go to the movies, I can't do anything. Every time I got nervous, I took a bath. I'm free of the Beatles because I took time to free myself mentally from it, and look at what it is. And now I know. So here I am, right?

### @ringostarrmusic
On this record I was mainly a time-keeper. It's very straight. It wasn't difficult at all. Very few fills. There's a few lifting the track occasionally, but my basic job on this record was just holding it down – wherever John wanted to take it.

### @seanonolennon
Production is so spare yet effective on Isolation. That organ and the little piano answer in the verses opens the whole thing up but you might not even know they're there. Whole album feels like master class in minimalism.

## 6. REMEMBER

### @johnlennon
In England, the Fifth of November is the day they blew up the Houses of Parliament. We celebrate it by having bonfires every November the fifth. It was just an ad lib. I was goofing about. I cut it there and it just exploded 'cause it was a good joke.

### @KlausVoormann
Ringo is rockin' like shit! I try to help the song to roll along.

### @ringostarrmusic
The tone of the drums was the tone we'd been using with the Beatles, really. They were very tight. They were very dead. With the old tea towels on top of everything. I would've just got into playing with that sound over the last couple of years.

## 7. LOVE

### @johnlennon
Love is a great gift, like a precious flower. You have to feed it and look after it. It has to be nurtured like a very sensitive animal because that's what it is. You have to work at love. You don't just sit round with it and it doesn't just do it for you. You've got to be very careful with it. It's the most delicate thing you can be given.

### @yokoono
Love is the energy that is really moving the whole world. Love is the creative energy and prayer is the poor man's weapon. With prayer and love we can really create the world. Please send out the strongest energy of love, peace and belief to the world.

## 8. WELL WELL WELL

### @johnlennon
We can't have a revolution that doesn't involve and liberate women. I'm always interested to know how people who claim to be radical treat women. How can you talk about 'Power To The People' unless you realize 'The People' is both sexes?

WAR IS OVER (IF YOU WANT IT): The Plastic Ono Supergroup at the UNICEF Peace And Love For Christmas concert, Lyceum Ballroom, London, 15 December 1969. Back row: Jim Price (trumpet), Bobby Keys (saxophone), Jim Gordon (drums), Klaus Voormann (bass), Bonnie Lynn (tambourine), Delaney Bramlett (guitar); middle row: George Harrison (guitar), Alan White (drums), Keith Moon (drums), Neil Boland (Keith Moon's chauffeur), Keith Robertson (photographer), Billy Preston (keyboard), Eric Clapton (guitar); front row: Legs Larry Smith (percussion), John Lennon (guitar, vocals), Yoko Ono (vocals).

### ⊚ @yokoono

John was a brilliant writer, a brilliant artist and a brilliant man, who believed in being truthful. More people should get down to being truthful to themselves. That is the most adventurous thing anybody can do.

### ⊚ @seanonolennon

Well Well Well is one of the meanest guitar licks dad ever played. You guys must've had fun playing that one.

### ⊚ @ringostarrmusic

Well Well Well – he just wound everything up. That's how he achieved most of those sounds. Louder was better. Distortion was good. John always wanted a lot of echo on his voice. He had a great voice and when he was singing, he gave all of that. I don't feel personally he was insecure about his voice. Everybody wants to be someone else, to be different.

### ⊚ @KlausVoormann

Again once that Ringo machine starts going, all you have to do is join in. To play with Ringo is like heaven! And John's rhythm guitar playing is the best I've ever heard.

## 9. LOOK AT ME

### ⊚ @johnlennon

Two years before I met Yoko, I was really going through a 'What's it all about? This songwriting is nothing. It's pointless and I'm no good, I'm not talented and I'm shit. I was just coming out of it before I met Yoko. She filled me completely to realise that I was me and it's all right. And that was it. I started fighting again.

## 10. GOD

### ⊚ @johnlennon

You're born in pain. Pain is what we are in most of the time, and the bigger the pain, the more gods we need. I had the idea: 'God is a concept by which we measure our pain'. When you have a phrase like that, you just sing the first tune that comes into your head. And then I just rolled into it – I Ching and Bible and the first three or four just came out.

### ⊚ @ringostarrmusic

John was always brave. I could always say that about John. He would put it out there, and the consequences sometimes were very harsh. But he would always put it out there. That's why you couldn't not love him, you know?

### ⊚ @seanonolennon

God was hardest to come up with a canvas for. The opening line alone is so philosophical. I don't know that I understand it 100% to this day.

## 11. MY MUMMY'S DEAD

### ⊚ @johnlennon

It helps to say, 'my Mummy's dead' rather than 'my mother died'. I never allowed myself to realise that my mother had gone. It's the same if you don't allow yourself to cry, or feel anything. Some things are too painful to feel, so you stop.

### ⊚ @yokoono

People are so frantic about Daddies because Daddies are the ones that are never home and they never got enough of Daddy and somehow there's a distance, so there's a mystery about them and mystique. It was that adoration and yearning for Daddy. Whereas Mummy was always there.

John & Yoko promoting their Plastic Ono Band albums whilst attending screenings of their films 'Fly' and 'Apotheosis' at the Cannes Film Festival, France, 17 May 1971.

## 12. GIVE PEACE A CHANCE (BONUS TRACK)

**@johnlennon**

The point of the Bed-In was a commercial for peace, as opposed to a commercial for war, which was on the news every day those days, in the newspapers. Every day it was dismembered bodies and napalm. And we thought, 'Well, why don't they have something nice in the newspapers?' It didn't matter what the reporters said, because our commercial went out irrespective.

**@yokoono**

All those Vietnam protests really changed the world. There was always that element who were really resisting it. That was the saving grace – that people were aware that they were that young generation who were really against it. And so it worked very well for the world. The Bed-In was a definite part of it. It was a statement on a very theatrical level and I think it was very effective.

## 13. COLD TURKEY (BONUS TRACK)

**@johnlennon**

Cold Turkey' is self-explanatory. It was the result of experiencing cold turkey withdrawals from heroin. Everybody goes through a bit of agony some time or another in their lives, whatever it is. 'Cold Turkey' is just an expression to explain the other side of life.

**@yokoono**

We were so totally scared. We thought it's an illegal thing, we can't openly go to hospital, they might arrest us. So we never even dreamt of going to hospital. We just cold turkey-ed. John had incredible will and once he decided to do something, he did it. Those 40 days were hard but we were totally clean.

**@KlausVoormann**

On this song, I played my bass part twice. One is on the right, the other one on the left. That gives you this hollow feeling. A feeling you have when you have withdrawal symptoms.

## 14. INSTANT KARMA! (WE ALL SHINE ON) (BONUS TRACK)

**@johnlennon**

I wrote it for breakfast, recorded it for lunch and we're putting it out for dinner. Recording it was great. I wrote it in the morning on the piano. I went to the office and sang it. We booked the studio, and Phil [Spector, producer] came in, and said, 'How do you want it?' I said, 'You know, 50s, but now'. He said, 'Right'. And 'boom!' I did it in about three goes.

**@GeorgeHarrison**

John phoned me up one morning in January and said, 'I've written this tune and I'm going to record it tonight and have it pressed up and out tomorrow. That's the whole point – "Instant Karma!" – you know?' So I was in. I said, 'OK, I'll see you in town.' I was with Phil Spector and said, 'Why don't you come to the session?' There were just four people: John played piano, I played acoustic guitar, Klaus Voormann on bass and Alan White on drums. We recorded the song and brought it out that week.

**@yokoono**

John was a brilliant man with a great sense of humour and understanding. He believed in being truthful and that the power of the people will change the world. And it will. All of us have the responsibility to visualise a better world for ourselves and our children. The truth is what we create. It's in our hands.

# *Ocean Rain*
## Echo & The Bunnymen
Korova 1984

There is something truly powerful about the atmospheres Echo & The Bunnymen create in music. Out of the darkness, the Liverpool band had the ability to conjure horizon-filling sounds that both swooned and devastated listeners. A swell of heavy emotions and big sounds, Echo & The Bunnymen also possessed a lightness of touch when they needed it which allowed them to truly soar. *Ocean Rain* is a tremendous demonstration of Ian 'Mac' McCulloch (vocals/guitar), Will Sergeant (guitars – **@Will_Fuzz**), Les Pattinson (bass) and Pete de Freitas' (drums) ability, as both their songwriting and their arrangements truly have the power to move. The album is also proof of the band's aspirations, as aided by cellist and arranger Adam Peters (**@theapereport**) there is an impressive orchestral finesse to its songs. Yet the strings and chimes were no bolt-ons or embellishments: they were key to The Bunnymen's widescreen vision, as Sergeant and Peters explained as they pricked below the surface of this stunning record.

PHOTOGRAPHY:
Brian Griffin

⊕

Space hoppers. Echo & The Bunnymen backstage in Chicago in 1984.

## 1. SILVER

### ◉ @Will_Fuzz (Will Sergeant)

This came from a very simple chord structure that I had. I think we were given three weeks to do the recording. The place had a very old feel a bit like the BBC. Lots of old equipment around. Bill Drummond and the Label found a very traditional studio in the heart of Paris. Studio Des Dames. Mac loved the romance of Paris and was convinced it would add something to the vibe, it did.

## 2. NOCTURNAL ME

### ◉ @Will_Fuzz

We were trying to sound like a Russian balalaika band on this one. Well me and Les were. We had been on a winter holiday to the USSR 1983 and it had a big Influence on us. When we were writing Nocturnal Me well before it had words we called it the Russian one. This must have rubbed off a bit on Mac as he gets very soviet Red Army choir by tracking the vocals on the outro.

## 3. CRYSTAL DAYS

### ◉ @theapereport (Adam Peters)

Mac great singing. Believable. Amazing guitars. Light. All multitracked cellos. About eight thousand of them. We were recording at Studio Des Dames. The French engineer Henri got a great sound out of the big old reverb.

## 4. THE YO YO MAN

### ◉ @Will_Fuzz

This is a waltz so take your partners. More eastern influence on this.

### ◉ @theapereport

Sparkling piano stars.  Recorded the cellos in the old reverb tank in the Paris studio. Had to climb down into it with all the spiders webs in there.  It was like recording in a submarine or a swimming pool.

## 5. THORN OF CROWNS

### ◉ @Will_Fuzz

We needed another track as the album was a bit short. We said we'll just make something up... It was all about dynamics on that one, ebb and flow. It has a nice Doors feel here and there.

### ◉ @theapereport

Originally it was a live jam on a Bo Diddley riff. That middle section is exactly what Bunnymen sounded like live.  The takedown. Sometimes would go on for ten minutes.  Explorations.

## 6. THE KILLING MOON

### ◉ @Will_Fuzz

Recorded Crescent Studio in Bath before we went to Paris, this set the vibe, where we were headed next musically. The Intro was just something I did when we were tuning up and getting ready to do the backing track. David Lord the producer spotted it and when we had gone out to the local curry house, he spliced up the little intro. Is Mac right to say it's the greatest song ever written? He has a point, I think...

### ◉ @theapereport

Perfect structure. Perfect song.  Perfect arrangement. Best vocal.. ever. Everyone playing at the top of their game.  We are so young and brave and wide eyed   Reaching for horizons. Something unspoken and magical happened in those days and it's all there in this music. A conspiracy of silence in the studio. You are what you play. What a thing. Brings a tear to my eye sometimes.

## 7. SEVEN SEAS

### ◉ @Will_Fuzz

We had a meeting with some French arranger bloke to talk about strings orchestration etc. we went for some food at lunch. He had worked with Serge Gainsbourg or Jacques Brel. Me and Mac didn't like him. We Didn't want him to do it was a last-minute thing we were nearly done in Paris and time was running out. Adam Peters had worked with us on Killing moon and was versed in writing for Orchestras. We Korova, the label, we got him to come over to Paris. While we were recording Adam was in the lounge with a piano writing the orchestra parts, he would take little motifs tunes embellish them. We were finding it hard to visualise but Adam knew what he was doing. Adam was working all hours to get all the parts written and we went to another studio to record all the strings. I lay on the floor on some old carpets while the orchestra and Adam conducted. It was magical.

←

Big Mac. Ian
McCulloch
performing live.

↓

Sailing the seven
seas. Ian McCulloch,
Will Sergeant, Les
Pattinson and Pete
de Freitas at the
Kinkakuji Temple
in Kyoto in 1984.

### 8. MY KINGDOM

**@theapereport**

I remember Will blowing my mind with the guitar solo. I seem to remember he was playing through a radio or something like that. Total drug song. "I chop and I change".

**@Will_Fuzz**

I had an old radio from the 30s. I had discovered you could use it as a guitar amp. I routed my acoustic though the amp. The acoustic sounded fuzzy through this old radio. I used it on the solo for my kingdom. It's hard to believe it's an acoustic. I was after the power of when the guitar appears from nowhere in Love's song A House is not a Motel.

### 9. OCEAN RAIN

**@Will_Fuzz**

This was not my favourite at the time, I've since come to love this track for its dynamics. from so quiet to so bloody loud. Also I think this one of many of Mac's best performances.

**@theapereport**

Electric cello noodlings and piano to start. Les on double bass and the orchestra to take over. Mapped it all out. It ended up a perfect marriage of instruments. Orchestra quietly enters doubling Will's trem chords. Fearless orchestral playing on the melody. Purposely overdoing it and it sounds fantastic...never melodramatic, always honest. Brave. A great recording. Truly.

### 10. ANGELS AND DEVILS (BONUS TRACK)

**@Will_Fuzz**

We had a day off in San Francisco and Bill organised that we should go into the studio and record a beside. We jammed around a sort of Velvets style chord sequence for a while. It soon came into shape. The Late great Alan Perman who was our sound man from the gigs was drafted in to be in charge of the recording. I remember some lad hanging about that had red punk rock trousers on zips and shit all over the place. God knows why? Love this Tune, we were trying to be the Velvets or I was anyway.

# *Fat Pop (Volume 1)*
## Paul Weller
Polydor, 2021

⚑ Similar to the Listening Party team, Paul Weller (**@paulwellerHQ**) was a man who got busy during the pandemic lockdowns. He not only joined us to revisit *Cafe Blue* by his old band The Style Council (see *The Listening Party* volume 1) but he also brought things right up-to-date making his 16th solo album despite the trying conditions. Indeed, Weller not only engaged with the present, but with *Fat Pop (Volume 1)* there are glimpses of the future too, as the record saw the former Jam frontman working in new ways and with new forward-thinking collaborators such as Tom Doyle and Anth Brown of the visionary Electric Music AKA and a certain Leah Weller… his daughter.

Revealing the inner workings of *Fat Pop* in the week of its release, Weller wondered aloud during the Listening Party if this might be his final solo album, but with the teasing "Volume 1" subtitle and the fact the record went straight to Number 1 in the UK – meaning Weller has now topped the chart in five different decades! – we have a suspicion that there will be more Listening Parties and records to come.

ARTWORK:
Alex Borg

←
**@Tim_Burgess**
A brilliant album. A perfect listening party. I grew up with Paul Weller as a hero. And he still is. It's an honour to also think of him as a friend. A true genius and a beautiful person. Thanks Paul.

### 1. COSMIC FRINGES

◉ **@paulwellerHQ**

Started off as a kind of Stooges type song, all punky guitars, etc. Which didn't really work so I stripped it all away and made it more "electronic" and sparse. The character in the song is made up but I was imagining some couch-potato useless twat with all the opinions, views and attitude but who ultimately does fuck all about any of it – apart from venting their spleen on the net. It's meant to be a fun/silly sorta tune. I can hear a bit of glam-rock in it, but also taking in Motorik, Giorgio Moroder and punk. I think it's a modern take on a punk track!

### 2. TRUE

◉ **@paulwellerHQ**

It is a duet with me and Lia Metcalfe from The Mysterines. She's great. She came to the studio and we cut it live together. She's very talented and very together.

### 3. FAT POP

◉ **@paulwellerHQ**

This is my favourite on the album I think, because it's so different. This was Stan's [Kybert, co-producer] backing track and mostly me playing with Stan sampling what I'd played and reconstructing it. Very clever. I was hearing [Cypress Hill's] DJ Muggs vibes in it, whose work I've always liked.

### 4. SHADES OF BLUE

◉ **@paulwellerHQ**

I had the verse words and a kinda arrangement but I couldn't find the chorus, so my daughter Leah came up with the chorus lyrics and helped with the vocal arrangements. She's great and really focused on her music. [Ocean Colour Scene's] Steve Cradock is producing her album at the moment and I gotta say, what I've heard of it is sounding great.

◉ **@Tim_Burgess**

Amazing work Leah Weller. Your Dad's not bad either…

Popmaster. Paul Weller onstage in Southend in 2021.

Shades of blue. Paul Weller photographed just before the release of *Fat Pop (Volume 1)*.

## 5. GLAD TIMES

✔ @paulwellerHQ

Here's another tune I've written with Tom Doyle and Anth Brown [of Electric Music AKA]. We all wrote Movin' On from True Meanings together too. They sent me the backing track probably two years ago so it's taken me this long to finish it properly! They're a very talented team and I'm hoping we'll do more music together. This is a nice "Marvin" type groove (well, in my mind!) - soulful.

## 6. COBWEB/CONNECTIONS

✔ @paulwellerHQ

When I told my team that I was gonna make a record [around the lockdown] they were sceptical, but in the face of adversity… etc. Stan Kybert told me "it's a lot of work" but, as I told him, the hard work had already started by me writing the songs. That's the real hard work, in my opinion. But unless you are a writer, I think it's difficult to see that.

## 7. TESTIFY

✔ @paulwellerHQ

As soon as that first lockdown was announced last March and all of our touring plans were off the map, I decided to try and use my free time wisely! I thought "Fuck this, I'm going to make an album!" I already had 4/5 songs that were recorded after we'd completed On Sunset (2020) including Failed and In Better Times. We also had some unfinished backing tracks Testify, Fat-Pop & Glad Times.

## 8. THAT PLEASURE

✔ @paulwellerHQ

During the first lockdown of last year I would record my songs against a click track (a time-keeping device) and then send that off to various members of my band for them to record their parts. It was the first time I've recorded that way so that was cool for a while (good to try different methods) but definitely not any substitute for us all being in the same room, smashing it out!

## 9. FAILED

✔ @paulwellerHQ

… Same as the "streamed" gigs – we can't wait to get back on them old boards!

## 10. MOVING CANVAS

✔ @paulwellerHQ

I had loads of little ideas on my phone too and scraps of lyrics, so I decided to get them together and finish them. I think having so much free time also meant I had more time to think, stop and look around. Look at myself, look at those around me too.

## 11. IN BETTER TIMES

✔ @paulwellerHQ

I don't know if I'll make any more records after this one; it's hard to say at the moment. This is my 16th solo album! I can't believe it! I often think that after I finish an album – there's so much more involved in making [and] putting out albums these days. The music business has changed so much in the last few years, I don't really recognise it anymore. Thankfully, there's still great music being made and I'm sure that will always stay that way. But generally I don't think people invest in music like we did before streaming/downloads etc.

## 12. STILL GLIDES THE STREAM

✔ @paulwellerHQ

Here's one I wrote with Steve Cradock. He sent these lyrics/poems he'd done and I switched it around to suit the melody and arrangement on this very rough idea I had. I love this tune and I'm really glad me and Steve have written something together that we're both really proud of. I don't know what Steve was thinking when he wrote these words but, for me, I formed this story of a migrant worker working our streets, cleaning up our shit and I tried to imagine the person's life leading to them coming to this country. Poverty and/or war drives most people out of their countries in search of safety, solvency, a roof over their heads etc. When I hear people talk about foreigners taking our jobs I have to laugh. What jobs exactly?! Road sweepers, bin men, hospital ancillary staff, traffic wardens – poorly paid jobs that no one wants to do in reality, but all of those jobs and people are vital to our society and we should be grateful to them. "Be careful what you ignore. Look for greatness in the small." That's me saying don't disregard these people – everyone has a role to play in our society.

# *Intruder*
## Gary Numan
BMG, 2021

Such is the fickleness of fashion, there was a time when many supposedly discerning music fans considered Gary Numan over. Despite the obvious, electronic-driven inventiveness of his music, and the interesting places he drew lyrical inspiration from – and let's not overlook the fact he was a qualified stunt pilot too! – the Londoner was largely shunned… except by other electronic musicians who recognised and celebrated his influence. Now with the likes of Nine Inch Nails' Trent Reznor paying their dues, rightfully Numan's album releases have returned to being a real event… and none more so than *Intruder*. Calling on the talents of Gazelle Twin (see page 158) and his own daughters, the record's narrative around climate change and a decaying earth took on extra significance with its release within the Covid-19 pandemic. Eerily prophetic and wonderfully sonic, Numan (**@numanofficial**) and producer Ade Fenton (**@AdeFenton**) provided a glimpse behind *Intruder*'s future sounds.

**PHOTOGRAPHER:**
Chris Corner

LISTENING PARTY
**22 MAY 2021**

### 1. BETRAYED

**@numanofficial**
Sets up the theme for the entire album. At first we were young, pure, & the Earth worshipped us, gave us everything we needed. But as our numbers grew so did our greed & arrogance. Now we bring pain & death & the Earth is betrayed.

### 2. THE GIFT

**@numanofficial**
The Gift is about Covid seen as a weapon sent by Earth to fight back against us. It starts by talking about it as a gift, hinting at a danger within it. As it progresses it gets more direct, more angry, with the chorus shouting out its frustration & hurt.

### 3. I AM SCREAMING

**@numanofficial**
I tried to write a lyric that would not only express the feelings of the planet but also have another, separate meaning. The Earth is talking about its sadness that we, so self-obsessed, are ignoring its screams.

### 4. INTRUDER

**@numanofficial**
This one shows the Earth absolutely done with us. It wants to fight back, it wants us to hurt, it wants us gone. All of us. We are the Intruder the album sings about.

### 5. IS THIS WORLD NOT ENOUGH

**@numanofficial**
Okay, I've heard all the James Bond jokes :) The thing is I wrote this when the news was full of the latest Mars mission & so for the Earth to be asking Is This World Not Enough made perfect sense. I forgot the ? on the title.

### 6. A BLACK SUN

**@numanofficial**
My daughter Persia wrote this when she was 14. I added the chorus, lyric and vocal melody but everything else is hers. She was writing it for her own album but let me use it for Intruder instead.

### 7. THE CHOSEN

☑ @numanofficial

The lyric is perhaps the most direct attempt to explain how incredulous the Earth is that we continue to ignore its many warnings, and how it has washed its hands of us. Once we were The Chosen, but soon we will die, and it will forget we ever existed.

### 8. AND IT BREAKS ME AGAIN

☑ @numanofficial

Another double meaning lyric. Firstly the Earth is torn. From being angry & sure that we have to be gone, to a wave of sadness & regret that it's come to this. Like a loving parent with an ungrateful child grown into a cruel adult. But also, how I feel about the possibility of losing [his wife] Gemma. I'm actually haunted by fears of death these days. Of losing the people I love. It stops me sleeping and is beginning to find its way in to many of the things I write.

### 9. SAINTS AND LIARS

☑ @numanofficial

Looks at people's willingness to believe in a God, & the corrupting nature of religion, but not see what's staring them in the face. Gazelle Twin [see page 170] and Persia and Raven sing beautifully on this.

### 10. NOW AND FOREVER

☑ @AdeFenton

I fucked this one up a little bit in the first version I sent to Gary. I'd made it a little too Bladerunner, so he got a bit grumpy and I tried again. As often happens, he was right.

☑ @numanofficial

I didn't get grumpy. I merely pointed out that it was SHIT!!!!!!!! and needed to be looked at again :) I love the feel of this one.

### 11. THE END OF DRAGONS

☑ @numanofficial

I love dragons. I choose to believe they were real. My house is a shrine to dragons. I wanted to draw a parallel between our persecution of dragons & their demise to what we're doing to the planet. Dragons lost, the Earth won't.

### 12. WHEN YOU FALL

☑ @numanofficial

Religion, hatred & prejudice. Another mass shooting (I live in the US), politicians offering their thoughts & prayers & little else. White supremacy torch lit marches, unchristian Christians. What's the planet to make of that?

↓

Intruder alert. Gary Numan onstage in San Francisco in 2002.

☑ @numanofficial

The idea for the album came from a poem my daughter Echo wrote when she was 12. Without it *Intruder* may never have been made.

# *Audioweb*
## Audioweb
Mother Records, 1996

A fax from Joe Strummer… now there's a unique punk rock artefact if ever there was. And Manchester band Audioweb were its grateful recipients. Still interweaving indie dance with dub, hip-hop loops and reggae flavours, its easy to see why The Clash frontman – who had covered Junior Marvin's Police And Thieves on his own debut – would appreciate Robin File (guitars), Maxi (drums), Martin "Sugar" Merchant (vocals) and Sean McCann's (bass) vibe. So why was Strummer faxing Audioweb about their urgent cover of Bankrobber? Robin File (@_Audioweb) revealed all in a Listening Party for Audioweb's eponymous debut.

ARTWORK:
AK47

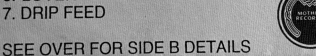

CHOP EM OUT CHOP EM OUT
TRINITY MEWS, CAMBRIDGE GARDENS, LONDON W10 6JA
Telephone: 0181-960 8128

AUDIOWEB

# AUDIOWEB

**"ALBUM MIXES"**

SIDE A:
1. SLEEPER
2. INTO MY WORLD
3. JAH LOVE
4. YEAH
5. WHO'S TO BLAME
6. LOVER
7. DRIP FEED

SEE OVER FOR SIDE B DETAILS

SIDE B:
1. TOWN
2. OTHER SIDE OF LIFE
3. DIVIDE
4. BANK ROBBER
5. TIME
6. FAKER

MOTHER RECORDS

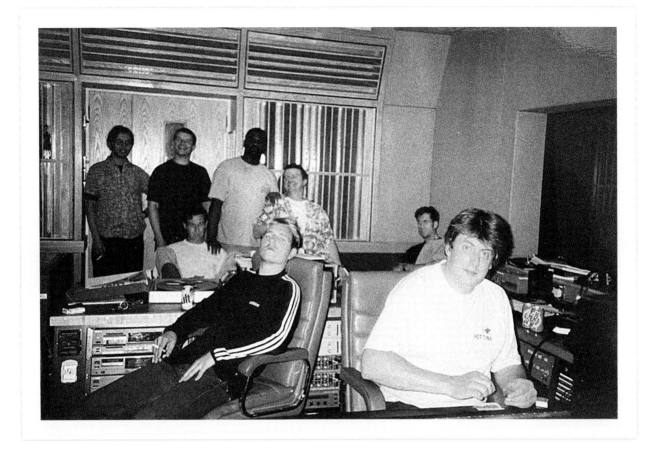

LISTENING
PARTY
13 JUNE
2021

↑

In control. Audioweb
shared a studio pic
from the sessions of
their debut album.

←

The net. Audioweb
backstage in
Cambridge in 1996,
along with an early
promo cassette of
their self-titled
debut album.

## 1. SLEEPER

✓ @_Audioweb

We wanted to make people dance, and if you
make them dance, you've got a chance. The hook-
line is there, and you could hit that groove and
melody. The guitar riff is and always will be a
monster. The release got a lot of traction early
doors. Part of our team was influential & respected
plugger Scott Piering, which lead to John Peel
playing it. That's the way to open a record, right?

## 2. YEAH?

✓ @_Audioweb

Out and out Rock n Roll meets Dancehall. Rock n
Soul. Written in a Levenshulme basement. Martin
brought some contemporary Dancehall records to
the table, which referenced Bogle, a dance
technique originating from Jamaican culture. We
dropped a hip-hop beat on it, and there we had it,
heavy! Lyrically this was a statement to the press
situation we faced at that time.

## 3. INTO MY WORLD

✓ @_Audioweb

The first of the Audioweb tunes, written early on in
the Sugar Merchant's days, and one we all felt very
comfortable with bringing into the new setup. Sean
had a little acoustic guitar line that went from A to
G that he used to fool around with. We put a break
under it and the track was cemented. It became a
live favourite and a buzz to play, you could feel the
energy in the crowd. Locked in. Percussionist Chris
Cruiks provided Tibetan Monks sample on this,
adding something different.

## 4. FAKER

✓ @_Audioweb

It started off with a loop of Whole Lotta Love and a
Beastie Boys break. We messed around with the
Led Zep riff until you could barely work out what it
was (not sure we even kept it!). We were locked in
the room until we figured it out. The killer guitar riff
was written in Robin's Didsbury flat. Probably the
last song done for the album. Definitely a contender
for the track that took the most time to construct.
Hour after hour in the studio.

↑

@_Audioweb
"So, who's to blame?"
Audioweb live.

## 7. JAH LOVE

☑ **@_Audioweb**

Once we took the horn break from Shinehead we knew something was cookin', boiled over when Sean added the bass. Big power guitars recorded in Sheffield, all done before the rest of the band arrived at the studio, simple but effective. Sometimes you would try and find a part for hours and get nothing. Come back fresh the next day and bang. Kev had an idea of setting different size tom's up in the live room and Maxi would be running along them doing long fills that we cut up. It gave a good effect in the end.

## 8. BANKROBBER

☑ **@_Audioweb**

Bankrobber was actually just a live jam to start with. The original demo is a dub version, but after time it got faster and faster, and more punk. Martin put the Sensimilla tags at the end and it breathed a life of it's own. We were at TFI Friday to perform it and after sound check we got a TV exec come in and tell us we'd been pulled from the show. EMI had been on and said we didn't have the right to perform it unless we had permission from the band. Luckily our manager at the time had a connection with Joe Strummer and I think drove to his house to get his blessing. A while later we got the fax from Joe to give us permission to play the song on the show that night.

## 5. WHO'S TO BLAME

☑ **@_Audioweb**

Done largely in Sheffield in the downstairs studio. It all started to click when Robin pitched down the guitar chords using the tremolo arm on his Stratocaster. The lyrics ring true today, and they stand the test of time. "Money can feed your ego", right? Personally think Martin's lyrics are up there with his best on this track.

## 6. TIME

☑ **@_Audioweb**

Written and recorded in the studio at Manna. The weather outside was cold and snowy, it made us feel a little isolated from Manchester life. Some of the lyrics actually came from that. Even though we were living out our dreams, there were times you missed the home comforts. Whilst recording we hit the zone with this track, and we felt straight away this was going on the record. The thought process was this would be a hit at student club parties, something we'd all be into.

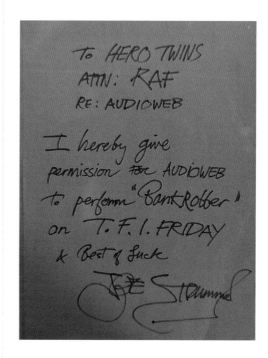

To HERO TWINS
ATTN: RAF
RE: AUDIOWEB

I hereby give permission for AUDIOWEB to perform "BankRobber" on T.F.I. FRIDAY & Best of Luck

JOE STRUMMER

@_Audioweb
The thought process was this [Time] would be a hit at student club parties, something we'd all be into.

## 9. LOVER

✅ @_Audioweb

Lover is written about a horrible event of obsession and possession, which resulted in the perpetrator being extradited from the US after leaving his victim in a suitcase in the boot of a car at Manchester Airport. Nuff said… Sean drove this one, there was a heated debate over the irony of the keyboard sound, John Quarmby, who's a very talented jazz keyboardist, couldn't get his head around it. The chords were off a Yamaha QY10 - a pocket midi sequencer, if you had a massive pocket, it came in a VHS videotape case! The fact that it's paired with Kev's CS80 which is the seminal synth used in Bladerunner is a fun fact, right!? The battle lasted a while, Sean stood firm. Even though John lost the battle, with compromise from Sean, he did a great classical arrangement for the end of the song. A very conscious track. For some reason I think Richard Hawley was there when Maxi was recording it because he ended up jamming with him. And the vocal at the end where Martin laughs. Just an ad-lib but sounds so fucking great. The way it comes in from Lover.  And yeah, we don't talk enough about the loops. That was always such a massive part of it. Crate digging for breaks. Then putting 808 hi hats and kicks on stuff to toughen them up, then Maxi drumming on top for the skips and feel.

@_Audioweb
[Yeah? was] Written in a Levenshulme basement. Martin brought some contemporary Dancehall records to the table, which referenced Bogle, a dance technique originating from Jamaican culture.

The fax from Joe Strummer allowing Audioweb to perform Bankrobber on TV.

# *The Trojan Story*
## Various Artists
Trojan Records, 2021

One of the most ambitious and longest Listening Party to date, Trojan Records don't do things by halves. Still, what would you expect from a label with a catalogue as priceless theirs? Responsible for helping the world to discover ska, rocksteady, reggae and dub music for the first time as well as introducing music from the Caribbean to the globe, the iconic record label celebrated its 50th birthday with compilation *The Trojan Story*. The Trojan Records team (**@trojanrecords**) were understandably determined that no track featured would miss out when they staged their party, so while it might be the lengthiest Listening Party, thanks to glorious grooves and sweet sounds included, it certainly didn't feel long. In fact, whether via vinyl, CD or streaming playlist, the label's illuminating track-by-track is one that is perfect to indulge in time and time again.

**ARTWORK:**
Dave Fields

---

**LISTENING PARTY
24 JUNE 2021**

### 1. LORD TANAMO: INVITATION TO JAMAICA

⊘ **@trojanrecords**
Starting off with one of the most important Jamaican musical pioneers, Lord Tanamo with Invitation to Jamaica.

### 2. DERRICK MORGAN: FAT MAN

⊘ **@trojanrecords**
Fat Man is one of Derrick Morgan's earliest hits, originally released by Simeon Smith – a significant figure on the islands music scene through the early 60s.

### 3. JACKIE EDWARDS: TELL ME DARLING

⊘ **@trojanrecords**
Jackie Edwards was one of Jamaica's finest crooners, his voice smooth and suave and imbued with a very polished sweetness.

### 4. OWEN GRAY: RUNNING AROUND

⊘ **@trojanrecords**
Owen Gray is one of the original Jamaican singing pioneers, an underrated but masterful vocalist.

### 5. JIMMY CLIFF: MISS JAMAICA

⊘ **@trojanrecords**
The legendary Jimmy Cliff is a household name in reggae today, but this track from 1962 takes us to his beginnings, when AGED 14 (wow), he recorded for the legendary Leslie Kong, the producer that he would work with until Kong's death in 1971.

### 6. DERRICK & PATSY: HOUSEWIFE'S CHOICE

⊘ **@trojanrecords**
FUN FACT – This track was initially called 'You Don't Know (How Much I Love You)' but it was so popular on the radio in Jamaica that a RJR DJ always referred to it as Housewive's Choice due to the endless requests from housewives for the record.

### 7. THE CONTINENTALS: GIVE ME ALL OF YOUR LOVE

⊘ **@trojanrecords**
No one really knows who The Continentals were, its one of the many mysteries of early Jamaican music.

### 8. OWEN GRAY: DARLING PATRICIA

⚬ @trojanrecords

Owen Gray is an extremely versatile vocalist, he can often be seen still performing this classic number during his live performances while displaying his wicked dance moves, known to Jamaicans as "dropping legs".

### 9. STRANGER COLE: ROUGH AND TOUGH

⚬ @trojanrecords

Rough and Tough is one of Stranger Cole's classics. He always strongly believed that the track was one of the first ska songs to emerge from Jamaica.

### 10. KENTRICK PATRICK: MAN TO MAN

⚬ @trojanrecords

Creator [aka Kentrick Patrick] recorded the timeless early reggae masterpiece, Kingston Town – a song subsequently covered by the chart-topping UK reggae group, UB40.

### 11. STRANGER & KEN: UNO-DOS-TRES

⚬ @trojanrecords

Here Ken Boothe is heard in his very youthful approach, harmonising alongside #StrangerCole, with their combined voices making a charming contribution to the male vocal duo format that became hugely popular in Jamaican music at this time.

### 12. AL T. JOE: SLOW BOAT

⚬ @trojanrecords

Al T. Joe almost always sang in a fashion patterned after his idol, Fats Domino, one of the prominent musical kings of New Orleans, whose music proved hugely popular and influential in Jamaica.

### 13. DUKE REID'S GROUP: RUDE BOY

⚬ @trojanrecords

It has always been common for Jamaican producers to release sides with a different moniker for the line-up of players, so Duke Reid's Group could be anybody at any given session.

Telling. Jackie Edwards outside the Royal Albert Hall in London.

### 14. HIGGS & WILSON: GONE IS YESTERDAY

✅ @trojanrecords

One of the earliest singing duos in Jamaica, Joe Higgs and Roy Wilson are probably best known for their massive hit Oh Manny Oh. They recorded this particular track under the guidance of manager Edward Seaga, who also governed as Jamaica's fifth Prime Minister.

### 15. LORD TANAMO: I'M IN THE MOOD FOR SKA

✅ @trojanrecords

Lord Tanamo's best known recording, which features the true inventors of ska music, the beyond legendary Skatalites.

### 16. THE BABA BROOKS BAND: VIRGINIA SKA

✅ @trojanrecords

This track was actually mislabelled on the original Trojan Story in 1971. We can assure you that this track is definitely called 'Virginia Ska', and not 'Yeah, Yeah' by the Riots as it may be referred to (by mistake). Ooops.

### 17. JUSTIN HINDS & THE DOMINOES: SATAN

✅ @trojanrecords

Justin Hinds was a devoted #Rastafarian and his faith reflected greatly in his lyrical content that was permeated with Biblical content and parables.

### 18. BABA BROOKS & HIS BAND: ONE EYED GIANT

✅ @trojanrecords

While Oswald 'Baba' Brooks may not be as much of a name as the Skatalites, with whom he sometimes played trumpet, his contributions are more than essential in the history of Jamaican music.

### 19. JOE WHITE AND CHUCK: EVERY NIGHT

✅ @trojanrecords

This was the first record Graeme Goodall released on his #DoctorBird label in 1966, and was a monster hit in the Jamaican market. It sold in such quantities that had the sales been accurately reported to the charts, it would have certainly shown up on the hit parade.

### 20. BABA BROOKS & HIS BAND: KING SIZE

✅ @trojanrecords

Baba Brooks, back again with King Size, in a sound that is reminiscent of a herd of cantering horses, with a wood block trotting along in the mix together with an organ, an instrument not often heard in ska up until this point.

### 21. THE ASTRONAUTS: SYNCOPATE

✅ @trojanrecords

The Astronauts' Syncopate is a rather unusual, but highly enjoyable piece showcasing a gorgeously executed guitar feature, complete with whammy bar tugging.

↓

Get the message.
Dandy Livingstone.

Play your cards
right. Desmond
Dekker (centre)
with The Aces.

**22.** WINSTON & GEORGE: KEEP THE
PRESSURE ON

✓ @trojanrecords

One of those 1966 tracks that sounds like it has
one foot still in ska, with the other one moving
forward into #rocksteady, performed by Winston
Weir and George Agard – the latter also known as
George Dekker joined The Pioneers years later.

**23.** THE TECHNIQUES: OH BABE

✓ @trojanrecords

Originally a regional hit for its writer, New Orleans
performer Chris Kenner, and then a national one
for Fats Domino, 'Sick and Tired' was a big seller
in Jamaica throughout the late Fifties, as reflected
in the number of cover versions by Jamaican acts.

**24.** THE ETHIOPIANS: TRAIN TO SKAVILLE

✓ @trojanrecords

Despite the song's title, this is most definitely
rock steady rather than ska.

**25.** DANDY LIVINGSTONE: RUDY, A
MESSAGE TO YOU

✓ @trojanrecords

Dandy found himself wearing many hats as a
singer, producer, songwriter and musician, as well
as performing other duties at Trojan Records in its
early stages.

**26.** HONEY BOY MARTIN & THE VOICES:
DREADER THAN DREAD

✓ @trojanrecords

Honey Boy enjoyed stints as vocalist in one of Lynn
Taitt's pre-Jets combos, the Comets as well as with
Hugh Hendricks & the Buccaneers, but here he
fronts Tommy McCook & the Supersonics, featuring
Taitt.

**27.** THE THREE TOPS: IT'S RAINING

✓ @trojanrecords

It's Raining by The Three Tops with Tommy McCook
& The Supersonics came out on the first British
Trojan series, with the label erroneously crediting
the group as the Tree Tops.

**28.** THE ETHIOPIANS: THE WHIP

✓ @trojanrecords

Featuring a rhythm that, over the years, has
frequently been 'versioned' by numerous Jamaican
performers.

**29.** DESMOND DEKKER & THE ACES:
PRETTY AFRICA

✓ @trojanrecords

Lynn Taitt, and his band the Jets, with pianist
Gladdy Anderson, PLUS Desmond Dekker and his
sweet-as-dripping-honey vocals, the Aces' exact
harmonies, and gorgeous horn lines = a perfect
rock steady tour-de-force.

### 30. ALTON ELLIS & THE FLAMES: ROCK STEADY

**@trojanrecords**

This kind of tune was a perfect vehicle for Alton's soulful phrasing and expressive crooning; indeed, he may be the most soulful singer to ever come out of Jamaica..

### 31. EWAN & JERRY: ROCK STEADY TRAIN

**@trojanrecords**

The short-lived pairing of Ewan and Jerry take us on The Rock Steady Train, assisted by Bobby Aitken and his Carib Beats.

### 32. SUGAR SIMONE: KING WITHOUT A THRONE

**@trojanrecords**

King Without A Throne was produced by Sugar Simone himself under his real name, Keith Foster, but saw release as Sugar Simone on Island's Sue imprint in 1967.

### 33. PHYLLIS DILLON: PERFIDIA

**@trojanrecords**

Phyllis Dillon, widely heralded as 'The Queen Of Rock Steady', recorded some of the most enduring titles in the genre, filled with romance and innocence.

### 34. ROY SHIRLEY: MUSICAL TRAIN

**@trojanrecords**

Roy Shirley, the self-proclaimed 'High Priest Of Reggae' was an exceedingly colourful and flamboyant character in the Jamaican pantheon of musical heroes.

### 35. DERRICK MORGAN: DO THE BENG BENG

**@trojanrecords**

Derrick Morgan hits a strong up-tempo rock steady groove, ably backed by Lynn Taitt and The Jets for Leslie Kong.

### 36. LYNN TAITT & THE JETS: WAY OF LIFE

**@trojanrecords**

We finally get to hear a solo outing by the man himself, Lynn Taitt. A nice easy medium/slow tempo rock steady finds saxophone man Karl Bryan blowing over the proceedings.

### 37. TOMMY MCCOOK & THE SUPERSONICS: SECOND FIDDLE

**@trojanrecords**

Here we find Tommy McCook and his Supersonics grooving in 1968 as rock steady began shifting into #reggae with various instrumentalists starting to flirt with little detailed rhythmic changes.

### 38. LEE 'SCRATCH' PERRY: PEOPLE FUNNY BOY

**@trojanrecords**

Lee has long since seemed determined to create a completely different sound from all of his contemporaries, experimenting in the studio, sometimes utilising everyday objects such as bottles and cans, and, in the instance of People Funny Boy, a crying baby.

### 39. THE TENNORS : I'VE GOT TO GET YOU OFF MY MIND

**@trojanrecords**

Formed in Kingston in the mid-Sixties by George 'Clive' Murphy and Maurice 'Professor' Johnson, The Tennors originally billed themselves as the Tennor Twins, becoming The Tennors after Norman Davis joined them to complete a line-up.

### 40. THE MAYTALS: DO THE REGGAY

**@trojanrecords**

Believed to be the first recording to use the term 'reggay' (later to be spelled reggae), the track intros with a ringing and bombastic snare drum roll, after which we're off into the reggae journey, guided by the now legendary Maytals, led by the unique talent of Toots Hibbert.

### 41. THE SLICKERS: NANA

**@trojanrecords**

The Slickers were the Crooks brothers, Sydney and Derrick, along with Winston Bailey, and over the years following their formation did see some line-up changes. They are probably best known for the rude boy anthem Johnny Too Bad.

### 42. DELANO STEWART: TELL ME BABY

**@trojanrecords**

Winston 'Delano' Stewart began his musical career in a duo with B.B. Seaton as 'Winston & Bibby', a pairing that soon after led to the formation of the Gaylads, following the recruitment of a third singer, Maurice Roberts.

### 43. THE REGGAE BOYS: MAMA LOOK DEH

@ @trojanrecords
Another Pioneers-related affair under the auspices of Joe Gibbs, this time billed as The Reggae Boys. The group comprised the trio of George Agard, Glen Adams and Alva 'Reggie' Lewis.

### 44. THE ETHIOPIANS: HONG KONG FLU

@ @trojanrecords
Hong Kong Flu has a relentless and driving quality with Leonard Dillon and his Ethiopians singing beautifully about a miserable subject. Makes us wonder if Dillon were still here, would he be singing about the Covid 19 virus with his typically joyous approach?

### 45. THE MAYTALS: PRESSURE DROP

@ @trojanrecords
One of the more well-known songs in the Maytals' deep catalogue, which carries the typical electrifying sound of the group from this time with Toots laying his Otis Redding influenced deep gospel and soul-inflected vocals over a great performance by Leslie Kong's Beverly's All Stars.

### 46. THE SOUL MATES: THEM A LAUGH AND A KI KI

@ @trojanrecords
Once more, Hippy Boy regulars, Glen Adams and Alva 'Reggie' Lewis go under cover with George Agard of the Pioneers on this long-term boss reggae classic from early 1969.

### 47. THE MELODIANS: WALKING IN THE RAIN

@ @trojanrecords
Although best known for their classic Rivers Of Babylon, leading vocal group, the Melodians recorded an array of sublime sides, notably for Duke Reid's Treasure Isle and, of course, Leslie Kong's Beverley's label, for whom they cut this typically lilting number in 1970.

### 48. CARL DAWKINS: SATISFACTION

@ @trojanrecords
Carl Dawkins is one of the most unsung vocalists from Jamaica and also one of the most emotional. His voice is filled with agony, anguish, and deep soul, embodying a rawness and torment that could be compared to Otis Redding.

### 49. THE MAYTONES: BLACK AND WHITE

@ @trojanrecords
Written in 1954 by David Arkin and Earl Robinson, with the latter recording his own version in 1957, a year after Pete Seeger first recorded it. Sammy Davis also covered.

### 50. THE CHARMERS: RASTA NEVER FAILS

@ @trojanrecords
The Charmers on this track are none other than the great Ken Boothe, one of the top echelon Jamaican singers of all time.

My single is dropping. The Maytals in 1970.

# *Any Other City*
## Life Without Buildings
Tugboat Records, 2001

**ARTWORK:**
Hayley Tompkins

A brief moment of energy and artistry, like their songs, Life Without Buildings' sole album *Any Other City* – indeed, the Glasgow band's entire career – is a testament to embracing the forces of creativity. A collection of fragile, spiky, yet happy and warm songs, urged on by frontwoman Sue Tompkins' seemingly chaotic yet precisely crafted lyrics, the four-piece flared brightly for a brief moment before slipping away into other projects. Just a year after *Any Other City*'s release Tompkins and bassist Chris Evans returned to visual art, drummer Will Bradley became a writer, while Robert Johnston embraced graphic design and released music as Robert Dallas Gray.

Yet Life Without Buildings story does not end there. As their music found a new outlet when the song The Leanover became the soundtrack for a huge TikTok trend led by the singer Beabadoobee. Inspired by this interest, and a repressing of *Any Other City* on vinyl, Tompkins (**@SueTompkins2018**) and Johnston (**@rdg_music**) staged a kinetic Listening Party to celebrate LWB's flash of sonic sweetness.

LISTENING PARTY
8 AUGUST 2021

### 1. PS EXCLUSIVE

✓ **@rdg_music (Robert Johnston)**
This almost wasn't on the record – it was due for release in October 2000 but it got moved back and we went back in and did PS Exclusive perfect opener I think, almost like a northern soul stomper, and Sue's lyric is like a statement of intent.

### 2. LET'S GET OUT

✓ **@SueTompkins2018**
I wanted to do a song where u could call it by short hand xxx yay LGO. Used to bounce up and down in the cupboard recording box I loved it.

### 3. JUNO

✓ **@rdg_music**
Some people said we were math-rocky or kind of 90s emo or something – I guess Juno is the closest we get to that, a big Mission Of Burma/Sonic Youth rock epic. love the drums.°

### 4. THE LEANOVER

✓ **@SueTompkins2018**
I liked saying words I liked. So random but v deliberate yay!!! Always singing in the breakdown bits woooooo.

✓ **@rdg_music**
The Leanover is always going to be my favourite. It was the first thing we did that made us think we actually were making our own sound. the way Sue works around the beat still amazes me, and again the drums are just so musical. It sounds like walking in a city at night, to me.

### 5. YOUNG OFFENDERS

✓ **@rdg_music**
Trying to be The Jam and The Smiths and The Heartbreakers all at the same time.

### 6. PHILIP

🔵 **@SueTompkins2018**

If I ever listen to our songs this is the one I put on. I was always thinking about science, I love science, but can't do it alllll?!! 37 percent in chemistry at school. Scared of physics and electricity but loved it too.

### 7. ENVOYS

🔵 **@rdg_music**

We hardly ever played envoys live because it was so hard to get right, but it's become one of my favourites. Sue's lyric and performance on it is just extraordinary.

### 8. 14 DAYS

🔵 **@rdg_music**

14 days is a really fun pop song, kind of modern lovers-ish. I really like the guitar solo, they all looked at me like I'd lost my mind when I was playing it in the control room but it worked.

### 9. NEW TOWN

🔵 **@rdg_music**

The songs kind of fall into two categories, the guitar tunes I brought in, which tend to be melodic and a bit fussy maybe, and the ones that came out of chris playing a groove. this is the classic example of a 'chris' song. Such amazing lines that stick in your head for your whole life, "I saw you today, you were like snow." Never quite occurred to me how exhausting these songs must have been to sing.

### 10. SORROW

🔵 **@rdg_music**

Incredible lyric and vocal performance. I don't know if my memory's faulty on this but I *think* this was pretty much the first time we played this right through, we were just following vocal cues from sue for when to change.

🔵 **@SueTompkins2018**

Some sort of balance between happy and sad erased memories. Keep X ING.

**@rdg_music**
Us in Australia...

# *Fever Dreams*
## Villagers
Domino, 2021

🎤 The inheritance of a rich musical tradition can be both a help and a hinderance. With Irish folk stretching deep into the mists of time, underlining the country's inspiring musicality, for an aspiring songwriter such a heritage offers both confidence and a sense of possibility, yet also the potential to make finding your own place in the music world a challenge. It is therefore a testament to the artistic vision of the current crop of artists emerging from Eire that it boasts so many distinct, original voices. Villagers, led by Conor O'Brien (**@wearevillagers**), have been a key driving force in this resurgence. Among the first on the scene to adopt folkish cues but then mould them into a contemporary sound that is truly their own, O'Brien's songs forge Irish creativity as much as they revel in it. Villagers' fifth album, Fever Dreams, is a prime example of this, as intimate folk instincts provide the foundations for a series of intoxicating, sprawling tracks that atmospherically envelop the listener. So lie back, relax and enjoy a Listening Party that saw Conor O'Brien's "dreams" come true.

**ARTWORK:**
Paul Phillips

⬇

Conor O'Brein live on stage in Berlin, accompanied by drummer Berndan Doherty.

## 1. SOMETHING BIGGER

⊘ **@wearevillagers (Conor O'Brien)**

Floating in a liminal space, beckoning you to come inside. Hiya!

## 2. THE FIRST DAY

⊘ **@wearevillagers**

We put the drums through a Minimoog while Ross [Turner, from Dublin band I Am The Cosmos] recorded them live and fireworks were exploding in my brain. It was a good day. The additional brass and woodwind took it to another dimension.

## 3. SONG IN SEVEN

⊘ **@wearevillagers**

This begins with a voice memo from my phone of [Villagers' bassist] Danny Snow telling me that the song is in 7/8. I'm in love with his bass line. You may be excused for thinking that there are translucent singing angels laced throughout this final section but it is, in fact, seven layered vocal takes from the one-and-only Aoife O'Sullivan.

## 4. SO SIMPATICO

⊘ **@wearevillagers**

So Simpatico was a tough nut to crack. It went through so many stages. I was listening to lots of [soul singer] William DeVaughn, trying make something as magical and groovy.

## 5. MOMENTARILY

⊘ **@wearevillagers**

I kind of feel like this is the moment that the album really settles into itself. The initial rush of the first few songs dissipates in a haze and you are left with this stark romantic backbone, which was there all along.

## 6. CIRCLES IN THE FIRING LINE

⊘ **@wearevillagers**

Any song that permits me to rock my Telecaster and scream about society's ills should be cancelled and shamed immediately, in my personal opinion.

## 7. RESTLESS ENDEAVOUR

⊘ **@wearevillagers**

I whispered directions into everyone's headphones in real-time as they were exploring unfinished ideas with a loose blueprint. I love this jam so much. It's the seventh song too. We recorded the album in [producer/engineer/artist] Brendan Jenkinson's freshly conceived studio in Dublin. It is to his credit that the free flow of ideas was captured and organised so adeptly.

## 8. FULL FAITH IN PROVIDENCE

⊘ **@wearevillagers**

I recorded this at my piano in my apartment during the first lockdown with a little zoom recorder.

## 9. FEVER DREAMS

⊘ **@wearevillagers**

More liminal space means more encounters with the number seven, lushly accompanied by the string arrangements of Mr. Gareth Quinn Redmond [Dublin-based ambient musician].

The voice here is a processed recording of [journalist] Siobhán Kane reading her interview with [American singer] Linda Perhacs during a lockdown livestream – one for all you trivia geeks. The final section is populated many magic people who sent recordings of themselves repeating the incantation "The More I Know, The More I Care" (which was the album's working title for a little while).

## 10. DEEP IN MY HEART

⊘ **@wearevillagers**

The more I know, the more I care. [American writer and activist] James Baldwin once said, "Love is a battle, love is a war, love is a growing up". I would tend to agree, especially with the latter.

The musicality and sensitivity in all of the players really gets me in this one. "When tragedy brings us a melody/Your majesty hits like a dart / Deep in my heart…"

# Buena Vista Social Club
## Buena Vista Social Club
World Circuit, 1997

PHOTOGRAPHY:
Susan Titelman

The very existence of the Buena Vista Social Club is a timely reminder of how to make the best of things when they don't go as expected. Originally supposed to be the focus of a collaboration with Cuban musicians, highlife artists from Mali and the much-revered American slide guitarist Ry Cooder, the entire project was almost scuppered when the Africans were refused visas and so could not attend sessions at Havana's EGREM studios in March 1996.

Rather than abandon the whole thing, Cooder and producer Nick Gold from World Circuit – the record label that had organised the recordings – thought on their feet. They instead switched the focus to the Cubans, all the finest exponents of the island's *son cubano* sound, and in seven days the pair made a record that would transform the global appreciation of this most infectious and joyful of music.

Because of other countries' frosty relations with Cuba's communist regime and various economic boycotts, many of the musicians who were Cuban stars in the 1940s and '50s at the *son cubano* peak were barely known outside their homeland before *Buena Vista Social Club*'s collection of local standards and film music was released.

After these sessions in a studio still decked out with 1950s gear RCA had installed before the country's revolution, members of the 'Club finally enjoyed the long overdue musical appreciation they deserved. Wim Wenders' 1999 documentary told their story, while all the leading musicians went on to have hugely successful solo careers. To celebrate 25 years of *Buena Vista Social Club*, the team at World Circuit (using **@BuenaVistaSC**) opened their archive to host a listening party that took us right back to those special days in Havana.

Night clubbing. Compay Segundo (centre) and other members of Buena Vista onstage in 1998.

**@BuenaVistaSC**
Chan Chan is perhaps the most well known track from the album, which was recorded in 1996 at EGREM's studios in Havana.

LISTENING PARTY
**21 SEPTEMBER 2021**

### 1. CHAN CHAN

✔ **@BuenaVistaSC**
Chan Chan is perhaps the most well known track from the album, which was recorded in 1996 at EGREM's studios in Havana. It was clear from the atmosphere of the recording sessions that something very special was taking place. When the legendary [Cuban trova guitarist] Compay Segundo arrived in the studio, he played Chan Chan, one of his own very recent compositions, becoming the first song recorded for the project. Eliades Ochoa sings lead vocals with Ibrahim Ferrer, backed by Compay's congas.

### 2. DE CAMINO A LA VEREDA

✔ **@BuenaVistaSC**
De Camino A La Vereda was written by Ibrahim Ferrer in the '50s, around the time he was touring Cuba on a carnival float with Pacho Alonso. After years singing with Benny Moré & Los Bocucos, by 1996 he had given up his singing career. Ibrahim was born at a social club dance in Santiago in 1927, which he later took as a signal that music was his destiny. Ry Cooder referred to Ibrahim as 'the Cuban Nat King Cole' for his smooth tenor voice.

### 3. EL CUARTO DE TULA

✔ **@BuenaVistaSC**
The majority of the musicians involved were celebrated veterans of the Cuban music scene of the 1940s and '50s. They had never played together before they made this album – although many of them did know each other from their past musical lives. El Cuarto de Tula features Ibrahim Ferrer, Puntillita Licea and Eliades Ochoa on vocals, improvising lyrics laced with sexual innuendo in the Santiago (Eastern Cuba) tradition. The extraordinary solo on the laúd (a small twelve string instrument similar to a lute) is played by Barbarito Torres.

### 4. PUEBLO NUEVO

✔ **@BuenaVistaSC**
Pianist Rubén González was regarded as one of Cuba's national musical treasures. He was instrumental in creating the modern Cuban piano sound, having played and toured for years with legendary Cuban band leaders Arsenio Rodríguez & Enrique Jorrín. In the years leading up to the Buena Vista recordings, Rubén had given up playing due to arthritis. He was always the first at the studio every morning, waiting for the doors to be unlocked. Once inside he would rush to the piano and play.

### 5. DOS GARDENIAS

⊘ **@BuenaVistaSC**

Dos Gardenias is a classic bolero featuring the great Ibrahim Ferrer on vocals. Ibrahim knew this piece from his days singing with the great Benny Moré, at Club Alivar in the 1950s. Incidentally, the iconic album cover image was taken by Susan Titelman on the 2nd day of recording, as Ibrahim is about to enter the front door of EGREM's Areito studios. During the Buena Vista recordings, Ry Cooder asked if there was a soft voice to sing a bolero. Barbarito Torres suggested Ibrahim. Juan de Marcos González walked the few blocks to look for him and persuaded the reluctant singer to come to the studio

### 6. ¿Y TÚ QUÉ HAS HECHO?

⊘ **@BuenaVistaSC**

¿Y Tú Qué Has Hecho? is a delightful guitar duet between Ry Cooder and Compay Segundo. Compay plays the "armónico", a small guitar with seven metal strings which he invented in the 1920s to combine the characteristics of the Cuban 'tres' and guitar. The song was written in the 1920s by Eusebio Delfín, a good friend of Compay's. When talking about this song Compay Segundo said ' You mustn't forget tradition… why? Because if you forget tradition, you're forgetting history.'

### 7. VEINTE AÑOS

⊘ **@BuenaVistaSC**

Veinte Años is the only song on the album to feature a woman – the wonderful Omara Portuondo. This duet, with Compay Segundo, was recorded in a single take. Omara was working on her own album in EGREM's Areito Studio B. By chance, she bumped into Ry Cooder and Juan de Marcos González, who were in the middle of recording Buena Vista Social Club downstairs and invited her to sing on the record.

### 8. EL CARRETERO

⊘ **@BuenaVistaSC**

Before heading to Cuba, Ry Cooder, Nick Gold and Cuban bandleader Juan de Marcos González had been exchanging cassettes of repertoire they hoped to record. El Carretero is one of the few songs that had been originally intended for the sessions. Originally written by Guillermo Portabales in the early part of the 20th century, this song is a typical 'guajira' sung by Eliades Ochoa, who is deeply immersed in the 'guajira' tradition and wears his cowboy hat to identify himself as a country man.

**@BuenaVistaSC**
In the years leading up to the Buena Vista recordings, Rubén [González, pianist] had given up playing due to arthritis. He was always the first at the studio every morning, waiting for the doors to be unlocked. Once inside he would rush to the piano and play.

Ibrahim Ferrer and Omara Portuondo at New York's Carnegie Hall in 2001.

### 9. CANDELA

◎ @BuenaVistaSC

Ibrahim Ferrer's effortless vocal improvisation skills are beautifully exhibited on 'Candela' – with its lyrics about everyday life, and added sexual innuendo. Ry Cooder's comments sum up the vibe of the sessions beautifully: "The musicians were wonderfully good. So, naturally, when you're with masters, you know you're alright because they're going to play well, it's going to be terrific whatever they do."

### 10. AMOR DE LOCA JUVENTUD

◎ @BuenaVistaSC

Compay Segundo provides guitar and his famous 'second' vocal on Amor de Loca Juventud. A great innovator and composer, Compay was one of Cuba's longest living, most charismatic and brilliant musicians. Compay is Cuban slang for Compadre (friend) and Segundo refers to his trademark bass harmony 'second' voice, which he employed with his Los Compadres duo, formed 1948. He left Los Compadres in 1955 to form his own group, Compay Segundo y sus Muchachos.

### 11. ORGULLECIDA

◎ @BuenaVistaSC

Orgullecida has a ragtime/early jazz feel which is beautifully captured by 'Guajiro' Mirabal's trumpet. Compay Segundo was particularly delighted by Ry Cooder's 'cowboy' guitar solo.

### 12. MURMULLO

◎ @BuenaVistaSC

Murmullo is a romantic ballad inspired by Hollywood musicals [and] features Ibrahim Ferrer on vocals, accompanied by Rubén González's beautiful piano playing.

### 13. BUENA VISTA SOCIAL CLUB

◎ @BuenaVistaSC

The name 'Buena Vista Social Club' was inspired by a real Havana club that operated in the 40s and 50s. This song was written by bass player Orlando 'Cachaíto' López's uncle Israel ('Cachao'), the co-creator of the mambo, about the original club. This instrumental recording, which opens in danzón rhythm and moves into a mambo section, features an extended improvisation from Rubén González on piano.

### 14. LA BAYAMESA

◎ @BuenaVistaSC

The closing track from the album is 'La Bayamesa'. The lead vocals here are by Manuel 'Puntillita' Licea, one of the great soneros who made his name in the 40s and 50s singing with the big Havana orchestras. The lyrics tell the story of a woman from Báyamo, the first town to be liberated in the revolutionary war of 1868, who burns her house down to avoid letting it fall into the hands of the Spanish.

# Huffy
## We Are Scientists
100%, 2021

One of the overlooked gems of the modern BRIT Awards is Arctic Monkeys' acceptance speech for Best British Breakthrough Act in 2006. On an NME tour at the time, they couldn't attend the ceremony so sent a video instead which featured California's We Are Scientists accepting the award on their behalf… wait a sec, wasn't it the Brits? If music hadn't called them, then it's likely Chris Cain (bass) and Keith Murray (guitar/vocals/cheekily doing the talking for the Arctic Monkeys) would have penned a Seinfeld-like sitcom by now, such is the band's offstage wit and humour. In front of a mic, though, they're all about joyous, passion-filled tunes. This Listening Party gave the pair (both **@wearescientists**) an opportunity to combine both these facets, giving us a heart-moving and humorous playback of seventh album *Huffy* that should win an award too.

**ARTWORK:**
Keith Murray & Chris Cain

(far left)
**@wearescientists**
Much of this record was labored over in Sunny Miami. Here's Keith's southern studio.

(left)
**@wearescientists**
This was taken – pretty sure – moments after we got Pandemonium in the bag.

## 1. YOU'VE LOST YOUR SHIT

**@wearescientists**
TIM TWITTER LISTENERS: Have you lost your shit yet? If no, you missed the starting bell. This is our favorite song on HUFFY. Downhill from here. It began with a way more specific pronoun (she/he/they), but we made it "you" so everyone could feel implicated. The bridge was originally six times as long. We reined it in to make it radio-playable. But they ignored our invitation.

## 2. CONTACT HIGH

**@wearescientists**
The owner of Atomic Heart, where we recorded most o the album, gave Keith a baggie of mushrooms – that was a lyrical inspiration for this one. (He has not yet ingested them; waiting for them to age properly). This one wasn't going to be a single, but our German label head, Mareike, told us that the Germans would love this track. Indeed, it has done better at radio in central Europe than any other song (in music history!)

## 3. HANDSHAKE AGREEMENT

**@wearescientists**
This machine is the secret to the sound of Handshake Agreement...

## 4. I CUT MY OWN HAIR

**@wearescientists**
This was written pre-Covid, and would have been considered one of the most inventive lyrical confections of modern rock. Instead, once the world started home haircutting, we raced to release it so that it wouldn't seem like old news. For the video, Chris tried out the thing Keith had been doing for years. It was rad. He still does it today.

## 5. JUST EDUCATION

**@wearescientists**
Just Education was slated to be a single until Handshake Agreement displaced it. Still our drummer Keith's favorite track on the album. Our mixing engineer Claudius Mittendorfer wanted us to juice the bridge, so we added these barking seal vocals. He agreed it was a huge win for seals, and that the song was a little better.

## 6. SENTIMENTAL EDUCATION

**@wearescientists**
Just Education, of course, is just ONE of the two "education" songs on this record. Reader, there were 25 demos with that word in the title. This is Keith's wife's favorite song OF THE 100 DEMOS WE CONSIDERED for this record. (Flaubert [who wrote a novel with the same title] is actually her least favorite European author, ironically.) Original title of "Sentimental Education": A Coward's Bowels. Demo titles often change. A song on our album Helter Seltzer (Waiting for You) was original "Castrated Dolphin". We still consider it A Coward's Bowels...

## 7. FAULT LINES

**@wearescientists**
Most of HUFFY was self-produced, but we got Scott Storch (the Canadian Scott Storch [Chris in disguise] ) to helm this one — no idea how(!) He brought a certain blues-based swing to Fault Lines that the other tunes on the record kind of lack, for better or worse.

## 8. PANDEMONIUM

**@wearescientists**
Pandemonium, along with many of the tunes on HUFFY, originated as entries into the NYC Songwriter Challenge group we participate in.

## 9. BOUGHT MYSELF A GRAVE

**@wearescientists**
Bought a Grave is the only song on the record Chris lead-sings. This song was super-short at first, and we didn't know how to pad it out. The high-pitched auto-tuned vocals are one of the crown jewels in the WAS sound catalog. We're considering licensing it to Ford Motors. Nando's has also made a strong bid. This guitar symphony ending is what Keith's music would sound like if he took mushrooms every day

## 10. BEHAVIOUR UNBECOMING

**@wearescientists**
Behavior Unbecoming was the subject of FIERCE conflict with our label due to our controversial american spelling of "behavior".

# *Hi*
## Texas
BMG, 2021

✦ There can't be many albums that credit both RZA and Richard Hawley as co-writers. Still, with the Wu Tang Clan leader and the Sheffield rock'n'roll kingpin both sharing a love of old skool grooves (different skools, same swing), Texas were clearly on to something when they took a collaborative approach to their tenth album *Hi*. Sparked into life when the Glasweigan band found unfinished recordings for the sessions of their all conquering *White On Blonde* record, having worked with their past selves, Sharleen Spiteri (vocals/guitars), Ally McErlaine (guitars), Johnny McElhone (bass), Eddie Campbell (keyboards), Tony McGovern (guitars/backing vocals) and Cat Myers (drums) started to look further afield this time – even recruiting Altered Images/*Gregory Girls*' Clare Grogan for a duet, too. Celebrating the album's release Sharleen Spiteri (**@texastheband**) said hi to *Hi* with a listening party.

**PHOTOGRAPHY:**
Julian Broad

---

**LISTENING PARTY**
**14 OCTOBER 2021**

### 1. MR HAZE

🗨 **@texastheband (Sharleen Spiteri)**
The track that kicked off the writing of the new album. Originally we were making an anniversary record for White On Blonde & when we went into the Universal Vaults to find unheard versions of some of the songs we found three unfinished tracks. So we finished the chorus to Mr Haze, added a bridge, the sample from Donna Summer's Love's Unkind and thought, shit, this is too good to be a bonus track, hell let's write a new album!

### 2. HI FT WU TANG CLAN

🗨 **@texastheband**
After doing a documentary with [Wu Tang Clan's] RZA talking about our collaboration on Say What You Want, RZA said we should do another track. We had previously written Hi & we thought perfect, it's got the Morricone sound, the outlaw feel perfect for the Wu-Tang and of course has Kadeem Ramsay in the video with RZA!

### 3. JUST WANT TO BE LIKED

🗨 **@texastheband**
This is about social media and the pressure of constant acceptance, literally liking a photo, a comment, etc. Way too important in so many people's lives, causing doubt and unhappiness.

### 4. UNBELIEVABLE

🗨 **@texastheband**
The song talks about the destruction of your emotions and feelings. To let someone go and not be consumed by the fear of doing this and maybe by doing this is only when you reach the unbelievable, then rebuilding yourself and all around you.

### 5. MOONSTAR

🗨 **@texastheband**
Actually my fav track on Hi. Moonstar has got that kinda "brother where art thou" thing going on with the slightly off-kilter harmonies trying to find that church feel but with a constant acoustic simplicity to it.

### 6. DARK FIRE

✅ @texastheband

This is a track that we wrote with Richard Hawley. One of Richard's two in the morning calls with: check this out. Johnny, Richard and I wrote this very dark but beautiful song about relationships that are going through the mill and I guess relationships that have passed their sell-by date but there's still – a love.

### 7. LOOK WHAT YOU'VE DONE

✅ @texastheband

After performing at the Royal Albert Hall with [singer/actress] Clare Grogan, there was such a great blend, but also an unusual blend that we thought would work great on this song – throwing in another element of two women singing the lyric "look what you've done".

### 8. HEAVEN KNOWS

✅ @texastheband

Almost spoken rather than sung in places which isn't something I've done before. We are always trying to change it up, challenging ourselves to approach songs and sounds in a different way.

### 9. YOU CAN CALL ME

✅ @texastheband

[Soul and rockabilly label] Hi Records influenced but a more modern melody and vocal style, with the fast, staccato vocal. A lot of words firing fast at you!

### 10. SOUND OF MY VOICE

✅ @texastheband

This is the song to get an audience rockin! Recorded as a full band live – feel good and upbeat. Fast as fuck and a killer on my arm to play!

### 11. FALLING

✅ @texastheband

Has a Viking, Nordic feel. Like a great wave flowing over you. Hopefully creating a falling feeling. Hauntingly dark but the chorus hits and it is supposed to lift you from the fall.

### 12. HI (SINGLE MIX)

✅ @texastheband

This is the original recording before we gave it to Wu Tang Clan and it's really an insight to how you can change up a song with another set of ears that gives the writer a whole different angle to a song.

➡️ Texas' Sharleen Spiteri on stage in London in 2021.

# *Music Of The Spheres*
## Coldplay
Parlophone, 2021

⚓ Coldplay have become accustomed to all things big. Glastonbury's Pyramid Stage is their second home, stadiums usually host their own gigs and with their ninth studio album Guy Berryman (bass), Jonny Buckland (guitar), Will Champion (drums), Phil Harvey (creative director) and Chris Martin (vocals and piano) (all using **@coldplay**) sought out the *Music Of The Spheres*, no less. With a constellation of guests including pop star Selena Gomez, electronic visionary Jon Hopkins and the world's biggest boy band, BTS, the album certainly possessed the ambition to live up to its name and Coldplay's global reputation. "We always knew after [previous album] *Everyday Life* that we would be thinking about another tour," confirmed Berryman of this record's scale. "That always ends up helping to define the style of songs that go on an album. So with *Music Of The Spheres* there's some bigger, more anthemic songs which we felt might sound good in a stadium." In lieu of enormo-domes being available around the album's October 2021 release, the band did the next best thing and all crammed around a tiny keyboard to introduce *Music Of The Spheres* to the world… clearly they had a ball!

**ARTWORK:**
Pilar Zeta

Having a ball. Will Champion, Chris Martin, Jonny Buckland and Guy Berryman in 2021.

### 1. MUSIC OF THE SPHERES

◉ @coldplay (Chris Martin)

Our co-producer – the mighty Bill Rahko – used a speak & spell toy to create the opening words Music Of The Spheres.

### 2. HIGHER POWER

◉ @coldplay (Will Champion)

Higher Power was the first foundation stone of the record: It was the song that seemed to arrive in its most complete form and it provided something solid to build the rest of the album around. It features the wonderful Love Choir whose vocals provide so much drive and energy.

◉ @coldplay (Phil Harvey)

Higher Power was one of the first demos that chris presented. We recorded most of it on the first day with Max [Martin, producer]. I love how Jonny steals the show in the last third.

### 3. HUMANKIND

◉ @coldplay (Jonny Buckland)

Humankind was probably the hardest song to record on the album, just because we couldn't quite get the feel of it right until the end of the sessions. And then suddenly it all clicked into place and now we're really excited to play it live. It's like our tribute to Van Halen being played by New Order.

◉ @coldplay (Guy Berryman)

I think it was really important when we were auditioning songs to let Max hear them in the early stages, to comment and to help guide the actual selection of the songs and which ones he felt were the ones which were worth focusing on.

### 4. ALIEN CHOIR

◉ @coldplay (Will Champion)

It is a great moment in the record: Jon Hopkins helped us create a 'tail' at the end of Humankind which sounded like the song being sucked into a black hole and then we emerge in to the calm on the other side… thanks Jon.

### 5. LET SOMEBODY GO

◉ @coldplay (Phil Harvey)

Chris and I in particular have been big Selena Gomez fans for the longest time. She has such a unique, evocative, mysterious voice. When Selena performed Let Somebody Go with us on the Late Late Show I was so struck by her effortless charisma. I really love this song, particularly the explosive middle.

Ciao! Chris Martin performing live at Italian *The X Factor* in 2021.

### 6. HUMAN HEART

✔ @coldplay (Chris Martin)

This is Will's favourite song on the album. It only became great once Jacob [Collier, British musician], [duo We Are King's] Paris and Amber joined. It's so fun singing with them.

### 7. PEOPLE OF THE PRIDE

✔ @coldplay (Jonny Buckland)

Chris had the idea for the People Of The Pride verse when we were recording Viva La Vida, so it's been knocking around since then. It's been an idea looking for a song. It's definitely the heaviest song we've ever done. I think we were looking to make the song sound as intense as possible. Like a really concentrated guitar sound. Ironically quite a lot of the guitar was recorded on an acoustic.

### 8. BIUTYFUL

✔ @coldplay (Chris Martin)

Biutyful arrived when I was playing with different vocal sounds. We started working on it in the Everyday Life sessions, but we needed Max and Oscar [Holter, co-producer] to finish it.

✔ @coldplay (Jonny Buckland)

Part of Biutyful was recorded in Sweden in July 2020. That was one of the most magical recording sessions we've ever had. It was such a strange time with everywhere in lockdown but we just had so much fun recording. We were in Benny from ABBA's studio which was incredible and really inspiring and we just got so much done and had a really lovely time.

### 9. MUSIC OF THE SPHERES II

✔ @coldplay (Phil Harvey)

At the height of Covid restrictions, we were recording in the same hotel where Chris and I were staying. Chris asked the doorman to introduce Supernova 7 at the Music Of The Spheres festival [international album launch event]. We ran his voice backwards and through a few filters, and added a rapturous alien festival crowd.

### 10. MY UNIVERSE

✔ @coldplay (Phil Harvey)

About 18 months ago, I mentioned to Chris that some members of BTS had said they were into our band, and I'd heard a rumour they might like to collaborate. Four months later he called me super-excited – 'I've got the song for BTS!' – and played the demo over the phone. It was one of those brilliant moments I'll always remember. The band fleshed it out together and then Chris went to Seoul for 48 hours (most of the time in a quarantine hotel). [BTS member] RM did an amazing job with the Korean lyrics, and SUGA and J-hope totally nailed the breakdown. All 7 of their voices blend so well together, and with Chris'. This is me and my three boys' favourite song.

### 11. INFINITY SIGN

✔ @coldplay (Will Champion)

This features the largest choir we have ever worked with… the recording is based around a stadium show 'olé olé olé' chant. It attempts to imagine what a festival on another planet might sound like - Galaxtonbury!

✔ @coldplay (Guy Berryman)

I think for us the process of creating an album is always set in a kind of a predetermined visual landscape that we've created – a world – it just helps give us a framework into which we work musically. That was something we really started on Viva La Vida, and have kind of maintained for each album ever since. That's what led to the alien planets and languages on this album.

### 12. COLORATURA

✔ @coldplay (Jonny Buckland)

I really loved Coloratura before it got extended. It was my favourite song so I was a bit scared about changing it when Chris came back with this idea for the song going off in lots of different directions. But we just decided to go with it and follow where it took us. Coloratura's probably my favourite song ever to play live. There's so many bits. You can just exist in the song. You lose yourself in it.

✔ @coldplay (Guy Berryman)

We'd never really talked about doing such a long song before. It's the longest we've ever done. But it really does feel like the right song to end the album on.

Pick me! Coldplay bring *Music Of The Spheres* to the final of Italy's *The X Factor* in Milan.

# *Parallel Lines*
## Blondie
Chrysalis, 1978

The iconic sleeve, the equally iconic tunes… Blondie did not just make a record with their third album, they created a blueprint. Whether it is the infectious tunes, the skinny ties or the charismatic lead singer, the elements that have made the New Yorkers so cool have been copied time and again – often all at once – by acts trying to channel some of their metropolitan magic.

But there is only one Blondie, and 1978's *Parallel Lines* is a neat encapsulation of what made Deborah Harry (vocals – **@BlondieOfficial**), Chris Stein (guitar – **@chrissteinplays**), Clem Burke (drums), Nigel Harrison (bass), Jimmy Destri (keyboards) and Frank Infante (guitar) so great at this special time – and let's not forget album *Plastic Letters* was released the same year, while classics such as *Eat The Beat* and *Autoamerican* followed hot on the heels of this release. From the moment the handbreak is released, this album is straight no chaser all the way until its final notes. Brimming with energy and fizzing with melody, *Parallel Lines* blasts and beguiles as Harry's assured, irresistible vocals lead the way. The frontwoman also took the lead for the 1000th Listening Party, revealing how films, old TVs and a lost cat helped them create an album that set the standard for successive generations of New York bands.

**PHOTOGRAPHY:**
Edo Bertoglio

Rock 'n' roll to a tea. Debbie Harry having a cuppa in 1978.

Pooling their resources. Nigel Harrison, Frank Infante, Clem Burke, Debbie Harry, Chris Stein and Jimmy Destri at the Sunset Marquis in West Hollywood in 1978.

LISTENING
PARTY
**28 OCTOBER
2021**

### 1. HANGING ON THE TELEPHONE

**@BlondieOfficial (Debbie Harry)**
Ah, yes, The Nerves, the seminal, yet short-lived
Los Angeles power pop trio. We loved this song,
when we first heard The Nerves recording. Chris
and I played the recording while in the backseat of
a cab in Tokyo, the driver started tapping his fingers
on the steering wheel. We knew right then [it] was
a hit.

### 2. ONE WAY OR ANOTHER

**@BlondieOfficial**
This was Nigel's idea... riff... He came into
rehearsal one day and started playing it. The song
practically wrote itself. I was singing lyrics over
[the] band jamming, right there on the spot.

### 3. PICTURE THIS

**@BlondieOfficial**
An idea that came to me, Chris wrote the hook,
totality of its own, another song that existed [in]
my head. I wrote the lyrics, Jimmy wrote the verse
melody and Chris wrote the chorus. We all had
little pieces of one another's songs, just throwing
it all together... to make Picture This.

**@Tim_Burgess**
My fave. I asked Debbie to sign the 7" at Q AWARDS

←

Picture this. Blondie playing live in Los Angeles in 1978.

### 4. FADE AWAY AND RADIATE

✔ **@BlondieOfficial**

Chris wrote this song, Fade Away and Radiate. In the 60s 70s 80s TV channels went static [at] midnight, happened when the transmitter shut down. They would shift to white noise, I would fall asleep to the tv. Chris would watch me fall asleep each night in the white noise, it seems to have inspired him.

### 5. PRETTY BABY

✔ **@BlondieOfficial**

We saw the 1978 film, directed by Louis Malle... starring Brooke Shields, Keith Carradine, Susan Sarandon. I had met Brooke at a photo shoot by then, Chris wrote the music.

### 6. I KNOW BUT I DON'T KNOW

✔ **@BlondieOfficial**

Frank's song…

### 7. 11:59

✔ **@peter_beecham [fan]**

This album sounds just as amazing as the first time I heard it!

✔ **@chrissteinplays**

Thank you all for your support over the years too!

### 8. WILL ANYTHING HAPPEN?

✔ **@BlondieOfficial**

Another Jack Lee song that we liked a lot, we made a great connection with Jack.

### 9. SUNDAY GIRL

✔ **@BlondieOfficial**

A cross between visualizing a girl and my cat (Sunday Man), somehow these concepts collided and became Sunday Girl. Later on, Sunday Man ran away when we were on tour, he found a new home.

### 10. HEART OF GLASS

✔ **@BlondieOfficial**

Existed for such a long time as Once I Had A Love, didn't have the chorus, didn't have title or hook phase for a long time. We also didn't know there was a movie title Heart Of Glass. Mike Chapman loved the early demo versions.

### 11. I'M GONNA LOVE YOU TOO

✔ **@BlondieOfficial**

We had a misguided hunch this might get some serious radio attention, it went nowhere…

### 12. JUST GO AWAY

✔ **@BlondieOfficial**

Clearly, I was running out ideas at this point…

→

Parallel universe. Clem Burke, Nigel Harrison,Frank Infante, Chris Stein, Debbie Harry and Jimmy Destri outside Hollywood's ABC Studios in 1979.

# Non-Stop Erotic Cabaret
## Soft Cell
Some Bizzare, 1981

⚓ If the nocturnally-lit album cover wasn't hint enough, then even a cursory listen reveals a real after-hours, neon-drenched spirit of Soft Cell's debut album. Already pop stars – whether they liked it or not – by the time of its release, thanks to their iconic cover/reinvention of Tainted Love, Marc Almond (**@MarcAlmond**) and Dave Ball (**@softcellhq**) brought creatures of the night into the full glare of the spotlight with this candid musical account of what happens when the sun goes down. Driven by new synth tech that was blossoming in the early 1980s, plus Almond's sharply crooned narrations, this record was a vivid swirl of the different worlds that the pair found themselves moving through: from grimy bedsits, to iconic New York clubs and all the dark crannies in between. This approach also meant mainstream pop fans were confronted with alternative lifestyles and ways of thinking that were different to what Thatcherite society was prescribing at the time. "It all added to the spirit of Post Punk Art School Anarchy around Soft Cell," Almond told the Listening Party of the chaos that seemed to flow around the making of *Non-Stop Erotic Cabaret*. Happily, the playback of this glorious slab of synth-sleaze, was conducted in much the same vein.

**PHOTOGRAPHY:**
Peter Ashworth

---

**LISTENING PARTY**
**31 OCTOBER 2021**

### 1. FRUSTRATION

✅ **@MarcAlmond**
Dave wrote the original lyrics to Frustration. It was about his dad. Two and a half minutes of the most life changing music!

### 2. TAINTED LOVE

✅ **@softcellhq (Dave Ball)**
Gloria Jones' version was the first version we ever heard. I prefer the Ruth Swann version & Coil's not bad.

✅ **@MarcAlmond**
What we wanted to achieve at the time was we hoped would be a successful album to follow the huge success of Tainted Love and to represent Soft Cell in the best and truest way as we were at the time. It was all so hurried and frantic though. I wasn't needed in the studio that much.

### 3. SEEDY FILMS

✅ **@MarcAlmond**
What do you think of first when you think of Non-Stop Erotic Cabaret? I think of New York, the excitement of being there for the first time and recording there too. Life changing experience...

✅ **@softcellhq**
I think of the crazy times in the Some Bizarre office above the legendary Trident Studios, St. Anne's Court in Soho. And even crazier times running around New York nightclubs after working in Media Sound Studios in the daytime. My memories of the early 80s are very neon-lit and drug-fuelled with a disco beat.

### 4. YOUTH

◉ **@MarcAlmond**

This whole album tells a story. You can write a narrative about all the songs! This is the main character of the song looking back on his youth before he was a cross dresser and ended up in an S&M club with Sex Dwarves!

### 5. SEX DWARF

◉ **@MarcAlmond**

This was based on a newspaper tabloid @softcellhq – tabloid exploitation. The dwarf in the video stole the clip before it was released and gave it to the newspapers! We got raided and then I became a headline – Marc Drugged Girls In A Sex Dwarf Vice Den!! We'll probably get cancelled for this now! In fact for the whole album really!

### 6. ENTERTAIN ME

◉ **@MarcAlmond**

The album title came from a sign in Soho, back in the days when there were strip clubs. We thought it was a good way of looking at life at the time. The sex and sleaze behind closed doors and the pulled curtains of Thatcher's Britain.

### 7. CHIPS ON MY SHOULDER

◉ **@MarcAlmond**

This is about people who are just never satisfied. The pop star world we found ourselves in after the success of Tainted Love. A lot of these songs are about tabloids too, a reaction to what's going on behind the door in Margaret Thatcher's Britain. Non Stop Erotic Cabaret is really a post punk statement with a punk attitude.

### 8. BEDSITTER

◉ **@MarcAlmond**

I wrote this song in my bedsit in Leeds and it really was my life at the time.

### 9. SECRET LIFE

◉ **@MarcAlmond**

This song in a way is a preceding song to Say Hello Wave Goodbye about a politician's affair with a prostitute, his secret is he's also a cross dresser.

### 10. SAY HELLO, WAVE GOODBYE

◉ **@MarcAlmond**

I've got very cruel imitations of the last note of this song which is one of the greatest notes in pop music. David Gray of course did an amazing version of this and I also really loved Aha's version of it too as Morton Harket is one of my favourite singers.

↓

A fair cop. Dave Ball and Marc Almond.

# *Prioritise Pleasure*
## Self Esteem
Universal, 2021

Rebecca Lucy Taylor (**@SELFESTEEM___**) is a multi-media force. In her first band Slow Club, her vocal talent and her inherent musicality were there for all to hear.

Yet her personality and her full creative vision was not. However, in a series of social posts that followed the dissolution of that band, that showcased Taylor's painting and prose poem-like statements delivered as smart phone screen-grabs, a much fuller version of her artistry began to emerge. Thankfully, this self-expression also made its way on record as Self Esteem. Having drawn up the musical spaces her ideas could inhabit with debut album *Compliments Please*, *Prioritise Pleasure* delivered a truly vivid portrait of modern emotional life. A sights, sounds and smells depiction of dating boys and girls, attitudes between couples and the heart-breaking shrapnel that lingers long after the end of the affair, Taylor's incisive, candid words are accompanied by a swirl of sounds that streak through future-pop squelches, aggressive beats and soul-collapsing torch songs. *Prioritise Pleasure* is a true experiential album, and as you'd expect from an artist comfortable across a range of media, her Twitter Listening Party game is as honest, confessional and as funny as you would dare hope.

**PHOTOGRAPHY:**
Olivia Richardson

### LISTENING PARTY
### 3 NOVEMBER 2021

**1. I'M FINE**

☑ **@SELFESTEEM___**
Proud day in the studio this. Needed to tell my story somehow. Needed to get it the fuck out of my body. One day I'll write it all down but for now we bark. Men love to call women crazy. Well we are crazy, of course we fucking are, you would be too.

**2. FUCKING WIZARDRY**

☑ **@SELFESTEEM___**
When I wrote the lyric 'to even get near to me was some fucking wizardry' I said to Johan [Karlberg, producer], "ok good we have the 'so I'm gonna get drunk and slag you off' of the album." Ok full disclosure, I feel a bit silly about the bitchy lyric in this song. Chose to keep it in because as a time stamp it's interesting to me to remember how in my feelings I was. How gutted and hurt. So gutted and hurt, I'm being a rate cow. I'm interested in the way sometimes I'm the victim and sometimes I'm the cause. The fact that right and wrong is not as binary as we think. Maybe I'm over thinking it. I really liked this lad and it was very annoying!

**3. HOBBIES 2**

☑ **@SELFESTEEM___**
Run this screengrab? This is a sequel to the poem Hobbies on my first album performed by [actor] @Alessandro_Babs. Forever toying with whether casual sex is akin to playing badminton or not. At least they check I came y'know. cute. Modern dating is miserable.

**4. PRIORITISE PLEASURE**

☑ **@SELFESTEEM___**
Realised I don't shave my pubes for boys anymore and wrote a song about it. One day I'll release the audio of me singing in the string lines, trying with all my might to sound LIKE a sentient string. I really did think that one would be kind to me...

## 5. I DO THIS ALL THE TIME

✓ @SELFESTEEM___

I guess we need a whole separate evening for this one. maybe an ITV special? Too much to say about this one but the Easter egg is the beat sample is the same from the song Wrestling which was also the first song off my first record. I find Easter eggs dead spooky and exciting. When I used to sit and watch my brother play playstation games I got such a fucking THRILL when there were special things you found? So anyway, I do that in my songs for literally about 7 or 9 of you to notice. The string line is me ripping off Max Richter.

## 6. MOODY

✓ @SELFESTEEM___

Easter egg: the person I was sexting is the same person 'so I'm gonna get drunk and slag you off' [from In Time on debut album Compliments Please] is about. Don't book me on you MH talks cos I haven't solved mine bebe!

## 7. STILL REIGNING

✓ @SELFESTEEM___

Easter egg: I'm still banging on about the same lass She Reigns is about, shocker. It's vital that you have some alone times, luvs. You put up with so much less shit once you're not scared of being alone.

⊕

I do this all the time. Self Esteem, AKA Rebecca Lucy Taylor, onstage in Manchester in 2021.

## 8. HOW CAN I HELP YOU

✓ @SELFESTEEM___

Johan said to me 'write about being mad about not getting a mercury nomination' but I realised I'm MUCH MORE mad about everything else.

## 9. ITS BEEN A WHILE

✓ @SELFESTEEM___

I wanted to make a trap song about my ex girlfriend's acne. I sat in a bath in a cottage that [musician] Kelli Jaine Blanchett paid for me to go to and listened to [Kanye West's] I AM A GOD over and over and then this happened. I really need you to buy more albums so I can take Kelli to a cottage back. When we were in this cottage I spent the whole time with a silk cap on growing my hair cos I had been so sure my ex bf didn't want me cos of my short hair hahahahaha.

## 10. THE 345

✓ @SELFESTEEM___

Literally written in response to the thought process behind my last tweet.

## 11. JOHN ELTON

✓ @SELFESTEEM___

This is a song I wrote when I was in Slow Club, ehhehe. You see they all have kids. Or at the very least they get married. They really get the fuck over you. You disappear completely. Packed up. Neat little box. No bow. But me? I'll carry the scraps of you. Whether I know they are there or not. Shine a light on me like when they do the UV thing on Hotel Inspector. Shine that UV light on me and yeah theres the old cum stains, but theres also you. Your hand prints.

## 12. YOU FOREVER

✓ @SELFESTEEM___

This was the only head scratcher on the album. It was Lion King musical in demo form but I wanted Robyn Dancing On My Own, and it took us ages but we got there.

## 13. JUST KIDS

✓ @SELFESTEEM___

I hate sayings as lyrics usually, but fuck me I've been the biggest square peg in a world of round holes for 35 years. Mmm round holes...

# Lost In The Dream
## The War On Drugs
Secretly Canadian, 2014

✠ "We're rolling…" There is something uniquely evocative about The War On Drugs' third album. Its title, *Lost In The Dream*, speaks to this quality, this sense of its vividness but there is something about this record that just had to be experienced. From its opening notes to its final chords, *Lost In The Dream* not only inspires mental pictures of sweeping American vistas and detailed landscapes, but it also conjures up the spirit of blue-collar life, the steel mills and truck stops, the roadside diners and the endless stretch of the freeway.

This unique sonic alchemy is achieved by the songwriting and production ideas of the band's leader, Adam Granduciel. In places he is happy to allow his music to sprawl, occasionally to become almost ambient, yet underpinning all this movement are melodies and lyrics attuned with Dylan and Springsteen's attempts to grasp and portray American life. With much of the material infused by Granduciel's struggles to adjust to everyday life after touring – he felt depression and paranoia after spending most of 2011 on the road – the source for the record's sense of movement and its thoughtful lyrics might be clear, but *Lost In The Dream* is anything but a simple response to these issues. As Granduciel (using @TheWarOnDrugs) revealed as he recounted the work behind the record, getting *Lost In The Dream* was a mammoth artistic undertaking, which explains why listening to it proves a consistently rewarding experience.

**PHOTOGRAPHY:**
Dustin Condren

⊕

Living the dream. Adam Granduciel onstage in Bergen in 2014.

## 1. UNDER THE PRESSURE

⊘ **@TheWarOnDrugs (Adam Granduciel)**

We're rolling. I remember when Dave Hartley did the bass to this. Mitch easter's Fidelitorium in NC. Brad [Bell engineer] cool had just eaten a suicide hot wing. Dave was finding his pocket on a short scale Tiesco bass. Jon Natchez drove to Philly for an afternoon and composed that amazing saxophone line in his Camry #legend. For me, the first 5 minutes of the song can't exist without these last 3. All the guitar on this song is the first guitar I ever owned – my harmony bobcat.

## 2. RED EYES

⊘ **@TheWarOnDrugs**

I woke up on my couch in a state of full blown panic and meltdown and then I started strumming these verse chords and singing this melody. I already basically had the rest of the song but no verse… North Carolina played a big part in this record. We considered Asheville and Durham our home away from home.

## 3. SUFFERING

⊘ **@TheWarOnDrugs**

Almost track 1!! We've only played suffering a few times but it remains one of my favourites. Guitar tone inspired by Robbie Robertson's Black Box built by Garth Hudson. We recreated it in Asheville's Echo Mountain [studio]. [guitar pedals] Jesse Turbo Fuzz into Jesse Turbo Green Ringer into Space Echo into Leslie. It goes without saying that Jeff Zeigler played a huge role in the creation of this record's vibe/mood. Some incredible engineering on this… unparalleled IMO.

## 4. AN OCEAN IN BETWEEN THE WAVES

⊘ **@TheWarOnDrugs**

A totally different version existed until a week or two before we had to be done. Didn't have that midnight vibe yet. Went back to Uniform Recording [in Philly] and recorded and mixed this in three days. Our assistant engineer at echo mountain in asheville ended up playing drums on this song and Living In The Dream. Jon Ashley. Trying to channel Sir Elton on these outro vocals. Abrupt ending inspired by plastic ono band… Remember.

## 5. DISAPPEARING

⊘ **@TheWarOnDrugs**

Originally it was gonna end early but I remember driving through Philly in my van at 2am and the rough mix just kept going and it was a moment that put the record in focus for me – I went home that night and did all the slide and lead parts. I like that we didnt fade Disappearing.

## 6. EYES TO THE WIND

⊘ **@TheWarOnDrugs**

I remember doing these vocals in Asheville with Dave, just listening for hours and being so patient and supportive as I worked it out over a few hours. Until mixing, these vocals had a fair amount of delay on them. [Mixer] Nicolas Vernhes heard a different kind of song and dried them up with a vintage UA 175b compressor. And I think that decision kinda changed my life. Also Charlie's [Hall] drums on this. First take, first impression. So good and pure. Always reminded me of [Bob Dylan's] Bringing It All Back Home or something.

## 7. THE HAUNTING IDLE

⊘ **@TheWarOnDrugs**

What can you say?

## 8. BURNING

⊘ **@TheWarOnDrugs**

My dad's favourite song – but my favourite chorus and my first high harmony. I had this keyboard riff for so many years before it ended up as Burning.

## 9. LOST IN THE DREAM

⊘ **@TheWarOnDrugs**

If you heard the insane drum machine pattern I wrote this to you may not like it as much. A couple lines of undefined words on this song but I like it…it felt right and true.

## 10. IN REVERSE

⊘ **@TheWarOnDrugs**

My favourite song of ours and one I'll never not play. Dave was on a cruise when I was mixing so he was eagerly awaiting ANYTHING in his inbox. He was coaching us from somewhere off the Alaskan coast. The beginning sounds like a light that's drifting, in reverse. I'm moving. So happy we get to perform this song. Thanks for hangin' with me on here.

# *Loveless*
## My Bloody Valentine
Creation, 1991

⚓ Despite its relative youth, My Bloody Valentine's second album has already acquired a trail music folklore that would put most 78s to shame. Tales of sonic perfection, demands for experimental equipment, a three-year gestation, sessions round the clock, tents in the studio and the infamous tale of record label Creation stealing master tapes from the studio as they tried to release the album in the face of spiralling production costs, have all attached themselves to *Loveless*' myth.

In some ways it is easy to see why My Bloody Valentine's record has attracted this extraordinary reputation. A body of shimmering noise, fragile melodies and sweet static, even two decades after its recording by Colm Ó Cíosóig (drums), Bilinda Butcher (vocals/guitar), Debbie Googe (bass) and visionary leader Kevin Shields (all using **@MBVofficial**), the records still sounds like a message from the future. However, this is a Listening Party, so hearsay and tall tales are for the rest. Instead, to mark *Loveless*' 30th anniversary, all the band were on hand to sherpa us personally through this unique masterpiece's sonic mountain range.

**ARTWORK:**
Designland

Blown on a wish. My Bloody Valentine pictured in 1992.

↑
Soundwaves. Famed for the intensity of their live shows, Kevin Shields and the band onstage in London in 1990.

LISTENING PARTY
4 NOVEMBER 2021

## 1. ONLY SHALLOW

### ✔ @MBVofficial

Kevin: Only shallow was recorded 2nd take. The last verse has the original guide guitar in the final mix, virtually all parts were always 2nd take for some reason, although we rarely did more that three takes of anything, never comped anything or fixed things. The main guitar part (where there is no singing) was two valve amplifiers with tremolo facing each other, played a few times then sampled and played backwards and an octave higher along with the original part, 'possibly'.

## 2. LOOMER

### ✔ @MBVofficial

Kevin: This song was recorded using a guitar that was my attempt to improve the Fender Jaguar, it had a Strat neck and Fender Lace active pickups, I dismantled it just after I recorded it. I was trying to make a sound like fire sounds, also train noises.

## 3. TOUCHED

### ✔ @MBVofficial

Kevin: This was originally made as a link between tracks but it was really its own thing so I got Colm to give it a title.

### ✔ @MBVofficial

Colm: Touched is story of a sexual encounter. The first part is anxiety followed by the release then the sadness and the title has another soft meaning. Written in two hours with string and timpani samples.

## 4. TO HERE KNOWS WHEN

### ✔ @MBVofficial

Kevin: This was first take on guitar, it was lucky as the engineer passed out around two minutes in while I was playing it, it put him in a mild coma basically, he had to go home afterwards. He was also smoking too much weed. This song was the one where everything went off the rails for awhile, two weeks trying to program a tambourine track which was then played by hand in 10m. Three weeks sampling guitar feedback. Two weeks on drum samples experiments.

## 5. WHEN YOU SLEEP

### ✔ @MBVofficial

Kevin: The main keyboard part of this song is made using samples of Bilinda's voice among other things, we did this a lot, usually a mixture of guitar feedback, Bilinda's voice, a flute sample and an oboe sample.

### 6. I ONLY SAID

○ **@MBVofficial**

Kevin: The main guitar on this was processed by hand using the parametric EQ on the recording console as a wah wah kind of effect.

### 7. COME IN ALONE

○ **@MBVofficial**

Kevin: The instrumental bit in the middle of this one took about 20hrs to record and because we kept going over the same part of tape so much it kind of wore that part of the tape out a bit. After getting over the shock we realised it was the perfect amount of sound change to allow the sampled part to come out properly.

○ **@MBVofficial**

Bilinda: I do really love Loveless and cherish those songs. I always enjoy singing them and if they mean a lot to other people it's probably because they were done with love and honesty. There were battles to get things done but Kevin took the brunt of all that and still remained positive about the album. We were a bit like ships in the night because I had my son to look after and didn't go into the studio until I did the vocals. I enjoyed writing the lyrics despite a sadness to some of them but the album is bigger than any of its parts and is timeless.

### 8. SOMETIMES

○ **@MBVofficial**

Kevin: Sometimes was unusual in that it was a song written and recorded near the end of the loveless sessions. I had wanted to write a certain type of song and just had to wait until it arrived (it finally did after about a year). The acoustic guitar is actually seven tracks each with a different sound panned like a fan left to right so it sounds like one track if that makes any sense? The distorted guitar is the re-amped acoustic thru our trusty Vox fuzz, this pedal was pretty much the only fuzz or distortion used on Loveless, I think.

○ **@MBVofficial**

Debbie: Here's a little Loveless joke from me: The making of Loveless was when Kevin started his infamous 'tent' building', constructing little dens out of blankets, curtains and foam… it was baffling!

○ **@MBVofficial**

Kevin: Doing the vocals for this one was the only time i built an actual tent in the live room, it did sound better this way.

### 9. BLOWN A WISH

○ **@MBVofficial**

Kevin: The recording for this was mostly done in a studio where [engineer and later acclaimed producer] Alan Moulder sometimes had to spray me with a light mist of water while I was recording to get rid of my extreme static, it was ruining the recordings so I had to be damp to play. I often wound up in a puddle of water by the time we finished recording.

○ **@MBVofficial**

Colm: One of the engineers broke down after a frequency disagreement and said all he wanted to do was open a pizza place.

(→)

**@MBVofficial**
This pedal was pretty much the only fuzz or distortion used on loveless, I think.

### 10. WHAT YOU WANT

✔ **@MBVofficial**

Kevin: The main memory of this song is that it was nearly scrapped because I couldn't get usable guitar sound for it, something to do with the tuning, it was saved by a vintage ampeg amp that used to belong to Black Sabbath. Doing the vocals for loveless was a fairly simple process although we did have to leave the studio we were in before we finished all the songs due to the studio cleaners coming in everyday at 7am, which was usually when we were just getting into recording, it was the only studio we had ever worked in that had daily cleaners.

✔ **@MBVofficial**

Debbie: In 1990 we took a break from recording to go out and tour to promote the Glider EP. The tour started in Ireland and was kind of disastrous. The first gig I seem to remember was at some student union place where they had no idea we were supposed to be there! The second place was booked in a pub, where the stage was so small we could barely fit the drum kit let alone the rest of our gear, so we couldn't play there either. Eventually we got to this place, I think it was in Tralee, where we just holed up in this hotel ballroom for a couple days, I don't even think we played a gig, I think we just hung there and Kevin spent most of the time painting a guitar and I spent a couple days trying to find a surge suppressor unit, which frankly in Tralee, in 1990 was about as successful as tracking down a dodo.

### 11. SOON

✔ **@MBVofficial**

Kevin: One of the main overriding memories from the recording of Loveless was this kind of overwhelming love and sense of protection for all the songs, like they were a bunch of living things. There was also an incredibly strong sense of how everything needed to be done, everything else was just a distraction.

Come in alone. MBV's Bilinda Butcher.

# *Beautiful Garbage*
## Garbage
Mushroom, 2001

⚓ Having produced Nirvana's *Nevermind* (see page 234), Butch Vig might have acquired a lifetime's worth of rock'n'roll folklore in one go. However, having written some of his own songs, the producer's urge to form a band – named after a studio insult "this sounds like Garbage" – proved too strong. With Vig behind the drum kit, Duke Erikson primarily on bass and Steve Marker on guitar, Garbage avoided the pitfall of simply being a producer's side project by uncovering one of the world's most iconic front people to lead the band, Shirley Manson.

With the Scot's vocals and lyrics giving Garbage a unique, visceral edge, the future-facing rockers soon became as big as many of Vig's best clients. Indeed, still together and making music, the quartet (all using **@garbage**) opted to celebrate the 20th birthday of their third album with a listening party that reaffirmed that Garbage are far from disposable.

**ARTWORK:**
Me Company

---

**LISTENING PARTY**
**9 NOVEMBER 2021**

### 1. SHUT YOUR MOUTH

✅ **@garbage**
Shirley: This is really about the growing resentment I met as our success continued to grow as a band. People say and do terrible things out of jealousy.

✅ **@garbage**
Butch: I love the drums in SYM, they were bussed through the Roger Mayer RM 58 compressor, lofi and crunchy. I still have it, it's crusty but it works! Duke played some stellar Wah Wah, and DJ Sloppy makes an appearance after each chorus. I think some of Shirl's lyrics came from too many people in the music biz giving us their "opinions" about what BG should sound like. "We don't give a f**king damn".

✅ **@garbage**
Duke: We discussed how, since the title was going to be Shut Your Mouth, the lyrics should be really 'wordy'.

### 2. ANDROGYNY

✅ **@garbage**
Shirley: So proud we were ahead of the curve in encouraging the mainstream acknowledgement of non-binary gender and sexual identities. We also fully support the LGBTQIA community. Always have. Always will. Androgyny is a hard song for us to perform live for some reason which is why we don't play it very often. Sometimes I think I am half boy half woman.

@garbage

Butch: One of the most eclectic tracks on BG, we intentionally wrote the verses chorus bridge with completely different vibes. That kind of set the tone for the whole album.

### 3. CAN'T CRY THESE TEARS

@garbage

Shirley: My favourite moment in the entire song is on the line "It's time that I told you so" during the double chorus at the end . That "so". It's a moment for me.

@garbage

Duke: The bridge is pure Shangri-Las.

@garbage

Butch: This is our homage to the fabulous girl groups of the late 50's early 60's, The Shirelles, Ronettes, Shangri-Las and Crystals. I believe this is the only song we've used sleigh bells!

### 4. TIL THE DAY I DIE

@garbage

Shirley: I think it was Duke who came up with the line " 'til the day I die" and the chords of the song but I can't be sure. I tried to match the lyrics to the rock and roll swagger of the music. The demo of this is really good. We really wanted to get a gospel choir to sing on the choruses for this song but for reasons too boring to explain here......it didn't work out.

@garbage

Butch: Duke playing a Keith Richards riff in the verse, going toe to toe with DJ Sloppy! I hear Shirl channeling some Chrissie Hynde into this track. We are all massive Pretenders fans! Little known fact: we brought a choir into Smart to sing on the choruses with Shirl, but they didn't make the final mix as we thought is was too out of context. Instead we mixed Shirl's BK Vox with a Mellotron.

Tales from the road. Images from the *Beautiful Garbage* tour shared by the band during the Listening Party.

### 5. CUP OF COFFEE

✅ **@garbage**

Shirley: Ugh. The saddest song in our entire discography. Even to this day I can get emotional whilst singing it live. It's is an amalgamation of numerous breakups I endured. Lost love sucks. This is my favourite slow song we have ever written. One day I want us to perform this with a live orchestra ….Nelson Riddle style.

✅ **@garbage**

Duke: Came up with the orchestral break idea in my little studio at home and wondered if I should show it to the band. Glad I did!

### 6. SILENCE IS GOLDEN

✅ **@garbage**

Shirley: This is a song dedicated to all victims of domestic and sexual violence. Listening to Silence Is Golden is still very hard for me. Sending you all so much love tonight in this tricky old world of ours.

✅ **@garbage**

Butch: We came up with the idea for this song in a van in Denver, after hearing Wings "Let Me Roll It" on the radio. I dig the meter changes in this, the front half is 6/8 and the end is in 4/4. It is tricky to perform live! Shirl's vocals on the outro, "Won't someone listen" starting when the ringy guitars kick in, are a first take. We had no idea what she was going to do, she sang so hard the vocal gets really distorted, but the performance was so kick ass we kept it.

### 7. CHERRY LIPS (GO BABY GO!)

✅ **@garbage**

Shirley: I was so inspired by the writings of JT Leroy during the making of this whole record. Cherry Lips was directly influenced by their novel "Sarah" and has become a kind of trans anthem for so many of our fans. Come on you know you want to dance. Strangely this song was licensed by a yogurt company in Italy. Nothing is stranger than life.

✅ **@garbage**

Butch: One of the things I love about this song is Shirl's vocal. We slowed the track down for her when she sang, so at regular speed it's pitched up quite a bit. Makes her sound like an alien. Which she might be.

### 8. BREAKING UP THE GIRL

✅ **@garbage**

Steve: Pop is not a dirty word.

✅ **@garbage**

Duke: A brazen attempt to write a catchy pop song!

✅ **@garbage**

Butch: It was tricky recording Shirl's vocals for this track. The arrangement we came up with, the 1st verse starts really low in her register, and keeps rising up through the song, even modulating up at the end. As I remember, there were a lot of takes!

✅ **@garbage**

Shirley: Either Butch or Duke came up with this title. I can't remember! Then I wrote around it's theme. I kept asking them what the title meant but they never were able to come up with a satisfactory answer. Duke thinks I hate this song. But I don't. I just don't love it as much as all our other children. My mum always used to tell me I'd better keep my shit together or I would end up in the gutter.

⬇

Words and music. Garbage shared this image to illustrate the writing of the lyrics for Til The Day I Die.

### 9. DRIVE YOU HOME

⊘ @garbage

Shirley: This song concerns the slow breakdown of a relationship. The misery and heartbreak of it all. It still kills me. Listening to Drive you Home still makes me feel a bit sick. It's so so desperately sad, but I still really love this vocal.

⊘ @garbage

Butch: I really love this track, there's a lot of vulnerability in Shirl's vocals and lyrics. I guess I'm a sucker for dark, bittersweet pop songs.

### 10. PARADE

⊘ @garbage

Shirley: This is the closest we have (in my opinion) ever gotten to writing a kind of hymn, a prayer or a mantra. I love this song. It's so full of joyful celebration.

### 11. NOBODY LOVES YOU

⊘ @garbage

Steve: What kind of music is this?

⊘ @garbage

Butch: Weird, listening to this now, I can hear a bit of a Radiohead influence in Duke and Steve's guitars. But wait, that's not weird because we love Radiohead. Also hear some Trip Hop textures in this. Lots of scene changes.

⊘ @garbage

Shirley: I was going through a painful divorce at the time of writing these words. I was drowning in shame, sadness and excruciating loneliness. The line everyone asks about in the break is "I cracked a piece of broken glass." Staying in love takes monumental effort.

### 12. UNTOUCHABLE

⊘ @garbage

Butch: As I remember, Shirl wrote these lyrics about a real jackass that we knew in the music biz. Who shall go nameless.

⊘ @garbage

Shirley: I live this song. I know EXACTLY who this song is written about but of course a lady never spats and tells. This is both a reprimand and a warning. This lady was not signing up for anymore bullshit after this. We wrote this whilst obsessed with Timberland and Dallas Austin. Still obsessed to be honest.

### 13. SO LIKE A ROSE

⊘ @garbage

Shirley: In the course of my lifetime I've lost far too many people I have loved to suicide. This song is in honour of all those who were far too fragile for this world.

The band taking their *Beautiful Garbage* to Tokyo.

# Laundry Service
## Shakira
Epic, 2001

**PHOTOGRAPHY:**
Firooz Zahedi

"Shakira's music doesn't sound like anybody else's, and she has invented her own brand of innocent sensuality," wrote Gabriel García Márquez after meeting the singer-songwriter around the turn of the century. With the esteem and admiration of the Columbian author of *One Hundred Years Of Solitude* – the two became friends after the interview – Shakira Ripoll's pop ascent should not be surprising, although in the increasingly borderless streaming age it is perhaps possible to forget how many Latin artists had struggled to turn popularity with home audiences into real international success.

In every sense *Laundry Service* is a true breakthrough record. The album – her fifth, but first to be mainly recorded in English – saw Shakira match her South American achievements around the globe, though she conquered worldwide pop charts by staying true to the character and uniqueness that had so enthralled Márquez. Celebrating 20 years since its release, Shakira (**@shakira**) gave *Laundry Service* a spin just for us.

**LISTENING PARTY**

**13 NOVEMBER 2021**

### 1. OBJECTION (TANGO)

**@shakira**
Objection was the very first song I wrote in English, on a mattress in the bedroom of my Miami apartment, with a thesaurus in hand, when I could barely speak the language!

### 2. UNDERNEATH YOUR CLOTHES

**@shakira**
We did the video with Herb Ritts, an iconic photographer whose black and white images I really loved and who I was dying to work with. I was a huge fan of Herb but after that shoot I don't think he was a huge fan of mine because I took seven hours in hair and makeup before shooting… I was nervous, ok??

### 3. WHENEVER, WHEREVER

**@shakira**
Whenever came out of me wanting to do a song with Andean sounds and instruments like the pan flute and the bombo leguero. I was in a moment where I was in love with Latin folkloric music and I wanted something that honored that.

### 4. RULES

**@shakira**
Rules was the song where I first performed playing drums on tour. I had played drums before but that was the first song where I played them onstage.

### 5. THE ONE

**@shakira**
The One was the last single off of Laundry Service. The power ballad Shakira, lol.

### 6. READY FOR THE GOOD TIMES

**@shakira**
Ready For The Good Times was one of the most fun for me to perform on tour – there was a dance that went with it that I really enjoyed. That tour – the Tour of the Mongoose – was my biggest tour yet and we had so much fun.

### 7. FOOL

**@shakira**
Fool is a song that I wrote with my drummer Brendan Buckley. He has been with me for almost

my entire career and we still do things together (like Girl Like Me), but this is one of the first we did, just me and him!

### 8. TE DEJO MADRID

@shakira

Te Dejo Madrid is one of the few Spanish-language songs from Laundry Service and it's still one of the most fun to perform. In Madrid especially!

### 9. POEM TO A HORSE

@shakira

This was me at the height of poetic hyperbole. Essentially I was comparing a love interest to a horse who couldn't appreciate what he had before him. I was using the writing device of personification, but in the opposite way.

### 10. QUE ME QUEDES TÚ

@shakira

Que Me Quedes Tu was a love song I did with Luisfer Ochoa, my longtime collaborator from

[Shakira's third album] Pies Descalzos to today. That song very much has the sound of what Luisfer and I do together.

### 11. EYES LIKE YOURS (OJOS ASÍ)

@shakira

Moody guitars, slides, the lyrics of that song also makes use of a lot of hyperbole. I guess I'm a hyperbolic person when it comes to love... Or in general. Ha!

### 12. SUERTE (WHENEVER, WHEREVER)

@shakira

I still write with Luisfer to this day, and it's one of the times when I feel the most free. Just him, me and an acoustic guitar.

### 13. TE AVISO, TE ANUNCIO (TANGO)

@shakira

Wow, it's been so long since I remembered some of these songs...this was so fun you guys, now time to get back into the studio.

Cleaning up. Shakira live in Los Angeles in 2001.

233

# *Nevermind*
## Nirvana
DGC, 1991

⚓ Where do you start when discussing the impact, legacy, or even just the songs on an album like *Nevermind*? Nirvana very much started as the outlaws, riders on the edge of culture when they made their second album – so much so that much was made when it finally went ahead of Michael Jackson to reach Number 1 on the American charts the year after its release – yet as it celebrated its 30th birthday with this Listening Party it is fair to say that music has been reshaped in its image. Whether celebrated or eschewed, Kurt Cobain's atmospheric vocal angst and candid songwriting, complimented by Dave Grohl's incredible drums and the bass playing of Krist Novoselic, have changed many assumptions within mainstream and alternative music as these underdogs came good. To understand how this iconic album came together, its producer Butch Vig (using **@Nirvana**) – now a member of Garbage (see page 228) – rewound to the sessions in 1991 that would come to define an era.

**LIC_Nevermind_Nirvana.jpeg**

**PHOTOGRAPHER:**
Kirk Weddle

---

**LISTENING PARTY**

**13 NOVEMBER 2021**

### 1. SMELLS LIKE TEEN SPIRIT

🔘 **@Nirvana (Butch Vig)**
What can I say about this song. It started a revolution, it changed my life. And probably some of your lives too. The first time I heard Teen Spirit live was in a rehearsal studio in North Hollywood it was the first song Nirvana played for me. I was blown away, paced around the room, taking the song in. When they finished Kurt said "what do you think?" I paused for a few seconds, then said "play it again. And they did. During the second pass I got focused and started scribbling down production notes. It was a monster of a song. And it was the first time I met Dave Grohl. I was impressed with how tight and LOUD he played. He clearly had elevated the band to a new level.

🔘 **@Tim_Burgess**
Smells Like Teen Spirit. Never short of fucking amazing.

### 2. IN BLOOM

🔘 **@Nirvana**
In Bloom was one of the 1st songs we tracked at [studio] Sound City because I was really familiar with the arrangement, it didn't need any tinkering. I tracked the heavy guitars using a Fender Bassman amp that I had rented, possibly using the Big Muff. I wanted a smooth, deep guitar tone. The Bassman to me kind of defined a "grunge" guitar sound. We added Dave's vocal harmonies toward the end of the sessions, after we had moved to Studio B. His voice really complimented Kurt's. The high notes in the chorus were right at the top of DG's range, his voice kept breaking up, I had him do a lot of takes. After each one he'd take a pull off a cigarette, then take a shot of Jack Daniels, pause, and say in a low raspy voice "I'm ready Butch." Needless to say, the session got a little crazy.

### 3. COME AS YOU ARE

 @Nirvana

Kurt recorded his guitar solo in two takes, as well as three takes of vocals. I told Kurt I'd like to dbl track his vocals throughout the entire song, at first he said no, thought it sounded "fake"...but I reminded him that John Lennon dbl tracked most of his vocals, and he acquiesced. I love the guitar "solo" in the bridge, it's basically following the vocal melody, the same approach we used in Teen Spirit. During the vocal overdubs Kurt accidentally sang the phrase "And I don't have a gun" too early before the last chorus, but I loved it, so we left it in the final mix.

### 4. BREED

 @Nirvana

Damn, this is f**king tight! What a KILLER riff! Mute the right speaker and listen to Krist's bass, it's insane! I panned the bass (run through a fuzz pedal) hard left, and the main guitar panned hard right. I was referencing the extreme panning on the first Ramones album. The guitar solo is so crazy, during the mix I grabbed the pan knob on the console and swept it left and right. There was no automation for that, I had to nail it every time, "old school."

### 5. LITHIUM

 @Nirvana

This was one of the hardest songs to record. The band did a lot of takes, they kept speeding up, and they were pretty loose. I could feel Kurt getting frustrated, and after the last aborted attempt, while the tape was still rolling, Kurt launched into Endless Nameless. I've never seen so much rage in a person's face, it was scary. At the end of the song Kurt smashed his guitar to bits. And that was the end of the session. I quietly pulled Dave aside and asked him if he'd ever used a click track. He said no, so I gave him my Roland Drum Machine, which had a shaker/tambourine loop, and asked him to try practicing with it. He did. The band came in the next day, and they nailed the song on the second take. Years later, DG told me I broke his heart that night. But he forgave me.

Come as you are.
Dave, Kurt and Krist.

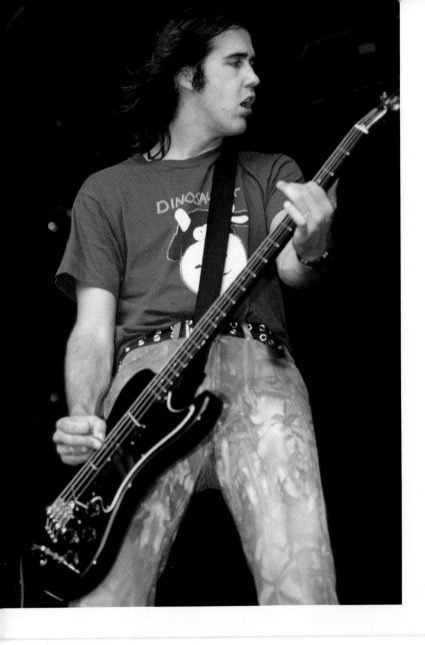

Getting shirty. Krist
Novoselic pays tribute
to Dinosaur with his
choice of t-shirt at
the 1991 Reading
Festival.

Jacket and Jeans.
Kurt Cobain
performing at
the 1991
Reading Festival.

## 6. POLLY

@Nirvana

This is one of Nirvana's darkest songs. This track
was originally recorded at Smart Studios in April
1990. Kurt playing a Stella guitar with only 5
strings that barely stayed in tune. The strings
were so old they didn't have any tone to them,
which gave it a dark, plunky sound. Kurt and Krist
recorded live, then we overdubbed lead and
harmony vocals, and then Chad Channing added
the cymbal crashes. There was point recording
Nevermind where we discussed if we should re-
record Polly. But we all agreed that, despite the
lofi sound, there was magic in the performance.
I'm glad we left it as is.

## 7. TERRITORIAL PISSINGS

@Nirvana

We wanted to add an intro to the song that would
be a counterpoint to the punk energy, so I
suggested "Why not sing something really lame?"
Krist went in and recorded a terrible rendition of
The Youngblood's "Get Together", an ode to the
60's if there ever was one. It's funny, and perfect!
The guitar tone on this is a mix of Kurt plugging his
Rat pedal directly into a Neve preamp and mixing
that in with his guitar amp. It's abrasive! Fun Fact:
I think the day we tracked this song, L7 stopped by
the studio. I sent out for B B Cue from Dr. Hogly
Wogly's, and by the time we finished getting a
master take, the food had arrived. When I walked
into the lounge, Nirvana and L7 were in the midst
of a food fight, it was crazy, chicken, brisket, beans
and coleslaw everywhere! I felt sorry for the studio
assistant who had to clean up the mess.

## 8. DRAIN YOU

@Nirvana

This was one of the songs we worked on quite a bit
in pre pro and during the sessions, it was really
arranged in the studio. After figuring out the verse/
chorus sections, we decided to let the bridge be a
"hypnotic breakdown" & layered a lot of abstract
vocal & sound EFX over DG's drum groove. Kurt did
3 vocal overdubs in the bridge w/ weird vocal
noises. We recorded a couple guitar overdubs with
the Mesa Boogie, but I didn't like the sound, so we
did one pass with the Bassman and dbled it with a
Rat/Bassman combo, we ended up with a killer gtr
sound for this song. Best lyrics ever: "Chew your
meat for you/Pass it back and forth/In a passionate
kiss/From my mouth to yours/I like you." Kurt
wrote the lyrics after meeting Courtney.

## 9. LOUNGE ACT

@Nirvana

Krist's bass really drives this song. In fact, through
all of Nevermind, his riffs are stellar: they are just
as hooky as Kurt's vocals and Dave's drum fills.
(Yes drums fills are hooks!) I recorded two tracks
of guitar with the Bassman, one clean and one
distorted. And I had Kurt overdub the "stab"
guitar before the chorus, I felt like it needed a jolt
of adrenalin. The vocals on this were tough, the
end choruses are just a bit out of Kurt's range.
But I think it gives the song a lot of urgency.

L7 drop by the studio for beers, BBQ and a food fight (see page 252).

Taking notice. A shot of Krist, Kurt and former drummer Chad Channing.

Putting your back into it. Kurt Cobain very much onstage at the Pukkelpop Festival in 1991.

### 10. STAY AWAY

@Nirvana

Another killer bass riff from Krist! I had Kurt overdub a "stab" gtr on this also, mixing it with so vocal "I Don't know Why"…it' pretty cool, very abrasive, it leaps out of the speaker. Fun fact: The original version I recorded at Smart was titled Pay To Play. Kurt changed the lyrics at the last minute the day we tracked at Sound City.

### 11. ON A PLAIN

@Nirvana

I LOVE Kurt's vocal melody juxtaposed over the guitar chords! It's pure pop! Great guitar tones, think it was the Bassman. And also great singing by Kurt with Dave on harmonies. It was effortless. In general, I don't like fade outs (although I have mixed my share of songs with fades), I think it's lame, a song needs an END right? But I think it really works great in this track, we're left with just Kurt and Dave's dreamy bk vox as the band drifts off.

### 12. SOMETHING IN THE WAY

@Nirvana

One of my fave songs on the album, and one of the darkest. I think Kurt had the fantasy he was the guy living under the bridge. This was the last and hardest song to record on Nevermind. We tried tracking in Studio A, but no matter how quietly the band played, the space was too overwhelming for the intimacy the song needed. After three or four aborted takes, Kurt came into the control room and started playing the song while lying on the sofa. So I put a 414 mic on Kurt and told him to play the song "how you hear it in your head." He did 3 takes that were soooo quiet, I felt like I held my breath during each performance. After extensive editing, we moved into Studio B and I had Dave and Krist overdub their parts. Also, really hard for them as they were used to playing live and had to adjust to Kurt's performance. I kept saying to Dave, "play more wimpy!" I had them do A LOT of takes. When we finally had the basic master we overdubbed vocals and added Kirk Canning on cello. I love how it turned out. I think it's the most intense song on Nevermind.

### 13. ENDLESS, NAMELESS (HIDDEN TRACK )

@Nirvana

This is entirely live, a take that erupted after several aborted attempts at tracking Lithium. I was smart enough to have kept the tape rolling. As many of you might know, Endless Nameless was added as a secret "bonus track" to the CD master. But was accidentally left off the first pressing because there was so much silence after Something In The Way, the mastering engineer Howie Weinberg didn't know the track existed! Thanks so much everyone! I hope Nevermind still touches you the way it does me! Be Safe!

# The Nearer The Fountain, More Pure The Stream Flows
## Damon Albarn
Transgressive, 2021

When you can count among your musical collaborators Tony Allen, Graham Coxon, Snoop Dog, Mark E Smith, Tina Weymouth, Ibrahim Ferrer, Alex James, Bobby Womack, Dave Rowntree, Little Dragon, Bobby Womack, Grace Jones and Mavis Staples... plus many more, you might have got to the point where you don't think you need to listen to your mother. Fortunately, that's not the case with Damon Albarn, as following his experiences with Blur, Gorillaz, The Good, The Bad & The Queen and a couple of original operas, it is Hazel Albarn he now has to thank for the title of this album after she recommended a piece of poetry to her son. The other influence the singer-songwriter has to thank for his second solo album is Iceland, where he has had a home for many years. His love for the country and its unique environment provided much of the backdrop as he composed tracks and songs for this sometimes dark, sometimes brooding, often tuneful and always beautiful record. Giving credit where credits due – *Hi, Mrs Albarn!*

– Damon Albarn (**@Damonalbarn**) led us through the musical landscapes *The Nearer The Fountain, More Pure The Stream Flows* has so stunningly carved out.

**PHOTOGRAPHY:**
Marton Perlaki

Pretty in pink. Damon Albarn performs solo at the 2021 Latitude Festival.

## 1. THE NEARER THE FOUNTAIN, MORE PURE THE STREAM FLOWS

### @Damonalbarn

An adaptation of a poem by John Clare called Love and Memory, the title of the song and the album is taken from a line in the poem. It was actually my mum who introduced me to him. She said, 'I think you'll like this guy.' He's a working-class poet in the 18th century, who was very into nature and allusions. So he always fascinated me. This particular poem really struck a chord with me, especially after my dear friend Tony Allen passed away last year.

## 2. THE CORMORANT

### @Damonalbarn

The Cormorant is probably my favourite thing I've ever done. I recorded it just as a vocal, sitting on a beach, watching this cormorant, who comes at about 4.30 every day when the sea's calm enough to do a bit of fishing. There was a cruise ship that had lights on at night and I imagined it being the last party on Earth out there. If you look at the same space for long enough, it reveals everything.

## 3. ROYAL MORNING BLUE

### @Damonalbarn

When it's raining and the temperature drops just a little bit more, a wonderful thing happens, it turns into snow, and then it slows down. The same wind. The same movement. But it slows down and then just becomes entirely different. The song opens with "Rain turning into snow…" because it's that moment, in all the darkness that we've experienced, that was such a beautiful, positive thing. I started off playing the piano with the orchestra, looking out the window on a very stormy day in Iceland. It was horizontally raining, obscuring the mountain. The sea is violent. It looks like it's boiling.

## 4. COMBUSTION

### @Damonalbarn

I started singing to pictures which my mum had shown me, drawings I'd done when I was about 7 or 8 years old. It was quite… Ian Dury meets some dodgy punk band. Three days I was doing that. It took me back into that period of my life and I remembered all this mad stuff that had happened. I didn't use the vocal in the end, but wanted to keep that energy because it was appropriate for the elemental aspect of the record to have that sort of volcanic eruption.

## 5. DAFT WADER

### @Damonalbarn

This song is a sort of journey back to Iran – a trip I made a few years ago that just had a profound effect on me. Iran is one of the most beautiful cultures I've ever had the privilege of exploring. The song detours into this Zoroastrian ritual – in the desert, they have the Towers of Silence, like huge circular pyramids. Traditionally, no one was allowed to go up them apart from a man called the nasular who was like the undertaker. I suppose in a way, it connects to the John Clare poem. It's not a morbid record, but it's definitely aware of mortality.

## 6. DARKNESS TO LIGHT

### @Damonalbarn

It's like the return of the empty cruise ship that I was imagining in The Cormorant. Simon Tong, Mike Smith and me – we were the band playing on the empty cruise ship, and this is one of the songs we're playing on it. The rhythm you can hear on this is one of the presets on my 1950s drum machine. In the absence of a drummer, I love a pre-set. I'm not really a programmer!

## 7. ESJA

### @Damonalbarn

Esja, that's the mountain we could see out of our window in Reykjavik. This is the same piece of music that you hear at the beginning of the record. We're following the outline of the mountain, but it's unadorned here.

## 8. THE TOWER OF MONTEVIDEO

### @Damonalbarn

This is about a building in Montevideo that had a real effect on me. It was built by an Italian architect called Mario Palanti in the 1930s. A beautiful building that had a cinema, a ballroom and a lighthouse on the top of it. When I stayed in Montevideo, I felt a strong presence of a ghost in the hotel. It's known for its ghost, so there was this moment, where I imagined a scene… I imagined myself on this empty cruise ship, in the band with the lighthouse from the tower shining a light through and I'm singing this song.

Northern lights.
Damon Albarn
onstage in
Manchester in 2021.

(right and belolw)
Drawings shared to
illustrate the genesis
of the song Particles.
**@Damonalbarn**
Particles starts from
a moment I had when
I went outside and it
was just a beautiful...

Room with a view.
Damon Albarn shared
the view of the mountain
Esja he can see from his
window in Reykjavik.

## 9. GIRAFFE TRUMPET SEA

@Damonalbarn

I don't know why I came up with this title. I was thinking of construction cranes – they always look like giraffes to me. One day in Iceland, I was looking at them and it felt like they were all singing to the sunset. I could hear this weird brass arrangement.

## 10. POLARIS

@Damonalbarn

Another Iceland song. The North Star, the Polar Star – a source point for navigation from the earliest times. In Iceland, when a storm comes in, birds get separated a lot because they just lose all orientation. That felt like it was true to what we were going through as well.

## 11. PARTICLES

@Damonalbarn

Particles starts from a moment I had when I went outside and it was just a beautiful, clear December night. I closed my eyes and I went, "I really wish the Northern Lights would appear". I opened my eyes and there they were. We're all in fear of particles. We wear masks to avoid other people's particles. But they are joyous – anything where change happens is necessary and part of what the universe is all about. We have to pull back and wait for beauty to follow. The phenomenon of the Northern Lights comes from solar winds, solar flares. When they hit the Earth's atmosphere, they die. But you get this chemical reaction which results in this incredible spectacle. That seemed to me an important note to end on.

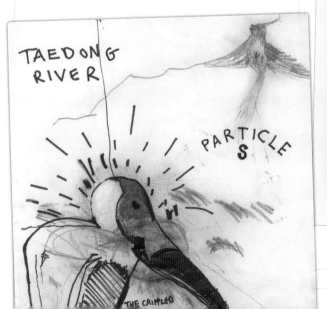

243

# Flying Dream 1
## Elbow
Polydor, 2021

✛ Every Elbow album feels like an achievement worth celebrating. It's not just the glorious, delicate music that seems purpose-built for filling ornate halls and striking basilicas, but the arduous journey the Bury group endured back at the start of the 2000s. Now Guy Garvey (vocals – **@Guy_Garvey**), Craig Potter (keyboards/producer – **@CraigLPotter**), Mark Potter (guitars – **@Elbow**) and Pete Turner (bass – **@peteelbow**) are soundtrackers of British life, but their first-ever record deal saw them dropped before they'd even released anything. These days, new Elbow's albums are an event, though the making of *Flying Dream 1* was more eventful than most. Written by the band remotely because of the Covid-19 restrictions, the group came together to record it at the improbable yet fitting Theatre Royal in Brighton (closed to the public due to lockdown rules). "Getting together with these lads and wandering through all our ideas in the theatre was one of the happiest times of my life," Garvey told the Listening Party confirming that out of adversity comes great feeling and strength.

**PHOTOGRAPHY:**
Dave Wilkinson

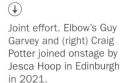

Joint effort. Elbow's Guy Garvey and (right) Craig Potter joined onstage by Jesca Hoop in Edinburgh in 2021.

## 1. FLYING DREAM 1

**@Guy_Garvey**

Dad was a proof reader at The Daily Mirror. Night work. During my mum's prayer group on a Tuesday I would silently slide down the stairs and try on the faithfuls hats and coats silently to make our Marcus laugh.

## 2. AFTER THE ECLIPSE

**@Guy_Garvey**

Got all the imagery for the first verse from an episode of [Melvin Bragg's] In Our Time on eclipses. Verse 2 was playing with my son in Ldown. Sonic Racing still a fave.

**@Elbow (Mark Potter)**

Mark Potter: This song is showcasing the amazing AlexReeves on drums

## 3. IS IT A BIRD

**@Guy_Garvey**

My wife nursed her mum to her death in our house. Diana Rigg [actor and mother of Garvey's wife Rachel Stirling] was indeed a warrior. My friend I'm extremely proud to say. I wrote this two days after she died. I was so proud of Rach that the sadness was tinged with relief.

## 4. SIX WORDS

**@Guy_Garvey**

Romantic memories of my beloved Prestwich in the autumn. From your lions to your Ostrich, I bloody miss you. Those amazing voices! Marrit! Hoop! Wilson! Ade! Forgedabowdeet!

**@CraigLPotter**

So lucky to have Jesca Hoop, Wilson Atie and Adeleye Omotayo on this.

## 5. CALM AND HAPPY

**@Guy_Garvey**

Me and Pete loved Brookside and Sheila Grant and my mum were the same person in my head. Love Sue Johnston

**@Elbow (Mark Potter)**

Late night calm n happy vibes.

**@CraigLPotter**

We had EVERYONE on twitter searching for a [keyboard] Celeste for this song (yes EVERYONE).

**@peteelbow (Pete Turner)**

My little boy Ted came up with the title Calm And Happy.

## 6. COME ON, BLUE

**@Guy_Garvey**

If my son's ever sad, this is to give him a cuddle. I mean the 'love transcends' line with all my heart.

## 7. THE ONLY ROAD

**@Guy_Garvey**

In this holiday fantasy I'm driving my family into Scotland where my wife's from. It's irritating to Rach that I'm at the wheel in the song because its bollocks. I'm a terrible driver. I love Scotland.

**@CraigLPotter**

Drum sound is ALL THEATRE on Only Rd. Took us a while to nail the direction on this one. 4 or 5 versions and a lot of scratching heads.

## 8. RED SKY RADIO (BABY BABY BABY)

**@Guy_Garvey**

Richard Swift was the coolest cat we ever toured with or even met! The end chorus melody is from his song Looking Back I should Have been Home More.

**@peteelbow**
My fav.

## 9. THE SELDOM SEEN KID

**@Guy_Garvey**

is a nickname I gave our friend Bryan Glancey. If he'd met my wife..... good lord.... My favourite elbow song.

**@CraigLPotter**
My first Clarinet arrangement!

## 10. WHAT AM I WITHOUT YOU

**@Guy_Garvey**

I felt like a lighthouse keeper through most of lockdown. The words to What Am I are kind of about my son but mostly about watching my Rach work miracles looking after her mum and son and I.

# St. Christopher
## Peter Capaldi
Monks Road Records, 2021

From world saving to world-class swearing, Peter Capaldi (tweeting from **@theblowmonkeys**) always makes his mark. The embodiment of both the 12th Doctor Who (or 13th if you count John Hurt's cameo) and *In The Thick Of It*'s government enforcer Malcolm Tucker, the Glaswegian actor has constantly proved his versatility, so when word emerged that he had been mucking about in the studio the usual course of groans that surround singing actors were absent. Capaldi, though, did not just have versatility on his side. His own collection of art rock records has been well-documented, while his recording attempts were helped by the frontman of British band The Blow Monkeys, Robert Howard (also using **@theblowmonkeys**), or Dr Robert for short. "I never expected to be making an album. I just liked playing with Dr Rob and talking about music," Capaldi told The Listening party, "For fun, I wrote a song. They recorded it in a day. Bang." Doctor Who fans will know about episodes such as The Three Doctors or The Five Doctors, when various incarnations of the character appear together. On this occasion, let it be known The Two Doctors really rocked!

ARTWORK:
Monks Road Records

LISTENING
PARTY
**21 NOVEMBER
2021**

### 1. BEAUTIFUL AND WEIRD

✓ @theblowmonkeys

Peter: A romance. That goes wrong. For various reasons. The intro poem bit was a very late addition. But I liked it was spoken word. I am an actor after all.

### 2. IT'S NOT OVER UNTIL IT'S OVER

✓ @theblowmonkeys

Peter: I think [it] might be about getting older. Escaping its expectations and constrictions. But in trying to, you might do stupid things… like making an album. But the truth is no one cares. So go right ahead.

### 3. IMPOSSIBLE YOUTH

✓ @theblowmonkeys

Peter: Throughout lockdown I'd keep seeing these young people doing wonderful things. Teachers doing incredible work. Medical students. Doctors. Artists. Musicians. Full of life. Inspiring. Invincible. Impossible.

✓ @theblowmonkeys

Dr Robert: Love the way he pronounces 'roared!' Lyrically he's so clever. No wasted words.

### 4. A LITTLE BIT OF CLASS

✓ @theblowmonkeys

Peter: This was about being a kid in the 60s, sing songs, all of that stuff. So I like that we had kind of period strings and old fashioned electric organ on it – thank you so much [The Style Council's] Mick Talbot.

@theblowmonkeys

Dr Robert: I heard it I knew it was a classic. And Mick Talbot is a genius on Hammond. A gentleman too.

## 5. THE GREAT MAGNIFICENCE

@theblowmonkeys

Peter: This might be [a] fairy tale. Or a folk song. Kind of. I copied some folky chords. But I couldn't leave them alone. I found this dirty big synth sound. In it went. The end, I said to Rob, should be like a synth is coming to get you. And it is.

The doctor will see you now. Peter Capaldi regenerates as an art rock star.

## 6. ATLANTA VACANT LOT

@theblowmonkeys

Peter: My apartment in Atlanta looked down on this empty lot. It was fenced off. All around it was busy. But the fenced off lot looked like the loneliest place on. Romy Deighton sings on it. She has a beautiful haunting voice. Thanks Romy. She's a star.

## 7. IN PERSON

@theblowmonkeys

Peter: This is about being famous. I go a bit Roy Orbison at the very end. I love Roy Orbison. In a museum in Nashville I saw his shoes. They were tiny. Yet impossible to fill.

## 8. IN EVERY FACE

@theblowmonkeys

Peter: Dr Robert's guitar here is lovely. I wasn't sure about the song. Then they added strings. Strings make everything sound better.

@theblowmonkeys

Dr Robert: I had to convince Peter to stick with this but I think it's one of the strongest on the album. Traces of Scott. Ben Trigg nails the string arrangement again. I had to record the guitar without Peter in the room. It worked.

## 9. ST. CHRISTOPHER

@theblowmonkeys

Peter: St. Christopher He had been a Saint from the middle ages. He was the saint of looking after people on their journeys through stormy waters. Then the Church decided he wasn't real. (!) But he couldn't be erased. Because people liked the idea of him. So he survived.

## 10. TAKE WHAT YOU NEED

@theblowmonkeys

Peter: This was the last thing I wrote for the album. We had seen such understanding and compassion in lockdown. And then the forces of selfishness and greed got going again. You know who you are. I am so lucky. By an accident of birth. Geography. Timing. Not everyone is so lucky.

# *Panic Prevention*
## Jamie T
Virgin, 2007

Arriving at early shows alone, with just an acoustic bass guitar, Jamie T cut an odd figure in and around West London. What could this skinny teen hope to achieve with a watered-down version of the instrument that is usually the butt of musician's jokes. Around half-an-hour later after he'd slaughtered a room of disbelievers by accompanying his sung almost-raps with his hand-picked bass grooves, there was no doubt this kid and his "clapped out bass guitar" were on to something.

However, when word got around after he signed a record deal that he was putting a band together, and his debut album would be something else, there were fears a special thing might be lost. Fortunately, the world has since learnt not to question Jamie T, and with its mix of home-made beats, scratchy samples and rapid-fire rhymes, by staying true to T's own expectations *Panic Prevention* proved a truly special debut. At once full of swagger and street boasts, while underscored with insecurities, mental health concerns and a wariness with the world, this is a multi-flavoured record that reflects oscillating confidence with which everyone embraces life. Intensely personal for Wimbledon-born Jamie Treays, it's sharp yet illuminated snap shots (imagine Hogarth's subject matter reinterpreted by JMW Turner) also chimed deeply with audiences. It's why as Jamie (**@jamietmusic**) held this listening party, 15 years to the day of its release, there was general agreement that we were celebrating the birthday of a modern classic.

**PHOTOGRAPHY:**
Tom Beard

---

**LISTENING PARTY**
**29 JANUARY 2022**

### 1. BRAND NEW BASS GUITAR

✔ **@jamietmusic**
Here come the croissants... Firstly, I would like to send all my love to Ben Bones who produced most of this album with me. Don't remember writing it but I remember recording it and that is one of my dearest memories. I can't remember the exact story behind fucking croissants but I remember it was fuckin funny at the time...

### 2. SALVADOR

✔ **@jamietmusic**
If your idols are so far away and their talent is un achievable for you. Do what I did. Try write "baby please don't go " by THEM and find originality in your failure.

### 3. CALM DOWN DEAREST

✔ **@jamietmusic**
I wrote most of these songs in my bedroom when I was 18 and recorded them at the same time. The lyrics were off the top of my head and yes I am trying to sound drunk... Or Maybe I was drunk

### 4. SO LONELY WAS THE BALLAD

✔ **@jamietmusic**
I'm proud of this one. It's about not wanting to go out but not wanting to stay in either. Basically still feel the same.

### 5. BACK IN THE GAME

✔ **@jamietmusic**
This is written about me and my brother living in Brighton. The protagonist. One of my favourites to play live.

### 6. OPERATION

🔘 **@jamietmusic**

This song was written start to finish in one go. I am so fond of it. Reminds me of Ben Bones a lot. We had no script or understanding and this is a great example. Fuck me can someone do me a favour and count how many times I say a variation of kick or kicking across this record? Need to settle a bet. "Ain't no abacus [but you can count on me]" line still makes me laugh.

### 7. SHEILA

🔘 **@jamietmusic**

Here come the Londons. I wrote this song for a girl called Laura. Last time I saw her was outside a bakery in Wimbledon and she boy'd me off. Cheers Laura!! Fucking over it. Donut. I like that this song means something different to different people. The characters are all versions of my best friends. Not telling you who is who though.

If you got the money. Jamie T signs on the dotted line.

By a whisker. Jamie T shared this photo of his home studio for *Panic Prevention*.

### 8. PACEMAKER

🔘 **@jamietmusic**

I distinctly remember recording this tune in my bedroom on my own and looking out the window and seeing a seagull and feeling alive as fuck. God I was a cocky shit. If you're the person who encourages their mate to fight someone bigger than them you're not good people. I want to put this one out to Chilli [Jesson] from Palma Violets. Love u Chilli.

### 9. DRY OFF YOUR CHEEKS

🔘 **@jamietmusic**

No one wanted this on the album. I did. Apparently it did well in Russia (meaning it got air play for a week) safe to say I felt vindicated. Someone told me once it was like I was shouting at them with this song. Wonder why?

### 10. IKE & TINA

🔘 **@jamietmusic**

Still wear my mum's ray bans and my dad's jacket. This is about my great friend Liquorice. Night busses and proper Mitsubishi's. Love you liq.

### 11. IF YOU GOT THE MONEY

🔘 **@jamietmusic**

Fuck knows what this is about but if you look in the video you will see a little known extra who ended up being in the powerhouse that is Mumford And Sons. My mate sometimes sends me pictures of myself from this time and just says da de do dah. Fuck off.

### 12. ALICIA QUAYS

🔘 **@jamietmusic**

Fuck last song already. I haven't listened to this album in it's entirety for a minute. New Year's Eve is shit, innit. Freestyle from start to finish. I really hate the last line in this song. I was young and dumb. We can only learn from our mistakes: still like the what am I thing. I was told I had to give insight into Panic Prevention but honestly I can't remember loads from this time. It was 15 fucking years ago. But I'm very proud of it and happy it resonates with so many people. Love you all. Get another pint on me. Night night x

# *Come Away With Me*
## Norah Jones
Blue Note, 2002

Having begun singing at an early age in school and church choirs, before going on to study jazz piano at the University of North Texas, Norah Jones might have been forgiven for filling her debut album with an anxious, nervous energy as she fulfilled what was clearly a life-long goal. Instead, *Come Away With Me* is a mature, tender collection of songs that charm and beguile with an assured gentleness. A mix of jazz and country-ish tones, the daughter of concert producer Sue Jones and musician Ravi Shankar finds her own path, imbuing songs written by herself and bandmates with the warm personality of her enveloping vocals. Exactly two decades on from *Come Away With Me*'s release, Jones (**@NorahJones**) returned to this precociously assured debut for an overdue spin. "Thanks to you for listening along, with me today," she tweeted, "and the past twenty years!"

**PHOTOGRAPHY:**
Joanne Savio

---

**LISTENING PARTY
26 FEBRUARY 2022**

### 1. DON'T KNOW WHY

**@NorahJones**
This song was written by my band mate, and old friend, Jesse Harris! This was the first thing we recorded while making some demos for the label. That's Dan Reiser on drums and Lee Alexander on bass. First take, all live. We later added the harmonies and doubled the guitar. We knew we could never beat this take.

### 2. SEVEN YEARS

**@NorahJones**
My bass player, Lee Alexander, wrote this song after seeing an old home video of me dancing as a little girl, in my own little world.

### 3. COLD COLD HEART

**@NorahJones**
We added this Hank Williams cover at the 11th hour to get a different feel on the album. I love this arrangement. Such a great song and so fun to play live.

### 4. FEELIN' THE SAME WAY

**@NorahJones**
Another Kevin Breit Guitar part from upstate NY. I think this is the fastest song on the record.

### 5. COME AWAY WITH ME

**@NorahJones**
I was inspired to write 'Come Away With Me' late one night on an old electric guitar after coming home from seeing different songwriters play at [NYC venue] the living room. This song felt more country than jazz, probably due to my limited guitar chord skills.

### 6. SHOOT THE MOON

**@NorahJones**
Jesse Harris wrote this song and plays acoustic Guitar on it. Producer, Arif Mardin always loved it.

### 7. TURN ME ON

☑ @NorahJones

This was another demo that we couldn't beat. We added my friend and piano teacher, Sam Yahel, on Organ for the final album. One reason I never could never let go of this version is the little vocal turn I stumbled into at 2:12 that I'd never done before and have never been able to do since! Glad the tape was rolling...

### 8. LONESTAR

☑ @NorahJones

Lee Alexander wrote this song, it's always been a special one for me to sing, being from Texas.

⊕

Shooting for the moon. Norah Jones at Los Angeles' Bel Age Hotel, the week before *Come Away With Me* was released in 2002.

### 9. I'VE GOT TO SEE YOU AGAIN

☑ @NorahJones

This track has Jenny Scheinman on the violin! I used to sing this song as a duet with Jesse Harris on his gigs. He wrote it for his band The Ferdinando's. Once he started playing in my band we started trying it different ways.

### 10. PAINTER SONG

☑ @NorahJones

Another gem written by Lee Alexander. It took me a long time to figure out these chord changes on the piano. Rob Burger is on the accordion. I've done this song mostly solo over the years. So different to hear the band version!

### 11. ONE FLIGHT DOWN

☑ @NorahJones

Jesse Harris wrote this song long before we started playing together. It might have been one of the first charts he gave me to learn when we first met in Texas, where I was studying Jazz piano at UNT. I remember being shocked when I asked him what he did and he replied, "I'm a songwriter". It hadn't yet occurred to me that that was a possible career!

### 12. NIGHTINGALE

☑ @NorahJones

This was the second song I wrote after Come Away With Me. I knew we needed a specific drum groove to help it take flight and Brian Blade delivered!

### 13. THE LONG DAY IS OVER

☑ @NorahJones

Another recording from the trip upstate New York with Craig Street Producing and Recording engineer, Husky Huskgulds. I love this one.

### 14. THE NEARNESS OF YOU

☑ @NorahJones

Producer, Arif Mardin, thought it was important to end the record with a solo piano version of one of my favorite old standards, "The Nearness of You," written by Ned Washington and Hoagie Carmichael.

# *The Line Is A Curve*
## Kae Tempest
Fiction, 2022

⚑ As a poet and a playwright, as well as a songwriter and MC, Kae Tempest (**@kaetempest**) is a pleasingly difficult artist to pin down. With Ancient Greek myth and vivid expressions of modern life among the things feeding these various works, Tempest's words spread out like a constellation, illuminating the dark and ill-defined corners of human experience with ideas and imagery that burns brightly. Having forged a long-standing music collaboration with acclaimed producer Dan Carey, on record and in song, and calling on guest vocalists such as singer-songwriter Lianne La Havas, rappers Confucius MC and Kevin Abstract, and Fontaines DC frontman Grian Chatten to add their voices to the tapestry of thoughts and feelings on fourth album *The Line Is A Curve*, Tempest's self-expression truly beguiles as stories and emotions compellingly intertwine with beats and synths.

PHOTOGRAPHY:
Wolfgang Tillmans

LISTENING PARTY
**13 APRIL 2022**

### 1. PRIORITY BOREDOM

✓ **@kaetempest**
This was the first song we wrote and as the rest of the album came together, I knew it should be the opener. I love how it's minimal and sparse but so layered and rich at the same time.

### 2. I SAW LIGHT

✓ **@kaetempest**
Met Grian [Chatten, Fontaines DC] years ago through Dan. I love Grian's presence on stage, his lyricism. For me he is a poet. A great one.

### 3. NOTHING TO PROVE

✓ **@kaetempest**
I love this song. It's the kind of beat Dan writes that immediately makes me makes me want to flow. The two verses are phonetically and syllabically matched and play off each other. It's an example of the form being as relevant to the lyric as the words themselves.

### 4. NO PRIZES

✓ **@kaetempest**
Lianne [La Havas] came down to the studio and started playing around with the hook. I had different verses for the song at the time but I wasn't really happy with them. She found the melody and we fit the words to it. And as she began to sing this chorus round and round, I started to think in pictures. I realised the song should be three verse portraits, framed by Lianne's hook.

### 5. SALT COAST

✓ **@kaetempest**
This is a love letter to the UK, to the land, the people, the soil, the concrete. Whenever I'm done in, I try and head to the edge. I like to stand on the beach and look back at the cliffs. It reminds me that this place is made of chalk and clay and rock, and that the cities we live in are not as permanent as they feel.

### 6. DON'T YOU EVER

⊘ @kaetempest

We [Daisy Beau and Luke Eastop, co-writers] were in a band together when we were 19, and I've never forgotten this song. I asked them to come into the studio and put a version of this down. We played a session together for the first time in almost 20 years. Dan sampled the session into his MPC and produced the beat out of it.

### 7. THESE ARE THE DAYS

⊘ @kaetempest

We wrote this in lockdown. It was the first time we had been able to get together in ages. It was hot outside and the city was still and I was so happy to be back in the studio with Dan at last.

### 8. SMOKING

⊘ @kaetempest

Confucius MC is someone I started rapping with at 16. I've studied his rhyme style since we were kids, he's a foundational presence in my creativity and one of the best rappers in the UK for me, it was right for him to be on this track. Killed it.

### 9. WATER IN THE RAIN

⊘ @kaetempest

This is a crucial moment in the album. For me, this is pure Dan Carey. The layers, the chords, the sensitivity of his writing, the way he responds to my lyrics.

### 10. MOVE

⊘ @kaetempest

At this point in the album, we need to shake things. This is a galvanising moment where I tell myself no matter how hard it might be, it's not over.

### 11. MORE PRESSURE

⊘ @kaetempest

This song feels like coming up. It's an endless crescendo. Unresolved harmonies that keep building.

### 12. GRACE

⊘ @kaetempest

This started life as a voice-note Dan sent to me over lockdown. Him picking his guitar. Looking for connection in the same way I was with the verse in Smoking. The lyric is like a prayer or something. A request. A promise.

Kae photographed by Wolfgang Tillmans.

# Index

**Music Venue Trust**

Music Venue Trust is a UK registered charity which acts to protect, secure and improve Grassroots Music Venues (GMVs). These venues have played a crucial role in the development of British music over the last 50 years, nurturing local talent, providing a platform for artists to build their careers and develop their music and their performance skills. As well as being a vital part of the UK's cultural infrastructure, GMVs are social hubs, providing important meeting places for communities and contributing to the local night-time economy.

MVT represents over 900 venues across the UK, members of its Music Venues Alliance. Prior to the creation of MVT in 2014 these venues were overlooked and under-represented, failing to be credited for their valuable work by governments or the wider music industry. Happily, this has changed in recent years and we are building a powerful movement, assisted in no small measure by artists who champion the venues which helped them build their career and fanbase.

Since Covid-19 closed venues across the land in March 2020, MVT's work has been practical: gathering data to lobby for support, helping venues apply for funding, supporting people to deal with crisis situations and providing advice and solidarity. It has also been about profile-raising and campaigning: the #SaveOurVenues campaign was launched in April 2020 and raised over £4 million for Grassroots Music Venues. Key to this success were artists such as Tim Burgess, KT Tunstall, Frank Turner, Arctic Monkeys, IDLES, and Billy Bragg explaining how important GMVs are to them. When an artist with a loyal following stands up for a cause it makes a huge difference. Tim is loved and trusted by many, so every mention of MVT, grassroots venues or #SaveOurVenues remains priceless.

Post pandemic MVT continues to support Grassroots Music Venues, especially though our Emergency Response Service, giving bespoke support to any venue in danger of imminent closure. It helps pay for the charity's team and specialists who support our work with expertise in planning, licensing, legal issues, acoustics etc. We work with venues to access funding, offer training, share information and work with all layers of government across the UK. The last few years have shown how powerful our music community can be when musicians, fans and venues come together. GMVs are facing a huge range of challenges, from audience recovery to noise complaints to the implications of the cost-of-living crisis, so MVT's work is as necessary as ever.

For further information about MVT see: musicvenuetrust.com

If you would like to help please visit: https://mvtdonations.goodcrm.co.uk/donate/o/ CA624ecc0abb5739.75683993donate-now